PLAYS TWO

Torben Betts

PLAYS TWO

INCARCERATOR
FIVE VISIONS OF THE FAITHFUL
SILENCE AND VIOLENCE
THE BIGGLESWADES
THE LAST DAYS OF DESIRE

OBERON BOOKS
LONDON

First published in this collection in 2001 by Oberon Books Ltd.
(incorporating Absolute Classics)
521 Caledonian Road, London N7 9RH
Tel: 020 7607 3637 / Fax: 020 7607 3629
e-mail: oberon.books@btinternet.com

ISBN: 1 84002 200 0

Cover illustration: Andrzej Klimowski

Cover typography: Jeff Willis

Printed in Great Britain by Antony Rowe Ltd, Reading.

for my mother and father
with love and gratitude

Incarcerator

...messy, generous, explosive, sawing on the gut and a feast for actors...
PLAYS & PLAYERS

...packs a punch that leaves you staggering...savage and hilariously funny...a delight to watch...
LONDON METRO

...blistering...Betts is prodding around in our intestines and translating what he finds into taut, explosive verse...muscular poetry...an immensely promising talent destined for great things...
WHAT'S ON IN LONDON

...a full-bloodied verse drama...Betts's verse is fast and funny...hilariously grotesque...
THE TIMES

Betts has a finely-tuned ear for contemporary hypocrisy and a nice line in sardonic wit...
INDEPENDENT

...linguistically bold...Someone's bound to hail him as the new Berkoff...
INDEPENDENT ON SUNDAY

I emerged after three hours of cartoon savagery feeling punch-drunk...a bloodbath straight out of Jacobean tragedy...
Michael Billington, THE GUARDIAN

...Big, bold and ambitious...imaginative and extremely clever... a bright new play...Betts is a writer to watch... sharply humorous...wickedly funny...
THE STAGE

...explosive...hilarious...dangerous...a powerful production...
SOUTH LONDON PRESS

...Incarcerator is a must...wry tragedy is a play to revel in... the house applauded with vigour...
WANDSWORTH BOROUGH NEWS

Critics Choice...a hugely ambitious poetic drama... The best of the Fringe
TIME OUT

A Listening Heaven

A great new play...totally gripping...searing...one scene of quite shattering impact proves he is a real dramatist...I came out of the Lyceum exhilarated by Betts' heightened realism...
Michael Billington, THE GUARDIAN

...refreshingly bleak...a tour de force of gallows humour that runs the whole gamut of emotional warfare...
THE TIMES (Five Best Productions Nationwide)

...this fine tragi-comedy...like the best work of Edward Albee... a startlingly rich evening's theatre...beautifully articulated...
THE SCOTSMAN

...a fierce indictment of a smug, emotionally illiterate middle class that doesn't understand the destruction it wreaks on its young...has a shocking power...the production is first-rate...
John Peter, THE SUNDAY TIMES

...a heart-rending tragedy...unflinchingly mature...
THE STAGE

...one of Britain's most promising young playwrights...
SCOTTISH DAILY MAIL

A wonderfully accomplished first play.
Alan Ayckbourn

Critic's Choice: comedy from widely-tipped actor-turned-writer...
THE GUARDIAN

A master of dialogue, of the silences...a complex writer of misery pockmarked with painful comedy...
YORKSHIRE EVENING PRESS

...a fine and thought-provoking work...
YORKSHIRE POST

...joy turns to pain in a tour de force...Betts' tragedy leaves the whole audience stunned into silence...
EDINBURGH EVENING NEWS

(*A Listening Heaven* is published by Oberon Books in *Plays One* – ISBN: 1 84002 176 4)

Clockwatching

A strong well-written comedy...Harsher and darker than any (Ayckbourn) has written...has a toughness and energy that are very much Betts's...we may have, not a new Ayckbourn, but Ayckbourn's successor.
Benedict Nightingale, THE TIMES
(Five Best Shows in London)

...a brilliant orchestrator of pain...Betts's outstanding ability...magnificent...a superb disonant harmony...
Alfred Hickling, THE GUARDIAN (Nth)

A bleakly comic vision...Betts has a sharp ear for the bruising banalities of family life...very funny...
Michael Billington, THE GUARDIAN (Sth)

A pitch-black comedy...sharply observed...
Paul Taylor, THE INDEPENDENT
(Five Best Plays Nationwide)

...Betts's unhurried, unsparing vision of everyday hell is quietly compelling.
Dominic Cavendish, THE DAILY TELEGRAPH

...Greek tragedy remade for a modern audience...thoughtful and edgy...a major playwriting discovery...
Sheridan Morley, INTERNATIONAL HERALD TRIBUNE & SPECTATOR

...as bleakly comic as Galton and Simpson but with the final lemon twist of Harold Pinter.
YORKSHIRE EVENING PRESS

...hilarious...beautifully staged...
WHAT'S ON IN LONDON

A superb play.
SCARBOROUGH EVENING NEWS

...sad and grimly funny...one of the best three thirty-something playwrights...highly entertaining...extremely funny set pieces...
COUNTRY LIFE

...wonderfully funny moments...strong...very dramatic... extremely moving...
RICHMOND AND TWICKENHAM TIMES

...an engrossing and unexpectedly poignant play...Betts has a perceptive ear for dialogue allied to an expansive understanding of human nature...darkly comic and pervasively sad...
THE GREEN MAGAZINE

(*Clockwatching* is published by Oberon Books in *Plays One* –
ISBN: 1 84002 176 4)

Contents

with special thanks to
Nigel Barrett, Victoria Betts, Peter Craze,
Jessica Dromgoole, Dic Edwards, Charles Glanville,
Humphrey Gudgeon, James Hogan, Cathy King,
Michael Kingsbury, Andrzej Klimowski, Tom Morris,
David Pownall, Karen Rose, Yael Shavit,
Phil Temple, Philip Witcomb
and all the actors.

INTRODUCTION

David Pownall

On first encountering a playwright's work, a fellow author is made aware of instinctive movements within its feel and structure – either to escape from the stage and its restrictions, or embrace it, warts and all, desiring its roughness. The first kind inevitably give themselves away by sketching the ghost of a film or television series within what has been created. The theatre energy is false, even though the writing may be clever. The author is only present in this cleverness. So the identity is glib. Torben Betts is not one of these. He relishes the stage and lives by its laws – those harsh laws which compress action into meaning and, hopefully in the heart of the playwright, bring forth a moment of revelation. He naturally believes in the power of acting and the power of being within that transforming power. His presence originates in the stage, as a spiritual platform. In the case of two of these plays, at the time of writing the premieres have not taken place. Although lifting plays off the page is an art many of us imagine we have, I defy anyone to read *The Biggleswades* and *Silence and Violence* and foretell their impacts. We cannot determine the effect intellectually because it is not explicit in the design, even in the writing – it comes, I suspect, only to an actor receiving a performance script and underlining his part, sensing an energy field and an orientation of sense. Some time I must watch a Betts play in an enormous theatre and sit at the back. I've got a feeling his best work, when written, will have no problem in reaching me because it will be long-armed, passionate and made to carry.

The stuff of Torben Betts' imagination is foolishness as seen through the many shapes of fool. Not propelled by incomprehensible obsessions, or even the fatal flaws beloved of playwrights, they endure weakness, blunder, addiction to fashion and easy answers, blindness to consequences and all the other banal traits on the slag-heap of human petty sin. The garb his actors rage in is despair but they are always maddened by the memory of hope.

Alternatives pulse beneath everything he puts on the stage – the pulse of a better world he feels must be there – which can be revealed. Beneath all his excesses and errors, all his successful scenes and high points, beats the hopeful, moral heart. His skill in portraying the foibles of family life and all the associated stupidity and insensitivity has been agreed – but the plays in this volume go beyond those Ayckbournian frontiers. The sneer drops away and wilder expressions take over. In the mêlées and the madnesses more space is created – space he can fill rather than settling for containment.

'I shun the fake, the asinine...' says one of his characters in *Incarcerator*, as she attempts to purge herself of fashionable idiocies and stand alone. But she can't. The fakeness and asininity are in the air she breathes, whatever she looks at or listens to. There is no escape, only death. So the vision is a dark one – the despair is one we know only too well. Even after we've laughed at the jokes and shrugged off the bawdy and youthful burlesque, the question keeps being asked in whatever Torben Betts writes – how do we get out of this mess?

The other side of his coin is, of course – how did we get into this mess?

This is a particular strength in his plays; a powerful sense of horror at – what we have settled for as life. Out of this he spins webs of inanity, exploding webs which then reform into a greater web from which there seems to be no escape. The effect of life as we generally live it now on the natural mind is for him like watching slurry being poured into a spring.

What he restrainedly rages against is studded throughout his work – the spiritual sloth, the cowardly complacency, the self-destructive hunt for pleasure in the modes dictated by commerce and the media. One side of his divided writing persona presents this as comedy – without the happy ending – the other forces it ever downwards in the hope it will break through into a purified artesian well of the future.

At some point, if he refuses all the advice he's currently in receipt of – the two sides of the writer will...may...

perhaps…merge and help lift the theatre to another level. We can't remain in the one-way system of despair for ever (Why not? I find myself asking.) Using a rolling Bettsian metaphorical extension, the ring-road of non-communication and the cul-de-sac of sex and violence miraculously disgorge into it anyway.)

For all the talk of creative freedom, this remains a bullying, prescriptive age. The idea of a natural author, unattached, unhampered by discipleship, living inside our society and coming up with their unique interpretation of existence gets more out-of-the-question as each day goes by. The pressures of political correctness, corporate power, media-backed fashion and ventriloquistic money preaching its abominable sermons, are intense. This is not the era of the individual voice – especially a voice from the humane but unsentimental tradition blasted by deconstructivist despair, but – in the case of this playwright – it is the age of the come-back. He feels the tradition but changes its weaponry to something more up-to-date.

Torben Betts isn't afraid to disclose his subjective torments. Characters struggle to extricate themselves from suffocating mundanity, go mad when they discover the wadding is already within. He often strikes chords with characters outside their stage function, pleas and heartaches are expressed in language beyond the character's limitations as if some god were hereabouts, a rough deity directly in touch with the author. In the playlet (can't bring myself to call it a sketch) *The Invention of Morality* – which could be straight from a university drama competition on the one hand but his use of crassness saves it because the god is speaking – Flack, a security guard with wings, (not real ones but a metaphorical pair) pleads with a tabloiderthal colleague to break out of the prison which employs them:

> FLACK: …I can offer you nothing, nothing but your own freedom, your own agony. Think, if you can… Think, if you dare…

His answer is a head-butt – a blow not from an oppressive system but from the victim of an oppressive system who refuses to identify the force bleeding his brain white – the machines, the cameras, screens, loudspeakers which construct reality for us.

We are not threatened by this take-over, the playwright is saying, it causes no trepidation.

We are already inside it, looking outwards from the comfort of our surrender.

Having been tormented for thirty years by requests for one-line descriptions of plays and books written, life came much easier when approaching the five works in this volume. Thematic links are everywhere, the spider-mind at the centre of the web is knowable, his feelings frank within every paradox or contradiction he pursues. His concerns (ah, that word!) flash and rumble beneath that which sings and that which croaks – both being well represented in this selection.

Five Visions of the Faithful is a group of short plays delving into cruelty in all its guises; *Incarcerator* is a pastiche of a Jacobean verse revenge play set today with appetite as its target; *The Biggleswades* shows the married life of an obsessive, paranoid, dominant male who is terrified of the real world – including the reality of his submissive wife; *The Last Days of Desire* is a mock autobiographical dream of a terrorist playwright manipulated by the society he hates; *Silence and Violence* centres on a crazed megalomaniac couple ruling and ruining a country, who are screwing an image of themselves out of a heavily-abused sculptor.

All these plays are criticisms of what we might call love, or devotion, or passion, or commitment. However wrongly defined, in each case, because of greed or need or lust or sloth of soul, the love is hurtful to those in receipt. It is not love. It's a mess, a warping of truth, a pollution. If he weren't the playwright of the possible he is, shorn of all neatness and easy answers, his vision might roll up the future too much, bringing us overly close to our hypnotic, submissive suffering. But his zest for play and pitfalls is such, all I can do is look forward to what he makes of the rest of his writing life.

David Pownall
Guildford, 2001

INCARCERATOR

Characters

CHORUS
The Incarcerator

MORRIS
The Independent Man

JESSOP
The Lusty Youth

LIDDLE
The Innocent

SMITH
The Egotist

FISHER
The Frustrated Intellectual

Incarcerator was first performed at The White Bear Theatre, London on 6 September 1999. The cast was as follows:

CHORUS, Andy Hawthorne

MORRIS, David Hollett

JESSOP, John Lightbody

LIDDLE, Ben Casey

SMITH, Pauline Turner

FISHER, Lisa Reeves

Director, Peter Craze
Designer, Philippa Kunisch
Lighting, Mark Dymock
Sound, Derek Carlyle
Assistant Director, Hajdana Baletic

It subsequently opened at the Battersea Arts Centre, London on 16 January 2001, with the following changes to the cast:

CHORUS, Peter Kenvyn

LIDDLE, Nigel Barrett

SMITH, Sarah Edwardson

Designer, Mavis Howard
Composer, David Schweitzer
Assistant Director, Yael Shavit

First Prologue

The stage and auditorium are in total darkness. Soon, we hear footsteps down a corridor and the jangling of keys, the opening and then slamming of doors. The footsteps draw closer. Shouts. Keys. A door is unlocked and a thin strip of light floods across the stage. The shadow of the bars. The CHORUS, dressed as The Prison Officer, steps forward. He speaks in a slow, officious, monotonous drawl.

CHORUS: the inmates were lost
    at the time
    all were lost
    but some, they dared
    (or so it seemed)
    they were intoxicated
    by the taste of their own
    extinction
    they craved the stench then suffered
    alone
    underneath the smiling
    beyond the hacking laughter
    past the acquiescence
    and into...the pain

    the inmates were bewildered
    at the time
    but forging their groups
    they drowned out confusion
    (or so it seemed)
    they diluted it with friends
    and weekends away
    but some, they dared
    they rejoiced in anxiety
    revelled in the laugh's demise
    and fled the grasping hands
    of unity and
    meals for ten
    the inmates were despairing
    but many did not know it

they were distracted
at the time
from themselves
they left their homes
for comfort only
for entertainment only
but there were the few
but they were mistaken

their honesty for cruelty
their curiosity for self-loathing
their passion for insensitivity
their freedom-pangs for egotism
their silence for contempt
but there was contempt
contempt was all around
contempt it bled from the hearts of men
they were in contempt of themselves
at the time

the educators
communicators
disseminators
administrators
legislators
celebrators
but

the inmates were afraid
at the time
they trembled on the branches
of their lives
as the storms gathered
and the trees creaked
so they flocked together
at the time
and they sang
they sang to keep out the cold

the time itself was a sing-song time
a sing-song ding-dong clap-clap time
sing-song
sing-song
sing-song…

Scene One

JESSOP, in a state of panic, is changing into his wedding suit.
MORRIS, his best man, is watching him, lager in hand.

MORRIS: I tell ya, sunshine…fucking chill!
   You need to…
JESSOP: Fuck!
MORRIS: …calm down!
JESSOP: I will!
MORRIS: Your freedom's fucked but no-one's dead!
   No problem then!
JESSOP: Inside my head
   It feels like twenty voices scream:
   'Wake up, ya cunt! Don't live the dream!'
   I'm sweatin', mate! I'm shittin' rocks!
MORRIS: So cancel it!
JESSOP: Just…pass me socks!
MORRIS: A ring, a church, all blessed by God…
JESSOP: What time is it?
MORRIS: A firing squad
   Would shake a man up less than this!
JESSOP: I'm going for me umpteenth piss…
MORRIS: You infant!
JESSOP: (*Leaving.*) And so off I fuck!
MORRIS: I see the serpent Marriage suck
   The joyful juices from his heart,
   Now Cupid's loathsome, toxic dart
   Has pierced his breast, his youth is spent.
   Oblivious to Love's intent,
   Says 'Matrimony, bind these hands!
   I'll live a drudge to your demands!
   Shackle me! Denude my hopes!

Tether me with mawkish ropes!
Take my horizons, shrink them, please,
Into one room! You must appease
This selfless yearning for castration!
For servitude, emasculation!
For days of toil and nights of tension
...and saving up for that extension.'
This wretched tool, this creeping toad...

JESSOP: (*Entering.*) My bladder burns, but nothing's flowed.

MORRIS: Look, where's the father of the bride?
His shotgun's where?

JESSOP: The cab's outside!

MORRIS: Now listen, pal...just pause for breath
And think!

JESSOP: O, fuck!

MORRIS: It seems like Death
Has gripped you by the greasy nuts
And sapped you of your blood and guts
And now...

JESSOP: O, fuck! I hardly know her!
Who is she? Fuck!

MORRIS: Just take it slower!
It's just a day. A piece of paper.
Think of it as just...a caper.
A social custom, etiquette.
S'all bollocks, mate.

JESSOP: I'm deep in debt:
She's made me fork out seven grand!
Her daddy's skint!

MORRIS: Don't understand...

JESSOP: For string quartets, egg mayonnaise,
For salmon (smoked) and canapes,
For champagne, wine (both red and white)
And evening nosh by candlelight,
Some arsehole with his discotheque...

MORRIS: (*Offering beer.*) Look, have a...

JESSOP: (*Accepting.*)   I'm a nervous wreck.

MORRIS: You've borrowed from the bank more cash?
For fuck's sake!

JESSOP: Was a little rash!
  You've got to help me…
MORRIS: No can do…
  I bailed you…
JESSOP: I depend on you.
MORRIS: I lend you money every year!
  You owe…
JESSOP: Fuck me…I've got the fear.
  I promised her…
MORRIS: Just calm yourself!
  It's detrimental to the health
  Is all this stress!
JESSOP: I've…
MORRIS: Take control!
JESSOP: There's more fulfilment on the dole!
MORRIS: Just stop! Now think! What's happened, mate?
  You've changed, my son. You've changed of late.
  Where has he gone, that carefree cub,
  The life and soul of bar and club?
  Who'd break girls' hearts with just a smile,
  Who celebrated life? And while
  We other bastards sweated, schemed,
  You glided through your days? It seemed
  That God, his angels, Jesus Christ
  All wanted sex with you. Now, spliced,
  My friend, all that must stop.
  Some female's plucked you from the shop.
  Now, calm. That's it. Yes, have a breather.
  Those days are gone.
JESSOP: I won't deceive her!
MORRIS: Of course you won't. And nor you should.
JESSOP: I love!
MORRIS: I know…but weren't it good
  When, minted up, we'd prowl the night,
  And sniff out kicks and such delight
  As this rank place affords a lad?
  Those were the best days that we had:
  Like hawks, we'd first survey the scene,
  We'd pounce and then we'd reconvene

Next morning and discuss our kills,
Comparing notes.
JESSOP: Sad, childish thrills!
There comes a time for that to cease:
The loveless fuck, the girl as piece
Of passive flesh, the drunken spiel,
That spurting out of pain. I feel,
That now with her... It's more, it's love...
It's something I've been dreaming of
Since I was just a kid. No more
Foul fumblings on the floor,
No more cold nights on strangers' rugs,
And fake emotions fuelled by drugs,
No more false laughter, smiling, nodding
Just to get my desperate rod in!
I'm moving on, Stu. Moving out.
I'm growing up.
MORRIS: (*Aside.*) Just, hear him spout
That age-old lie, that lame excuse...
JESSOP: I'll put my life to better use!
MORRIS: Forget the debt then, seize the day.
You'd kill for her...?
JESSOP: O, I would slay
The man who dared to breathe
Unwholesome air on her! Unsheathe
My sword of honour, flashing keen,
Then hack the heart from out the fiend
Who'd threaten her with eyes of lust,
First slice his belly, then I'd bust
His teeth and gums, tear out his tongue,
I'd rupture kidney, puncture lung,
I'd gouge my eyes out with a skewer,
I'd drink the contents of a sewer,
I'd set my flesh and bone on fire,
Unclothed, I'd crawl across barbed wire,
I'd trample babies, OAPs
To place a plaster on her knees!
For her, I'd swallow powdered glass...

MORRIS: (*Aside.*) Perhaps he'd take one up the arse.

JESSOP: Her breasts could launch a thousand ships!
　　Her body! Christ, she does these strips,
　　These shows for me...they drive me wild,
　　She does the nurse, the nun, the child,
　　She does these voices, dresses up,
　　She dances just like this. I cup
　　A tit like this, our groins like so...
　　We fuck ourselves unconscious. O,
　　It's ecstasy, it's drugs, it's death!
　　I smell destruction on her breath,
　　I can't express...she is my life...
　　My soul, my heart, my flesh...

MORRIS:　　　　　　　　　　Your wife!!

　　(*A pause.*)
　　So come, dear friend, the hour is nigh:
　　You now must love...until you die.

Scene Two

A cell. Sparingly lit. The shadow of the bars. A bed with clothes lying on it. LIDDLE standing semi-naked. He is child-like, wide-eyed, in a state of excitement.

LIDDLE: No such thing as innocence. No such thing. I breathe... I breathe... (*Watches himself do so.*) A specimen in full working order. (*A pause. He begins to dress himself into jeans, T-shirt, jacket.*) No such thing as innocence. Freedom from...guilt. But this, this is safety, it's... But they're...ejecting me. Rebirth with a clean slate. I feel my way. From scratch. Inventing it only I... No such thing as innocence. No such thing. (*He stops. A silence.*) I have befriended the sun. The years I have watched her drift across the blue, watching her arc slowly upwards, minute by minute sometimes. Day after day and... Seasons and...the fall. Watching her fall. Watching the grace of it, knowing. That drift. That float. That... Timelessness...she's been a friend. At night, I'd wait for her return. Knowing that my birth approached with every… And now… The door of the cage is creaking open. I am cleansed. Washed of my sins and deemed fit to… Freedom. A member. I… (*Resumes dressing.*) A knight would, of course, have his squire. Polished armour, chain-mail. A spit and a rub. Ready to do battle. Fear in his bones but glory in his blood. A knight would have his squire, a knight would… Risking his life for a blush. For a look. (*He stands still for a while, deep in thought.*) I am a child. Only purer. A child…but more whole. I know nobody. I need nobody. I love… (*He resumes.*) No such thing as innocence.

CHORUS: (*As The Prison Officer, stepping out of darkness.*) What is liberty?

LIDDLE: The pursuit of happiness? (*The CHORUS laughs.*) The greatest happiness of the greatest number? (*No response.*) To take time over a crap? Read a magazine?

CHORUS: (*Helping him into jacket.*) There we go.

LIDDLE: The time to earn comfort, to hoard the fruits of your labour and…

CHORUS: Turn around.

LIDDLE: (*Doing so.*) The freedom to…to hold a woman, to…

CHORUS: (*After a pause.*) What then?

LIDDLE: (*After a pause.*) Love?

CHORUS: Confident?

LIDDLE: I think I stand every chance. (*After a pause.*) Peace? (*The CHORUS laughs again.*) To still the voices? To still the voices, my head soothed on the breast of a woman…

CHORUS: And money?

LIDDLE: Steal it?

CHORUS: (*Removing dust from jacket.*) Satisfaction through honest labour?

LIDDLE: I could become a prison officer!!

CHORUS: We wouldn't have you.

LIDDLE: Why not?

CHORUS: Too many questions.

LIDDLE: Too many questions… (*Thinks.*) See, I'm curious. I want…to know. I'm an infant. Ignorant infant. So far…so

far I am merely a reaction. This time…I want to know.
I'm innocent of life's…
CHORUS: No such thing as innocence.
LIDDLE: (*After a pause.*) No such thing.

Scene Three

SMITH stands before a mirror, giggling and preening in egotistical ecstasy with FISHER unhappily helping her into her bridal gown.

SMITH: My breasts are pert, my hair is neat,
    My peachy flesh is soft and sweet,
    My waist is slim, my hips quite broad,
    Was ever female so adored?
    My teeth perfection, glistening white,
    My belly smooth, my buttocks tight,
    My eyes are pools of liquid fire,
    I make men sweaty with desire.
    My perfumed skin a pure surprise,
    I love their gazes on my thighs,
    My shoulders neck are…
FISHER: Turn around!!
SMITH: In elegance, divine, profound.
    The pinnacle of womanhood…
FISHER: Listen, love, I think you should…
SMITH: I'm bashful, smutty, wild yet prim,
    I'll play both slut and cherubim.
    I'm innocence when that's required,
    (When not arousingly attired!)
    I'll laugh and fawn and flash my arse,
    As lusty youths display their brass,
    I'll lead them on then leave them short,
    Insisting that I can't be bought,
    Intoxicate them with a smile,
    A fringe-flick or a show of style,
    And now…
FISHER: You'll have to comb your hair!
SMITH: I'm crowned the Queen of Everywhere!
    A man who's handsome, young and doting…

FISHER: (*Aside.*) I'll split her skull for this foul gloating.
SMITH: ...is mine for keeps, to have, to hold...
FISHER: (*Aside.*) And shower her with plundered gold.
SMITH: Oh, darling, could this rapture be
 A gift from God? From Him to me?
 I feel so blessed, I feel such joy...
FISHER: (*Aside.*) They feed the dragon with the boy.
SMITH: That others live and never know
 This happiness, it grieves me so!
FISHER: (*Aside.*) And thus adieu to my fond hopes of love,
 As girlish laughter stupefies the mind
 Of man and reason leaves its dwelling-place,
 For lust to cloud the sense. O, flattery!
 False prophet who, with all its leopard stealth,
 Creeps up upon its unsuspecting prey
 And strikes. Its teeth clamped tight around the heart,
 It gnaws and sucks the blood of logic out
 And, in its stead, sends forth its rancid bile
 Of vanity and fakery! O, Christ!
 He's drunk with it and here resigns his life,
 Discarding truth for rutting in her bed,
 Rejecting friendship, intimate concerns,
 For idle babbling, baby talk and pats.
 Yet here am I, colluding in this game,
 With outworn camaraderie still bound,
 Now I...
SMITH: When looking on myself like this
 (I ask you not to take the piss)
 I'm not surprised that, since at school,
 I've always made the young bucks drool.
 I feel...turned on by my own form...
 I'm wet down there! I'm wet and warm!
 A lucky man is he tonight,
 Who'll haul this off and hold me tight,
 Who'll tear my bra off with his teeth
 And pulp and knead what's underneath,
 Who'll peel these stockings off and then...
 O, he's the merriest of men!
FISHER: I think...

SMITH: Please, darling, tell me true…
   (The truth is what is linked with you)
   Do you not think that he's a dream?
   The cream that's on the cream's own cream?
   The premium, the choicest cut,
   Sheer excellence in maledom?
FISHER: But…
SMITH: No buts! No buts where love's concerned!
FISHER: You know I…
SMITH: You who've not been burned
   By true devotion's scalding flame…
   O, bless you, babe…you're not to blame,
   But when you shine in love's delight
   You'll understand the sweetheart's plight:
   Sheer flawlessness, the lover's state,
   Just…quality…
FISHER: You might be late…
SMITH: The thought of him and his affection,
   His manners, his demure erection.
   The way it quivers, shy yet brave…
FISHER: (*Aside.*) And thus makes man the willing slave…
SMITH: I love to…
FISHER: Maybe we should go…
SMITH: A new life beckons!
FISHER: Maybe so.
SMITH: So, stand aside. I'm not afraid:
   A woman's born. Farewell the maid.

Scene Four

Outside. LIDDLE is squinting into the daylight, holding a small suitcase. He puts it down. Ponders the future. He is barefoot. The CHORUS, still as The Prison Officer, enters.

CHORUS: So…
LIDDLE: So.
CHORUS: Here we are.
LIDDLE: The end of the road.
CHORUS: The start of it.
LIDDLE: I shall miss you.

CHORUS: And I you. (*A pause.*) You will visit?

LIDDLE: Of course. (*A pause.*) Just look at that sky! Masses of it!

CHORUS: It's all yours.

LIDDLE: I could swim into it. Front crawl. Breaststroke. Dive under it. Drink it all in. (*A pause.*) I have grown... attached.

CHORUS: Nothing lasts forever.

LIDDLE: All good things come to an end.

CHORUS: Time waits for no man.

LIDDLE: (*After a think.*) A rolling stone... (*Breaks off in disgust.*)

CHORUS: Feel any different?

LIDDLE: (*After a think.*) Restored.

CHORUS: The first day of the rest of your life.

LIDDLE: Platitude, platitude...

CHORUS: Just a little coaching. A little preparation.

LIDDLE: (*Inhaling.*) Civilisation spread out before me.

CHORUS: Remorse?

LIDDLE: (*After a think.*) None.

CHORUS: Hatred? Anger?

LIDDLE: Not to speak of. You?

CHORUS: Rage unclots my blood. Dissolves the fat in my arteries.

LIDDLE: Think of me?

CHORUS: Often.

LIDDLE: Advice?

CHORUS: Don't believe in it.

LIDDLE: (*Decisively.*) Then I shall take it moment by moment.

(*A blackboard appears. The CHORUS begins writing with chalk.*)

CHORUS: (*At speed, as The Teacher.*) If you must talk to strangers, then please show that you care. Never bite the hand that feeds you. Be good, be polite. Always polite. Be nice. Nice. O, niceness, nice. Smile to hide your disgust. Drive on the left. Pubs close at eleven. Visit your mother. Forgive your father. Smile to hide your disgrace. Shake hands firmly. Look them in the eyes.

Never offend. Take care not to offend. Smile to hide your dissent. Work hard, be reliable and learn a few jokes. Tell a few tales and ask many questions, get them to talk and then smile to hide your disdain. Being evil, you must conceal. Blatant depravity will only alarm. You must conceal. Smile to hide your despair. (*LIDDLE practices his smile.*) Never look a gift-horse in the mouth. Do not walk by on the other side. Always count your blessings. One…two… three… four. One…two…three…four. (*More menacing, circling him, as The Sergeant-Major.*) You belong to an empire, one of the greatest empires the world has ever known and this empire did not grow out of nothing. It was made by your forefathers by dint of hard work and hard fighting, at the sacrifice of their lives…by their hearty patriotism. They say we have no patriotism nowadays, and that therefore our empire will fall to pieces like the great Roman Empire did, because its citizens became selfish and lazy, and only cared for amusements. I am not so sure about that. I am sure that if you boys keep the good of your country in your eyes…above all else!!…then she will go on alright. Shoulders back! Chest out! Shoulders back! Chest out! (*LIDDLE obeys.*) Stay alert to the pitfalls of the flesh and the evils of desire and you will find yourself grown into a fine…hefty…brawny fellow, accustomed to facing danger with a grin. With a grin. With a…grin!! (*LIDDLE grimaces at perceived dangers. A silence. The blackboard disappears. The Priest.*) May God go with you. (*A long silence as LIDDLE attempts to move.*)
LIDDLE: It's taking the first step…that's the hardest.
CHORUS: You are perfectly reconstructed.
LIDDLE: I am…attached I…
CHORUS: The only way is onward, go.
(*LIDDLE tries to put a foot forward.*)
LIDDLE: The future…begins…when…if…
CHORUS: Walk without thought. Let your instincts take over.
LIDDLE: (*On one foot.*) I am unable to…

CHORUS: This is your defining moment.

(*LIDDLE sways, unable to take a step. The CHORUS fades from view. LIDDLE, still on one foot, balances precariously. We hear wedding bells somewhere off. JESSOP bounds on, out of breath, covered in confetti, with suitcase. He swigs from a champagne bottle. He takes out his mobile and begins dialling. He stops when he sees LIDDLE and watches him with curiosity.*)

JESSOP: You alright?

LIDDLE: I feel a little…anxious.

JESSOP: You need a hand?

LIDDLE: Already I feel that the world is…what's the right word?…complicated.

JESSOP: Is that right?

LIDDLE: One would have supposed…and it's not something I have really given that much thought to… one would have supposed that something as seemingly simple as locomotion could be undertaken without quite so much…how shall we say?…without quite so much… deliberation.

JESSOP: Your leg fucked, is it?

LIDDLE: How, one is then inclined to ask, when the mind is assailed by so many uncertainties regarding the elementary process of putting one foot in front of another, how is it likely to operate when faced with the inevitable, the unavoidable confrontations with other creatures. The sizing up of other beings, the gauging of their intentions, if you will. (*He puts a foot out and prepares to take a step.*) Before, you see, it was merely a routine. Pacing around the yard, eyes on the heels of the man in front. We knew then that our circularities were meaningless and we counted down the moments, covering always the same bit of concrete, the same bit of shale. But things have changed. Already I feel the weight of the world bearing down upon me. (*A pause.*) Offer me a choice, I beg you.

JESSOP: (*Dialling.*) I'm busy.

LIDDLE: First things first then.

JESSOP: Heathrow.

LIDDLE: Sustenance.

JESSOP: We been waiting for ages. Ta.

LIDDLE: Succour. Shelter.

JESSOP: (*To LIDDLE.*) You sure you're…?

LIDDLE: And thank you, my friend. Thank you for your listening ear.

JESSOP: (*Exiting.*) Good luck.

LIDDLE: Such a nice fellow. There was something like kindness in his eyes. But now…yes. This. This. This is my defining moment. (*He stands, again on one leg, arms out, swaying.*)

Scene Five

FISHER alone, holding the bouquet. The bells ring close by.

FISHER: Dear Christ, dear Christ, what fraudulence is this?
A shameless, idle, narcissistic sham!
The vicar spews anachronistic piss,
Banalities disgorged *ad nauseam*!
While she, she simpers, simpers like a child,
She smiles and giggles coyly through her veil!
That organ droning out, I feel defiled…
Defiled by all these lies. Must life entail
Such agony? Yes, agony. And he,
Just stood there, grinning, vacant and bemused,
A cunt-struck hog, ensnared so easily,
Now doomed to live a life in pain, confused.
But I am free. Quite free. I know I can
Exist alone, heartwhole…without a man.
(*She exits.*)

Scene Six

SMITH and JESSOP on a beach. The sound of surf, seagulls etc. He sleeps.

SMITH: I love to lie upon a beach,
A dry white wine within my reach,
The sound of surf, the seagulls' swoop,

They dive and twist then loop the loop,
The sun's caresses, sand in toes,
This happiness just grows and grows!
I'm loved, I'm worshipped, I'm alive!
How other women can survive
Without the blessings I enjoy,
Without the house, the wheels, the boy,
Is quite beyond imagination,
Their lives sad puddles of stagnation:
No legs to flaunt, no looks to show,
No admiration...ever! No
Heads that turn in pubs and bars,
No lusty horns from pricks in cars,
No clothes, no flowers raining down,
No jewellery, no wedding gown,
No sex laid on when it's required,
The Gravebound they, the Undesired!
Poor wretched creatures! Suffragettes!
They boil and stew in their regrets,
As envy curdles through their veins,
They hiss and scratch and start campaigns,
Their passions always unrequited,
The Uninvolved, the Uninvited!
But me, Sweet Me, I'm full of lust!
My lover, though, is fit to bust...
I've fucked him raw and sucked him dry,
He must replenish his supply,
I've chewed his tongue and drunk his spit,
We celebrate desire! Submit
Us, therefore, if you will
To flaccid censure for until
That day our passion's spent
We'll fuck and fuck and fuck! Cement
Our marriage with this yearning,
And bollocks to your books and learning!
(*Rising.*) And now...I stand, this randy bitch!
One thing alone can soothe my itch!
(*Kicks JESSOP.*) Arise, arise...your damsel calls!

34

See where my good sir knight still sprawls!
A naked duel, a clotheless bout
Is on the slab!
JESSOP:　　　　My love, don't shout!
SMITH: Get on your feet, you piece of meat!
My hunger won't accept defeat!
So satisfy my appetite!
And stoke yourself up for the fight!
JESSOP: (*Rising.*) The ceaseless joys of panting youth...
SMITH: (*Aside.*) A man must suffer for the Truth.

Scene Seven

Various loud pub noises. The CHORUS as The Barman, polishing glasses etc.

CHORUS: I don't know what your problem is
your despondency is surely affectation
cheer up cheer up
smell the roses and smile
it's arduous to frown
so smile so smile
a little

I'd like to be an actor
but I don't know why
is it the love of applause
or some dazed perception of glory?
but where is my philosophy
my sanctuary
when the earth shifts
under my feet?
you need to get out more
live your life a little
cheer up cheer up
laughter is the best medicine
and the doctor cares
he cares
doesn't he?

aloneness they repudiated
they shouted it down with alcohol
...but the liquid evaporated
they flapped at it with reading
...but the knowledge was contaminated
their conspiracy of friends
...which disintegrated
sought refuge in memory
...but it faded
faded...
cheer up cheer up
cheer up cheer up
you need to get out more
you need to get out more
you need to get out more
you need to get out...
(*MORRIS enters.*)
(*As chirpy cockney.*) Awright, my son? Awright? Awright?
The usual, is it?
MORRIS: Course. Despite
The fact that drink's my curse.
It chains me 'ere.
CHORUS: Well, I've seen worse.
MORRIS: This piss-hole of the universe!
CHORUS: Fat fuckers who seek sanctuary
From this abyss, who come to me
Like orphaned babes in need of cheer,
Who long to simply disappear,
Who seek the void through wine and beer,
Who, crushed by life, bewildered, lost,
Upon the seas of heartache tossed,
Who, weighted down by paltry cares,
Or loneliness or dull despairs,
They crawl here from their stinking lairs,
And come for comfort liquefied,
They come to have their livers dried,
They come for frothy fun and then
They come to have their say. Poor men,
They come for company, collusion...

MORRIS: And you dish out this sweet illusion!

CHORUS: Indeed I do!

MORRIS: So fill 'er up!

CHORUS: He drinks the dregs of life's foul cup.

MORRIS: The day don't start until I sup.

CHORUS: He soothes the pain that gnaws his soul,
He longs for loss of self-control,
He aches for liquid self-esteem,
They drown in piss then drift downstream,
They...

MORRIS: Could we not please change the theme?
I come here for a quiet drink...

CHORUS: I merely wish to make you think...

MORRIS: You fleece us for these jars from hell,
Then take the fucking piss as well!

CHORUS: (Aside.) I'm never one to oversell!
This place, though...

MORRIS: Cheers.

CHORUS: ...it's such a dump.

MORRIS: I guzzle from your wooden pump,
And chew your nuts and smoke your fags,
And listen to your arsehole gags,
To eye up all potential shags
That often flit around these parts...

CHORUS: (Aside.) A weakness for stilletoed tarts
That flock to feast upon his loot,
Like vultures pecking at his suit!

MORRIS: This lonely bastard's institute
At least provides me with...

CHORUS: My friend,
You worry me. I can't pretend
It's otherwise. The things I've seen!
Your life an aimless, dull routine
Of alcohol. A libertine,
Who seems to live for sex and ale
And cash and sport. The Holy Grail
Of pleasures, fleeting. What of joy?
Of love eternal? Girl and boy
Together, sharing?

MORRIS: You annoy
 Me more like so I'm...
CHORUS: Think on this:
 Instead of pissed paralysis,
 Of loudmouthed leering every night,
 Of football beamed by satellite,
 Surrounded by such erudite
 And pudgy-bellied masterminds,
 These sub-moronic, drooling binds,
 Instead of strips of Turkish meat
 At closing time, which you excrete
 In lonely flats, the stale repeat
 Of sporty chat, of dull TV,
 Of sticky-paged pornography,
 Or tearful fucks which breed resent,
 A sweet existence could be spent
 Of mutual trust, of love, respect
 A burgeoning of intellect,
 Of home-cooked meals and, I suspect,
 A child or two to shape and mould
 Into the future. Growing old
 With dignity, simplicity,
 Protecting, nursing tenderly.
 A man is made through family
 A man is born...
MORRIS: You talk of love!
 You talk of chains!
CHORUS: I'm speaking of
 A change in lifestyle.
MORRIS: This is drink!
 And you're a barman, not a shrink!
 So, keep it shut! For I shall sink
 As much piss-poison as I please!
 I'll quaff until I'm on my knees
 And retching on your floorboards here!
 Love sucks!
CHORUS: I shouldn't interfere
 I know. It's just...
MORRIS: So much is clear!
 You talk of love!

CHORUS: I merely meant...

MORRIS: The married wanker's days are spent
In slavery, in self-negation,
A lifetime of asphyxiation,
Of pitiful emasculation.
Against his instincts he must live,
And from himself a fugitive.
Thus, in exchange for sex and meals
He is demeaned and thereby seals
His fate forever. Such ideals
Of enterprise, of challenge, fame
Are shattered and, each day the same,
He sadly shuffles t'wards his grave
With lowered head. I say... the slave
Who seeks out his own cell,
Who, shackled, spends his days in hell
Then shrugs, resigned, this fragile shell
Of family life his sole reward,
This man is death. Yes, plodding bored,
Bypassing risk and pain and lust,
They shit out offspring, bound and trussed,
Then hide in sheds.

CHORUS: So...

MORRIS: My disgust
For this conspiracy...
It leaves me breathless!

CHORUS: Obviously.

MORRIS: Twixt devil and the deep, blue sea
I must remain.

CHORUS: It seems that way.

MORRIS: So, no more talk of love!

CHORUS: Okay.

(*MORRIS exits.*)

(*Polishing glass.*) I am merely a provider of alternatives.
I feel it is a public service. I am concerned. I really am.
And hard it is in such a time as this to care about one's
fellows. I do love to see a bit of wriggle, though. I love
to see a man lash out. He runs a little wild, that one.
Holding on as long as he can. But the solitude, it bites.

It bites hard. In the end. (*A pause.*) Just as the poodle is
descended from the wolf, so we take the man and we
mould him to our needs. Ah, but...what comes here?
(*Enter FISHER.*)

FISHER: That I should feel and feel the pain I feel
 For such a worthless man. That I should love,
 And love the man I love! And this one life!
 Such misery I never could conceive,
 Such...hollowness. My thoughts all tend to him,
 Imagination conjures up such sights
 Of him and her! I must move on but how?
 How, when love is all we truly know,
 This true affliction all that lights the path...
 How then forget? How trust one's self again,
 Whose judgment seems so arbitrary and false?
 If love is dead then how does one survive?
 If love is dead, then what is there to trust?
 And could I be so wrong? He loved me, sure,
 As friends perhaps at first but signs there were
 That friendship moved to love, and love to...what?
 A child he is. A lovely, lonely child.
 Shall I then die without his tender lips
 Not ever touching mine? We had a love!
 Am I to live without him to my death?
 If love is dead... I can't withstand this pain,
 So now, within this breeding ground of grief,
 Fermented grape shall ease me to my bed.
 The devil take tomorrow. Red wine, please.

CHORUS: Cheer up, cheer up, cheer up, cheer up
 It might never 'appen, might never 'appen.
 Cheer up, cheer up, cheer up, cheer up
 It might never 'appen, might never 'appen.

FISHER: To be alone yet not to be alone,
 This is all I crave.

CHORUS: (*Pouring.*) Might never 'appen, might never 'appen.
 (*Enter MORRIS.*)

MORRIS: A toilet from the bowels of Hades!
 I had to use the fucking ladies!
 Puke on wall and mould on door,

40

With fag-butts floating on the floor!
What the fuck they pay you for?
CHORUS: A slopster, no. A barman, yes.
Quite simple.
MORRIS: It's a fucking mess
Out there. A damned disgrace!
A vile and loathsome, putrid place!
A swamp that... Don't I know your face?
Your what's-it's mate...?
FISHER: Don't talk to me!
Don't even dare to breathe...
MORRIS: I see...
FISHER: I'm here to drown my pain in wine
Alone!
MORRIS: Alright!
FISHER: So, fuck off!
MORRIS: Fine!
FISHER: I shun the fake, the asinine...
So, please!
MORRIS: My love...
FISHER: Don't My Love me!
You twat!
MORRIS: What stunning repartee!
CHORUS: What have you done?
MORRIS: I'm not to blame!
FISHER: You fucking men! You're all the same.
To you it's just a little game,
Like marbles, conkers or Meccano.
CHORUS: What she mean?
MORRIS: I'm fucked if I know!
FISHER: You're running scared from true affection!
You're cowards, liars.
MORRIS: Please, objection!
FISHER: Bound hand and fist to your erection!
MORRIS: Some of us can stand alone
And fight the fight!
FISHER: Like overgrown
Yet undersuckled juveniles,
You wink your winks and smile your smiles
And live like infants!

41

MORRIS: (*Aside.*)   She beguiles
   Me. Mesmerising!
   Christ, I'm sunk.
FISHER: And so, despising
   Men, their minds, their fickle hearts,
   I do declare…a new life starts:
   A life of…theatre, books, the arts!
   A life of study, solitude!
   A life that's mine!
MORRIS: If this is rude
   Then tell me, please, but…
FISHER: On your bike,
   You drunken…
MORRIS: Why do you dislike
   All men? Has someone done you wrong?
   Deserted you?
FISHER: Will this take long?
MORRIS: What sadness have you undergone
   To make you bitter, make you hate?
   You mustn't…
FISHER: Don't commiserate
   With me, you boy, you sheep, you lad,
   You trainee!
MORRIS: You just seem so sad,
   That's all.
FISHER: Don't patronise me… Dad!
MORRIS: You've come for company.
FISHER: What balls!
   I've come for this!
MORRIS: (*Aside.*)   Her spite enthrals
   Me.
FISHER: This alone!
MORRIS: Then why come here?
   Where death hangs in the atmosphere,
   Where piss-heads, in pursuit of beer,
   All belch their lives away.
FISHER: Please, go!
   Just leave me with my sorrows!
MORRIS: No!

FISHER: If I should die then who would weep for me?
    Who, with their bitter tears, would wet my grave?
    Whose life would shatter and by what degree
    Would others feel the loss? Would they engrave
    A platitude, a triteness on my stone?
    Some falsity churned out for lonely dead?
    'She died as she had lived: in peace, alone.
    God rest her soul forever.' Or, instead,
    Frail parents sighing, cursing at the strain,
    That all their joy should be concluded so,
    The thoughts and pleasures rotting with the brain,
    The essence of one life, one effort. Oh,
    That I, from all this anguish might find ease,
    And end my days in other lands than these.
    (*A silence. She finishes her drink and then departs. Another*
    long silence.)
CHORUS: Same again, my gawping friend?
    One more to make your gut distend?
    One more to…?
MORRIS: I am lost.
    I feel my spirit cracking with this flood
    Of longing. Woman! Woman! Woman!
    What have you done to me? Where have you gone?
    From what dark region have you come that
    Now you grace me with your presence here?
    See, I am cut and now my wretched soul
    Seeps out. It oozes like a slick onto the floor
    And shudders. She, on angels' wings, has flown,
    But left her imprint on my heart. Her voice
    Still ringing in my ears. I must depart
    And go to her. But what if she be cold,
    And my attempt at closeness be abjured?
    I'm sweating, shaking, panting with desire.
    My chest's in flames.
CHORUS: (*Proffering glass.*) So take a gulp!
MORRIS: She's turned my heart and soul to pulp,
    Her lashing tongue, her scorching eyes,
    They burn and blaze, dehumanise
    Me. I, unmanned, must take a breath!
    I feel me half in love with death. (*He exits.*)

CHORUS: As lager flows in golden oceans,
    I, alas, go through the motions,
    And serve a gagging multitude,
    With that which has been boiled and brewed –
    I revel in such servitude.

Scene Eight

SMITH, in bathrobe, is standing by a bed, on which JESSOP sprawls.

SMITH: This hankering! This throbbing zeal!
    This carnival of flesh! I feel,
    Alive! Alive! We two are one,
    And this our moment in the sun!
    He makes love like a Roman god,
    Such passion and such thirst. His rod,
    A stalk of lust, a sheer delight!
    (*Waking him.*) I'll want some more the same tonight,
    You tiger!
JESSOP: Surely, sweet, you jest!
    I need at least a fortnight's rest!
    You've ruined me! I'm ripped and raw!
SMITH: A honeymoon's created for
    Incessant nakedness and sex!
    We're bonding, darling!
JESSOP: Should I flex
    My mating muscle one more time,
    It's curtains!
SMITH: You are in your prime!
    You're ripe for plucking!
JESSOP: I'm still young,
    But this has aged me!
SMITH: Then your tongue,
    That like a lizard darts and flicks,
    Shall service me!
JESSOP: I'm twenty-six,
    But now a cripple here I lie…
SMITH: Ah, fuck you then!
JESSOP: Well, I can try
    But…

SMITH: Do you know how many men
  Would amputate themselves and then
  Would murder mothers to be here
  With me? Like this? A hemisphere
  Of frantic, wild, testosterone
  Would die for this!!
JESSOP: But...
SMITH: Had I known
  That impotence was all I...
JESSOP: What?!!
  I'm black and blue!
SMITH: My Lancelot!
  Just playing, babe. You have a snooze.
  I shall my own sweet self amuse,
  But think of you! My greatest lover...
  Almost. So...
JESSOP: You've had another
  Better? Have you? Tell me! Please!
  How many? Who?
SMITH: (*Aside.*)   I'm such a tease!
JESSOP: I cannot stand the thought...
SMITH: Relax!
JESSOP: You scratching other bastards' backs!
  You straddling them and grinding, oh,
  It stabs me here!
SMITH: Just let it go.
  It's over now.
JESSOP: The thought of you,
  With them inside...
SMITH: I never knew
  You had a problem...
JESSOP: Christ, it hurts!
  You ripping off their jeans and shirts,
  You, naked, writhing, carnal, hot
  With other men!
SMITH: Look, is it not
  A thing that's passed? I like to fuck,
  But now just you.

JESSOP: So, did you suck
   Them ever? Make them scream?
   Or did they… (*To self.*) Christ, my self-esteem,
   It plummets earthward. Did you moan,
   And smile and snarl and grunt and groan?
   How big were… Did they satisfy?
   Or were they…? Did you…? Maybe I
   Am as the rabbit to the ram?
   What size…?

SMITH: You want a diagram?
   Or shall I…?

JESSOP: No. Yes. I don't know.
   Just tell me, were they…

SMITH: Some like so!
   And some like truncheons, some like that!
   The athlete, the acrobat!
   From tip to base…from here to here,
   They'd plug and prod and persevere,
   They'd grind away until…

JESSOP: Enough!!
   You torture me!

SMITH: They'd overstuff
   Me with their love. They'd often…

JESSOP: Stop!

SMITH: And snake-like slither…

JESSOP: Let it drop,
   I beg you, please. I'll do my best.
   Just let me…

SMITH: Then I'll get undressed,
   And come to you, my husband dear,
   My poor, exhausted cavalier.

JESSOP: I love you, Vic. I really do.

SMITH: (*Aside.*) How sweet.

JESSOP: And I'll be faithful, true.
   I worship you. You're all I need.
   My loyalty is guaranteed.
   I'll never let you down, I swear.
   I love you like…

SMITH: And you'll take care
   Of me? Defend me? Love me?

JESSOP: Oh, by the sun that shines above me,
    You will never ever come to ill!
    There's not a man I wouldn't kill.
    You know that, love?
SMITH: And I'll stay true.
    I'll be the perfect wife for you.
JESSOP: Then kiss me. Let us always feel
    This passion.
SMITH: Boy… you have a deal.
    (*They kiss etc.*)

Scene Nine

A dark, rainy street. A wall. LIDDLE, alone and begging. A tin.

LIDDLE: I, the remnant. I, the slippery trash. The…
    superfluous man. Without training, without education…
    I crouch. I squat.
    (*Footsteps move from left to right, his eyes following them.*)
    The stare implores, the eyes meet in a clash of disgust,
    of mutual disgust. I, the shard. I, the singing fool with
    hands muddied, fingers yellowed, teeth blackened. I
    grope in the darkness…for choice. Choiceless, I drift…
    I float like the sun I…
    (*Footsteps move from right to left, his eyes following them.*)
    Something gnaws at the soul. Something…claws.
    There is an…ache…a…
    (*The sound of a coin dropping into a tin.*)
    How you spit! How you spit your self-loathing at me!
    Belched out of offices, farted out of factories… (*A pause.*)
    Honesty demands a downcast head and tear-filled eyes.
    (*Footsteps move from left to right, his eyes following them.*)
    The dictates of honesty, the…
    (*The sound of a coin dropping into a tin.*)
    You would nail me to this wall you…
    (*The CHORUS enters, as The Policeman. He shines torch.*
    He gives LIDDLE a wry look.)
LIDDLE: Got to start somewhere.
CHORUS: Your function?

LIDDLE: (*After a think.*) Massage?

CHORUS: Possibly.

LIDDLE: Can you help at all?

CHORUS: (*Bending knees in the time-honoured way.*) Self-reliance, lad. Self-reliance.

LIDDLE: Solitude was easier alone.

CHORUS: Make some friends, boy. Plenty of friends out…

LIDDLE: I know but…

CHORUS: Do not despair.

LIDDLE: But you said…

CHORUS: I said? I said?

LIDDLE: You said…

CHORUS: Irreverence, is it? A lack of respect?

LIDDLE: Not at all…

CHORUS: Don't answer back!!

(*A silence.*)

(*Quiet.*) Laugh.

LIDDLE: What?

CHORUS: Laugh, I said!

LIDDLE: Laugh?

CHORUS: Come on, lad. Come on! We don't have all night!!

(*A silence. LIDDLE attempts a laugh.*)

CHORUS: As if you mean it, boy!

LIDDLE: I can't I…

CHORUS: Laugh!!

(*A silence. LIDDLE attempts another more nervous laugh.*)
Do not laugh with anxiety! Laugh with your soul. Give your whole soul to me now in the laugh!

(*LIDDLE attempts again. The CHORUS takes out his truncheon menacingly.*)

LIDDLE: I need…help.

CHORUS: (*After a think. Dances stupidly, truncheon out. Sings.*)
Oh, a policeman's lot is not a happy one, happy one!
A policeman's lot is not a happy one!

(*A pause as he turns to LIDDLE expectantly. No response. Dances again.*)
A policeman's lot is not a happy one, happy one!
A policeman's lot is not a happy one!

(*A pause as he turns to LIDDLE expectantly. LIDDLE forces a laugh.*)
This will not do. This simply will not do.
(*LIDDLE stops. The CHORUS thinks.*)
An Englishman, a Scotsman and an Irishman all died and went to Heaven. Saint Peter greeted them and said to them, what kind of life have you led on earth? And the Englishman said…
(*LIDDLE forces a nervous laugh.*)
Not yet! Not yet! Not till I say! Not till I say! (*Pause.*) And the Englishman said…
(*LIDDLE forces another laugh. A menacing silence.*)
I shall go now. But when I return…I will be funnier and, rest assured, you will laugh. You will…laugh…along.
(*The CHORUS exits.*)
(*A silence.*)

LIDDLE: (*Syllable counting.*) Alone…all alone…forever alone.
In such…desolate days…I am always alone.
Cut off from the world…from the…discourse of man…
I feel all my life-juices…ooze down…the pan?
Like a…rudderless…ship on a colourless sea,
I drift with the wind…to the land…of the…of the free?
(*MORRIS enters, drunk. He sees LIDDLE and takes out money from his wallet. Taunts him.*)

MORRIS: Those days have passed when once I queued
In lines of loafers. Sad. Subdued.
Just waiting there to scrawl a name.
A nervous smile when my turn came.
That was my due. I staked my claim.
Self-conscious shuffles, eyes that said:
'We've only just got out of bed.'
An aimless tide of human fear,
Of stinking sweaters, soaked with beer.
Thinking: 'We're not really here.
It's just a phase we're passing through,
So bollocks to your interview!'
Such lethargy! Such wasted youth!
Such ignorance! And fear of Truth!
We fled from there with claw and tooth,

With cash for beer and fags each week.
Those days gone by were grey and bleak.
(*He slumps down next to LIDDLE.*)
But then...the Golden Age arose,
With opportunities for those
Who, not content to decompose
Before the TV every day,
Might, instead, come out to play.
And join the party in the street,
And say farewell to this defeat,
This sordid life, so incomplete!
(*The CHORUS now enters in Thatcher Mask.*)
CHORUS: One has no right to be content
And luxury's not heaven-sent,
So roll one's sleeves up! Knuckle down!
Off one's arse and sniff around!
Possibilities abound!!
MORRIS: (*Rising.*) So... out of jeans...
CHORUS: And into suits,
One sallied forth...
MORRIS: As new recruits,
With Bryl-creamed hair...
CHORUS: And polished shoes.
MORRIS: And into better times did cruise
Like warriors.
CHORUS: One's pores did ooze...
MORRIS: With hunger.
CHORUS: Pride.
MORRIS: We tripped on power.
CHORUS: One quickly scaled the Ivory Tower.
MORRIS: And such a sorry sight we saw:
CHORUS: One lived like that just years before!!?
BOTH: That stinking landscape of the poor?!
CHORUS: Obscurity one left behind
MORRIS: With all the stupid.
CHORUS: Weak.
MORRIS: And blind.
CHORUS: I, giant-like, the world did straddle.
MORRIS: I rode the globe without a saddle.
LIDDLE: The rest?

BOTH: Shit Creek without a paddle!

CHORUS: All dreaming, seeming broke and bored.

MORRIS: It's we who earn this just reward!
> For hours of toil...

CHORUS: And contribution!

MORRIS: Towards the Glorious Constitution!

CHORUS: One calls it Wealth Redistribution!
> (*The lady exits. A silence.*)

LIDDLE: Teach me then the ways of the world.

MORRIS: It is the mastery of solitude, friend. Of that I am certain.

LIDDLE: The mastery?

MORRIS: Wrestle it down. Bring it to its knees. Flip it on its back. And crush it.

LIDDLE: Crush the solitude?

MORRIS: Bring death into your life. Learn to die while alive.

LIDDLE: I see.

MORRIS: Remain alone. Steer a course between the pleasure and the pain.

LIDDLE: Yet I feel pain. It is starting to...let me find the right expression...it is starting to assert itself. And I thought...

MORRIS: Don't think. Learn to entertain.

LIDDLE: I am a beggar.

MORRIS: Sing, boy. Sing us a happy song.

LIDDLE: A song?

MORRIS: We all must work.

LIDDLE: (*After a think.*) But I...I...I do not love.

MORRIS: Then you are whole.

LIDDLE: But why must I work?

MORRIS: Money, old boy.

LIDDLE: Why do I need it?

MORRIS: Women, my friend.

LIDDLE: But why do I need them?

MORRIS: (*After a think.*) To keep out the cold. (*He exits.*)
> (*LIDDLE clears his throat.*)

LIDDLE: (*Nervously at first, without conviction, clapping hands.*)
> The more we are together, together, together
> The more we are together, the merrier we shall be,

For your friends are my friends and my friends are your
                                                    friends,
And the more we are together, the merrier we shall be!
(*A silence. Then the sound of a coin dropping into a tin. Soon
the coins are raining down. LIDDLE looks up in wonder.*)

Scene Ten

*JESSOP at work, behind his desk, listlessly tapping away at a VDU.
He continues for quite some time before it all becomes too much for
him. He screams with boredom and rage. He slumps on his desk. The
CHORUS appears from nowhere, now as The Firm's Man.*

CHORUS: It seems you have a problem, friend?
    You look...
JESSOP: You said you'd recommend
    Me for advancement, some promotion?
    I'm drowning here! I'm...
CHORUS: Such emotion!
    Really, please. No need to shout!
    Contain yourself, I beg...
JESSOP: No doubt
    You're doing nicely! Swanky pad
    In Putney, weren't it? Heard you had
    Yourself a nice new Audi?
CHORUS: I...
JESSOP: Deals sown up in China, Saudi...
    Fingers in assorted pies
    I'd heard, old chap.
CHORUS: Then you've heard lies!
JESSOP: I beg you, please...I need...
CHORUS: So loud.
    Decorum, friend.
JESSOP: Look, I'm not proud...
    I'm only asking what I'm due.
CHORUS: Just listen, please...
JESSOP: A pay-review,
    Another type of work, a change.
    A man's not born to rearrange
    This pointless bullshit on grey screens

And input data. It demeans
A fucker. Strangulation!
His life is leeched. Humiliation
Piled each day upon his soul,
Until he's broken. There's a hole
Right here. It's raw, it's aching.
Help me since my heart is breaking,
Breaking as my life sails by!
Christ, must I rot here till I die?

CHORUS: I sympathise with your complaint.
But the Samaritans we ain't,
However.

JESSOP: I'm in the red

CHORUS: But aren't we all?

JESSOP: Then p'raps I'm dead?
Cos this is never what I planned,
This drudgery.

CHORUS: Please understand...
Our business is to make hard cash
And not to make folk happy.

JESSOP: Smash
My skull then, chew my bones!
I can't keep up with Mr Jones!
I need more pay!

CHORUS: Well, that's a pity
As profits weren't...

JESSOP: This fucking city's
Let me down! I need a rise!

CHORUS: I'm sorry...

JESSOP: You legitimise
All forms of thieving, cheating, fraud,
But, smiling in your suits...

CHORUS: I'm bored
With this, I have to say.
If you don't like it here, don't stay.
You're just a pair of hands, that's all.
Your job a goodwill gesture.

JESSOP: Maul
Me, rip me, slice me, stab me!

CHORUS: Sorry, no...just doesn't grab me...
JESSOP: I've bought a house!
CHORUS: Congratulations.
JESSOP: I'm being buggered by inflation!
    Please...
CHORUS: I'm sorry...
JESSOP: Have a word
    With them upstairs?
CHORUS: A little bird
    Did mention...yes...a movearound
    Just might be in the offing.
JESSOP: Sound
    Them out then? Mention me?
    I'm really fucked!
CHORUS: Quite possibly.
JESSOP: Twixt you and me, I've just got wed
    And honeymoons... I mean, she's bled
    Me dry. I love her but...
    She's got these tastes. Though she's a cut
    Above your average wench...
    But how on earth I'm s'posed to quench
    Her thirst for love, her want, her need,
    Her man-consuming, violent greed,
    Her stamina...
CHORUS: (*Coughing.*) Now, that will do.
    We've wandered down that avenue
    Quite far enough. So, back to work.
    And tap away, you...office clerk. (*Exits.*)
    (*JESSOP resumes his fascinating task.*)

Scene Eleven

FISHER, at a table in a restaurant, alone and reading. A glass of wine before her. She reads for a time but her mind is restless. She puts book down. Sighs. Picks it up again. Reads for a while. Puts it down. She is disturbed.

FISHER: Oh, peace! Be still! Have done and let me rest!
    Like demons must you jabber in my brain?
    A thousand rasping whispers ebb and flow,

Returning all thoughts here. These words no cure:
The ceaseless pains of centuries of war,
The ruminations of the troubled mind,
Worlds word-painted by novelists long dead...
No remedy in this. What's this to me?
That masses suffered love or lonely lives,
That masses in their trenches wept and died,
That masses...God...I have so little time.
To live a life that's real is all I ask,
To feel the flesh that breathes beneath the mask.
(*Weighed down by shopping bags, SMITH enters and greets
her, before taking a seat.*)

SMITH: Oh, darling, babe...what's on your mind?
　　Cheer up, my sweet...

FISHER: (*Aside.*)　　　　O, womankind!
　　That you should...

SMITH:　　　　　Thought I'd find you here!
　　It's lovely. Quaint. Quite...

FISHER: (*Aside.*)　　　This veneer
　　Of courtesy must...

SMITH:　　　　　　...continental.
　　Lee loves his grub all Oriental.
　　But give me Paris, give me Rome!
　　Yes, give me class!

FISHER: (*Aside.*)　　　This gastronome
　　Who's spent her life in burger joints,
　　Who's sold herself...

SMITH:　　　　　He disappoints
　　Me...

FISHER: (*Aside.*) Masquerades now as some queen
　　Of taste.

SMITH: (*Opening bag.*) Now have you ever seen
　　A pair of shoes so debonair,
　　So stylish and so chic?

FISHER:　　　　　(*Aside.*) Despair
　　Now pulses through my weeping bones,
　　It's choking me.

SMITH:　　　　And look...
　　(*She takes more things out and witters and giggles to herself
　　throughout this next.*)

FISHER: She drones
    On with such… Oh, that I
    Should lose in love to such a one as this!
    She robs me of my solitude and love
    She murders. Her smiling… God, her laugh!
    Dissembling, you must cease for time is short,
    Each passing moment sucks us to our graves.
    Be truthful, say! Be truthful! End this sham!
    And yet she loves me. Me she loves, she needs!
    But, God…to rid myself forever from her grasp.
    So why this conscience binding me? Oh, please!

SMITH: …I've always loved these dungarees!
    Just for schlepping 'bout the house…
    There's Donald Duck and Mickey Mouse!
    And look at this! It's such a snip…

(*Change to JESSOP and MORRIS in an Indian restaurant. Appropriate music. JESSOP has a letter.*)

MORRIS: For fuck's sake, matie…get a grip!
    And let me look…

JESSOP: The fucking bank…
    They're joking, right? A schoolboy prank
    To get me panicked, make me sweat.
    They're evil cunts!

MORRIS: A debt's a debt.
    And you're not paying…

JESSOP: Listen, Stu…
    I don't know what the fuck to do:
    They say me heart's not in me job,
    Which I confess, but I'm no slob…

MORRIS: Of course you are!

JESSOP: I never shirk!

MORRIS: Like chalk and cheese are you and work!

JESSOP: I ask for more…they give me less:
    A part-time post!

MORRIS: (*Reading.*) They'll repossess.

JESSOP: So help me, please!

MORRIS: You're in the shit.
    There's no two ways about…

JESSOP: Permit
    Me, Stu…to beg a favour!

MORRIS: (*Aside.*) Beware of Wedlock the Enslaver.
JESSOP: I beg you...lend me five, six grand?
   You're Mr Wedge!
MORRIS: Lee, understand:
   You owe me three from last New Year.
   I stand your curries, stand your beer,
   Your friendship doesn't come so cheap.
JESSOP: I'm shaking here...I'm losing sleep.
   I beg you, friend! I'm on my knees.
   Advise me!
MORRIS: How? I can't.
JESSOP: Christ, please!
   There must be something...
MORRIS: Your wife's mate.
   You know her?
JESSOP: Yeah?
MORRIS: I want a date.
   (*A pause.*)
JESSOP: A date?
MORRIS: A date. And then we'll see.
   If you can pimp her out to me,
   If you can play the go-between
   Successfully...
JESSOP: Have you not seen
   Her? Seen her furrowed brow?
   She's not for you...
MORRIS: Look, anyhow...
   If you can...
JESSOP: I say, look elsewhere!
   She's trouble, Stu. She's...
MORRIS: I don't care.
JESSOP: She's well fucked up, a misanthrope,
   She's full of rage, a lost cause.
MORRIS: Hope,
   They say...it springs...
JESSOP: She's mad!
   She spits at love...
MORRIS: I've never had
   A feeling quite as strong as this
   For anyone. Love's precipice,

Which I have spurned, which I have shunned…
Which now I'm falling through. Outgunned
Completely… I'm a child.
She makes me timid she's so wild.
She's the one. I tell you, Lee.
That woman is the one for me.
So set us up, eh? Pull some strings?
Females are such special things…
She might prefer the subtle tack.
Though I shall have her…on her back.
(*Change to FISHER and SMITH in the restaurant. SMITH is still showing off her purchases. FISHER the picture of misery. The CHORUS as The Waiter standing by.*)

SMITH: …it's just you always seems so blue!
I'm worried, Lor. I fear for you!
Your head forever in your books…
You've got the brains, you've got the looks
So advertise them! Take more care!
You need more body in your hair.
There's beauty in your cheeks, your eyes,
You need to draw it out. Disguise
That blotch with rouge or cream
Since men like girls with self-esteem,
Who hold themselves with ease, with grace.
Don't end up on your own.

FISHER: (*To CHORUS.*) The plaice,
Please. And some garlic bread.

SMITH: To tell the truth, I have this dread,
This dread of being left alone…
And Lee, he's such… If I had known
How much he worries…

CHORUS: (*French.*)   And for you?

SMITH: Six months with him… (*To CHORUS.*) I'll have
                                    that too.
Just six months married…how he moans!
'A man's not made of gold,' he drones.
'We need to plan the future. Save.
'We need to get ahead.' I crave
More…playfulness, more joy, more zest…

I feel so shackled, so repressed.

We argue all the time. It's him!

He's such a… Well, you know how grim

He gets! How full of fear…

FISHER: (*Aside.*)   Dear Christ, she's vile. So insincere.

SMITH: 'The office, love, it's killing me!

I'm just too tired for love.'

FISHER: I see.

SMITH: Rolls over, farts then goes to sleep.

You think I'm in a bit too deep?

But, no, I love the title: 'Wife.'

(*Toasting.*) To Marriage and the Married Life!

(*Change to MORRIS and JESSOP, numerous empty pint glasses before them on the table, very drunkenly surveying menus. Their heads are dropping and they laugh wildly.*)

JESSOP: Right then…mine's a sheek kebab with a tasty
                                                                keema nan.

And a Chana King Prawn Special.

MORRIS: I'm a chicken tikka man!

A dozen spicy papadums…

JESSOP: With all that pickle shite!!

MORRIS: And pilau rice.

JESSOP: We'll have that twice!

MORRIS: A meal by candle-light.

It's tremendously romantic but the music's far too low…

(*Calling off.*) Can't you turn this bollocks off!?

JESSOP: (*Calling off.*)   And stick on Status Quo?

MORRIS: Or something like The Rolling Stones?

JESSOP: What about… Nirvana?

And two pints of the Elephant!

MORRIS: A Murghi Lamb Masala!!

JESSOP: This is a 'Taste of India'. The ambience must be
                                                                        right.

To recreate the Orient.

MORRIS: Don't give me all that shite.

JESSOP: And shall we share a vindaloo?

MORRIS: Let's have a phall, you queen!

I'd like to burn my balls clean off!

JESSOP: That's cooked with gasoline!

MORRIS: So...try me, dear!

JESSOP: And two meat phalls! With that aloo gobi stuff!

MORRIS: You hail from Ethiopia? Don't you think we've
                                                  got enough?

JESSOP: And Sag Paneer, Paswari Nan, boiled rice and
                                                  bombay duck!
     Plus six onion bhajis.

MORRIS: Fuck, my bowels are panic-struck!

JESSOP: 'Scuse me, bud...I'm fucking parched...I'm
                                                  gagging for a lager!

MORRIS: (*Aside.*) As life creeps on its petty pace...This
                                                  pointless, pissed-up saga.

Scene Twelve

*A park. Birdsong etc. LIDDLE sleeps on a bench. He wakes. Stretches.
He takes out polythene bag from his pocket. He takes some slices of
bread out and breaks pieces off. He throws one or two into the audience.
The sound of ducks frantically feeding. It dies down. He throws more
bread. More duck noises. Presently, SMITH approaches, at the end
of a run. She is exhausted and sweating, with Walkman wired up.
She begins to do her stretching exercises, her head bobbing to the
music. He watches her.*

LIDDLE: Is this then the cause? The cause of it all? (*He
     watches.*) The flexible spine, the muscles sliding over
     each other? The sweat glistening in the morning sun?
     Here. Now. Each moment, an opportunity lost. A
     moment, a moment of youth she...luxuriates. Perfection
     only... And all this belongs to another? What is he that
     I am not? (*He watches.*) And what does she think? What
     ideology guides her?
     (*Eyes closed and concentrating, he tries to get inside her head.
     Violent and pounding electronic music suddenly reverberates
     all around. LIDDLE sits rigid and tries to free himself. After
     a mental struggle, the music fades out. Oblivious, SMITH
     continues.*)
     The dance of her soul. (*A pause.*) I could swim with her
     in a sea of truth.

(*SMITH now sits beside him and takes a bottle of water from her back-pack. She drinks. He watches her. She is eventually unnerved by his stare and turns. He smiles. Her head is still bobbing to the music. They stare at each other. He slowly reaches out and removes her earphones. The sound of birdsong is amplified. It fades back. A long silence. She seems drawn to him.*)

SMITH: Speak.

(*There is no response.*)

Please. Speak.

Scene Thirteen

FISHER and JESSOP. He follows her as she walks away.

JESSOP: ...hard-working, rich, good-looking, young,
　　　He's in demand. He's quite well-hung,
　　　(He tells me.) Look, it's just one night.
　　　I promised him. He's nice, polite,
　　　He says he's got this thing about you,
　　　Says he just can't live without you!
　　　So...Laura, look! A favour, please.
　　　I'm swinging on this high trapeze
　　　Without a net. He's not so bad.
　　　He's loaded, love. Don't look so sad...
　　　Please, Laura...look...You're helping me!
　　　We're mates, I thought? Old Lor and Lee?
　　　Remember? Pals? From childhood days?
　　　We played in dens like castaways,
　　　We shared so much! We...

FISHER: 　　　　　　　　Christ, no more!
　　　You torture me! And now you'd farm me out
　　　To lonely friends. Is this how much you care?
　　　This child who I have listened to with love
　　　For all these years! Say what became of him?
　　　That blue-eyed boy, that giggling, fearless boy,
　　　For whom each day meant wonder and delight,
　　　For whom a minute felt like days or weeks,
　　　For whom each breath was promise of more bliss.
　　　What happened then? To fall from that to this?

JESSOP: They're sending letters, constant threats:
    A man has rights when free from debts.
    Until such time he's just a slug
    That's sliding down the hole he's dug...
FISHER: No more of this.
JESSOP: I've lost control!
    There's something chewing through my soul.
    Some tumour spreads beneath my chest,
    A constant ache. I feel oppressed
    By everything! I'm sinking fast!
    The Devil has my life. He's cast
    Me down. I burn in hell!
    I burn for love!
FISHER: I burn as well!!
    Yet you, yet you from self-regard are blind,
    You turn your back on truth and now you gag,
    You gasp for breath, you choke as choke you must,
    For butchering all hope! I'm tired of this.
    No more, no more. The game is up for me.
JESSOP: I beg you, Lor! I beg you, please!
    One evening of your life to ease
    The mounting troubles of your friend!
    One evening, please! Can I depend
    On you? He'll call tomorrow.
    Cheers, my love. (*Exits.*)
FISHER: And thus my sorrow
    Deepens. I bury now the corpse of love.
    The rotten corpse that putrifies and stinks,
    I tread the earth upon its fetid grave!
    From this day forth I disavow all hope!
    From this day forth I live my life alone,
    From this day forth I fly as free as air,
    Self-preservation be my only guide.
    Love cracks and splits then seeps away inside.

Scene Fourteen

LIDDLE and SMITH stare at each other. They seem unable to speak. After a time:

LIDDLE: These are only words, I know. But, in the final analysis, it seems that words are all we have. You see, the feeling I have here…and here…as I look into your face… I seem to…it is such a… Perhaps if I looked at it from a biological perspective, maybe that…? My body is signalling something, I… The animal in me calls to the animal in you…but it is… I feel a sweat and a shiver. Like a disease. Yet it is more than desire. Desire, yes… but more… Not so…not so elemental. It has a permanence. A timelessness, yes… Yes. But perhaps I overanalyse? God, do I have to deconstruct everything? No. No. It is simply this. (*A pause.*) I…love you.

SMITH: You what?

LIDDLE: Beyond the mere bestial stirrings of the loins, beyond the need for conversation.

SMITH: You don't know me…

LIDDLE: I look into your eyes and I know that I love. I do not know you. I do not need to know you. This moment now. I feel… I could look into your face forever. You are so…so extraordinarily beautiful.

SMITH: I…

LIDDLE: I offer you myself. I have nothing. I am nothing. Only…

SMITH: Who…? Why…?

LIDDLE: This is something beyond rationality, beyond the confines of cold logic. We do not need display, we do not need to compare our personalities. Let us be brave, my love. Brave. Leap into the unknown, leap into me. Be lost in me as I shall lose myself in you. We will live a life of mutual understanding and there shall be such deep and loving silences that will fall between us. Often they…

(*A deep and meaningful silence. They stare.*)

SMITH: Your face is so…

LIDDLE: My kisses will be worshipful, my love will shine forever.

SMITH: I feel like…
LIDDLE: You feel?
SMITH: Like a child I…
LIDDLE: Yes?
SMITH: You are…gentle.
LIDDLE: You feel like a child? I also. Always.
    (*A silence.*)
SMITH: (*Quiet.*) Will you hold me?
LIDDLE: You are so…so beautiful.
SMITH: Please.
    (*He opens his arms slowly, uncertainly. She slowly and shyly walks towards him. They are close. They stare at each other. She rests her head on his chest. He encircles her with his arms.*)
    (*Softly.*) Thank you I… Thank you. Thank you.

Second Prologue

The park. Birdsong. The CHORUS, as The City Gent, sits on a bench, behind his Financial Times. He is no poet.

CHORUS: time is a tramp
    which, like a fat hag in the… (*thinks.*) damp
    with bags by her side,
    dawdles on
    muttering curses
    now the urge of the unborn
    whispering through brains
    demanding their day
    their day in the… (*thinks.*)
    sun

    time is… (*thinks.*) a drunk
    which lurches and staggers
    from tree to tree.
    now the inmates multiply
    they bless the earth
    with replication
    more of the same

if you please
more of the same
they proceed
manacled by others'... (*thinks.*)
need

time is... (*thinks.*) a whore
which, exposing its bruised white flesh
to pot-bellied men,
rots on its stalk.
and some
where they ran raw
and bleeding from
dream of return
but looking down
is never wise
keep your eyes
fixed above you
look to the... (*thinks.*)
skies?

time is...time is...
oh, what is...time?
what is time?
now babies in their bunks
demand their stories
meaning is craved
the moral is given
like liquidised meat
it drips from their lips
they wake in the night
and are sung back to sleep
since mummy knows best
yes mummy knows best
your mummy knows
best
(*SMITH enters, pushing a pram. The set-up for.*)

Scene Fifteen

*SMITH stands looking lovingly into the pram. She has matured a
little. The CHORUS, still as The City Gent, looks up occasionally
during the following.*

SMITH: When I, midst cupboard, kitchen top and shelf,
    For arid, dragging hours on end alone,
    Whenever I in sadness curse myself,
    And then this uneventful life bemoan,
    Should Fairy Liquid, Flash or Harpic start
    To fill me with a sorrow stained by bleach,
    Then, inwardly, I gaze toward my heart
    And find a love no mortal can impeach.
    Let others fret, let others save the earth,
    Let others chew their fingers to the bone,
    Let others prove to others what they're worth,
    Let others charter territories unknown.
    For I with you am raised above such things:
    Such wealth as this makes paupers out of kings.
    *(The sound of canned laughter hovers in the air. She freezes.
    It fades.*
    *LIDDLE, more dirty and ragged than before, enters and
    watches the happy mother, as she coo-coos and baby-wabies to
    her offspring. Unnoticed, he walks up behind her. After a
    while:)*
LIDDLE: Please…don't fill its mind with such things.
    (SMITH turns in alarm.)
    So young, so young and so innocent. Dependent on you
    for…and already you start.
    (SMITH is in a state of shock.)
    You will allow me to look?
    (He peers into the pram.)
    The smile is good. The smile is already in place.
    *(He scrutinises the baby, whilst she watches him with
    uncertainty.)*
    It is mine? *(No answer.)* You have chosen to exclude me
    but part of me remained. *(No answer.)* This is my child?
    (No answer. He looks at her.) I have been thinking of you.

Since that day. (*No answer.*) You never returned. (*No answer.*) I wanted to thank you. (*No answer.*) You moved me on. You...unshelled me a little you...(*No answer.*) Yet you never returned. You never returned and I feel...well, it's here. And here. Even before the moment our lips touched and then parted, I loved. When our tongues I... You... I wanted to thank you. I wanted to...but you never returned. I have never...I had never...I should like to kiss you again...to make love with you...again. (*No answer.*) I should like to... (*A pause.*) This child, is it mine? (*No answer.*) Is it my own? (*He looks back into the pram. He seems moved.*) My heart...my soul is... my heart is punching through my chest, my...soul is lashing about, lashing about like an eel, like an eel in a bucket. My eyes are heavy, as if they would burst with... (*No answer.*) This child...is it mine?

SMITH: (*After a pause.*) I don't know... (*She makes to go.*)

LIDDLE: Stay.

SMITH: I must...

LIDDLE: We three...

SMITH: No!

LIDDLE: Why? (*No answer.*) Please, why?

SMITH: (*Looking him up and down in disgust.*) You are so... You are too... (*She hurries off. LIDDLE makes a move after her and then stops. He is in some anguish.*)

LIDDLE: Ah...she is like... I must have... (*He holds his chest as if to contain the pressure.*) No! I... To touch...to hold...Jesus... (*He sinks to his knees.*) Ah, her skin! The smell of her flesh! That flesh! And I love! God, how I love! How I want! But I am...innocent...oh, innocent...

CHORUS: (*Reading aloud, matter-of-fact.*) We are the progeny of killers. It's official.

LIDDLE: ...and the death of it all and the...

CHORUS: (*Shaking head.*) Genocide upon genocide upon genocide...

LIDDLE: And the ache of the flesh...and this unending loneliness...

CHORUS: So that we may live...

LIDDLE: And that child, so defenceless...

CHORUS: It seems we stole land…
LIDDLE: A wide-eyed pup so…
CHORUS: It seems we stole food…
LIDDLE: A grinning whelp and so…
CHORUS: And also lives…we stole lives it seems…
LIDDLE: …irreproachable of…yet…
CHORUS: (*Taking sandwich from lunchbox.*) But we must all rest easy now.
LIDDLE: …there is something inside…
CHORUS: (*Eating happily.*) What's done is done.
LIDDLE: …I feel it inside.
CHORUS: The walls are secure and the living is easy.
LIDDLE: Is it love or…?
CHORUS: And the chains do not chafe. They do not chafe at all.
LIDDLE: Is it violence or…?
CHORUS: (*Breathing in deeply.*) It's a beautiful, beautiful, beautiful day! Let us sing then in celebration. (*He clears his throat. LIDDLE on his knees in anguish.*)
O, what a beautiful morning!
O, what a beautiful day!
I've got the funniest feeling
Everything's coming my way!
(*Birdsong continues for a while as The CHORUS accepts some imagined applause.*)
I thank you…I thank you. No, really, please…
(*The CHORUS then stands and removes from his briefcase a white coat and stethoscope. He addresses the audience and walks across the stage to where MORRIS is now discovered, pacing with some agitation. This is the set-up for:*)

Scene Sixteen

CHORUS: I ask you now to change the scene
But use me as your In-Between,
As presently I don this coat,
Dispensing pill and antidote.
A doctor, yes. This suits me well.
A man of medicine…can't you tell?

This mere stage is my domain:
The enemy of death and pain.

MORRIS: Dr Simpson?

CHORUS: Mr Morris, now we mustn't mess about.

MORRIS: I don't think I can handle this.

CHORUS: Would you take your penis out?

MORRIS: I can't expose my member to a stranger just like that!

CHORUS: Mr Morris, please remember...

MORRIS: ...cos I feel like such a twat!

CHORUS: ...judging by the symptoms the disease that you have caught

Is by exposing...

MORRIS: Dr. Simpson!

CHORUS: ...it more often than you ought.

MORRIS: It started 'bout two weeks ago when I woke to find a pain
So unpleasant in my privates that I snorted some cocaine.
I dangled them in alcohol and smeared them with Deep Heat.
(Bet they could hear me screaming in the shops across the street.)
The pain defied description and the trauma made me weep,
Like salt on open wounds it was. I drank myself to sleep.

CHORUS: This organ, sir, it seems to be a symbol in itself:
It's riddled with infirmity...(*Aside.*) Just like the country's health.
Such genitals I've never seen, so pitted o'er with scabs:
Your testicles are turning green.

MORRIS: It's something worse than crabs?

CHORUS: Oh dear! Oh dear!

MORRIS: So, what's up doc?

CHORUS: Your sexual glands are rotting.
Boils are running chockablock past scrotum up to bottom!

MORRIS: So, give me ointment! Give advice! Get this awful pox off!

CHORUS: The best thing, mister, is... think twice before you get your rocks off! (*Exits.*)

MORRIS: My knackers are on fire! It seems they're burning
from within,
And the only way to kill the pain is drown myself in gin
Or snort up all my profits and lobotomise my brain,
I crave a sweet unconsciousness. Paralysis beats pain.
It seems as well that light relief from all this dreadful woe
Can be gained by having sex or masturbating so
I've dipped my wick unfettered into everyone I can
Into Cindy, Carol, Jackie, Lucy, Pippa, Marianne,
Mary, Maureen, Beccy, Sandra, anyone that's game…
And there was a tubby schoolgirl but I never asked her
name.
Totally anonymous and over in a flash…
And for all of fifteen seconds I forgot this fiendish rash.
So until this dickhead doctor here restores my damaged
pride
I must postpone the paradise of servicing my bride.
(*The CHORUS re-enters with a clipboard.*)
CHORUS: Your case is one, we all agree,
Of some immense perplexity.
It's sort of quasi-syphilitic,
The fungus strangely parasitic,
The like of which we've never seen:
Shingles, scurvy cum gangrene.
MORRIS: There really has to be a cure!
I long for tackle fresh and pure!
CHORUS: The closest illness to your pox
Is in a type of Arctic ox…
It's not unlike Mad Cow's Disease:
It eats you from inside.
MORRIS: Oh, please!
You have to dish out something quick!
You're paid, I think, to tend the sick?
CHORUS: I'm baffled, I'm afraid, my friend,
And all that I can recommend
Is abstinence from sex. I think
You also should lay off the drink.
MORRIS: You'd rob me of the one great pleasure
With which I fill my days of leisure?

And booze is such an anaesthetic.
Sobriety is so...synthetic!
CHORUS: Otherwise just hope and pray
That this foul ailment goes away.
And if your mental functions fail,
Your anger builds, your breath grows stale,
Your speech starts slurring, passion surges;
You can't control your violent urges,
Then God be with you and your kind:
To slow destruction be resigned.
MORRIS: (*Aside.*) I'll tempt and taunt this thing called Death.
I'll scorn it till my dying breath!
CHORUS: One more thing...the tests we ran...
MORRIS: Misfortunes without end?!
CHORUS: Show... you are a sterile man.
MORRIS: (*After a pause.*) I must misapprehend!
CHORUS: A sperm count of the lowest kind.
MORRIS: My manhood is in doubt?
Masculinity undermined?
CHORUS: A spermatozoa drought.
MORRIS: A seedless grape?
CHORUS: You're firing blanks!
MORRIS: No fatherhood for me?
CHORUS: Nature says to you: 'No thanks. Don't want your
progeny.'

(*The CHORUS exits.*)
MORRIS: My bonfire's well and truly pissed on.
But there's one thing I do insist on:
I will never change my wicked ways
Despite the hell of this malaise.

Scene Seventeen

*JESSOP anxiously circling a desk. He is looking round the room,
which belongs to The Bank Manager.*

JESSOP: It's nice in 'ere! So fucking nice!
And fucking cheap at half the price!
A nice computer, banker's chair,
That scent of violence in the air!

(*The CHORUS as The Bank Manager appears unseen.*)
(*Picking up photo frame.*) Ah, a photo of his fucking kid!
So well-fed, fat. And God forbid
That he should lose his residence!
This freckly fucker! We, in tents,
Will beg for coins as Daddy passes
In his Merc! These little arses!
'Father, I should like these shoes,
This school, this car!' They schmarm and schmooze,
And Ma and Pa just rain it down
On fat-faced Freddy! I could drown
This brat, this ginger nonce,
This speccy, spoilt and smirking ponce,
Drown him, wipe off that fat grin
With head-butts, knuckles. Scar his skin
With knives and razors, fangs and teeth,
I'd peel it off and, underneath,
Where pulsing muscles, throbbing fat
And tissues twitch, I'd…
CHORUS: (*Sitting.*)   Thanks for that.
I'm sure my boy, though barely eight,
Has not deserved to draw such hate
From strangers yet?
JESSOP: It's just my joke!
He looks a nice and playful bloke,
A freckled, ginger ray of fun,
A cheeky smile.
CHORUS: My youngest son.
We're very proud.
JESSOP: I bet you are!
CHORUS: On Harrow's list.
JESSOP: The fond papa!
(*The sound of canned laughter hovers in the air. They freeze.*
It fades.)
Oh, he'll do well. He's got that look!
The glasses, see? He likes a book,
I bet?
CHORUS: A sportsman too.

JESSOP: Ah!

CHORUS: Midfield but he scores a few.
    A good left foot, tenacious, strong
    We're very proud.

JESSOP: It can't be wrong
    To hope your child does…

CHORUS: (*Examining papers.*) Let me see…
    It's Mr Jessop…?

JESSOP: Yep, that's me!
    See, as I say, I used to play…
    Centre-forward but…

CHORUS: Okay!
    Now…yes, it seems that you're the sort
    Who like their dwellings free?

JESSOP: I thought
    That we'd agreed…

CHORUS: Now, we've been kind.
    We've waited patiently. Declined
    Our rights to repossess…
    I have to say though, nonetheless,
    The time has come to…

JESSOP: Hear me out!
    Unless you want a bloodied snout!!
    Just joking, no… Look, listen, please!
    (*Genuflecting.*) No pride, see? Look, I'm on my knees…
    I need two months, I've done the sums!
    Two months!

CHORUS: (*Aside.*) See how this fool succumbs
    To sluttish hope.

JESSOP: I've got a son!
    He's just this big! He's not yet one!
    You know the score! You've been there too!
    Just tell me what the fuck to do!
    Parenthood is…work is… Mate?
    The bollocks piles up on my plate!
    I need a hand!

CHORUS: Some dignity
    Might just be useful here.

JESSOP: (*Rising.*) I see.

CHORUS: I'm sorry, sir…but that's your lot.
 We want our money back. We're not
 A charity, a free-for-all.
 It's business, sir. And please recall
 The terms we laid out at the start…
 You have to play the game.
JESSOP: My heart
 Is thrashing like some cornered rat,
 My throat's gone dry.
CHORUS: (*Aside.*) Well, fancy that.
JESSOP: My ribs are creaking with the strain!
 My heart is bursting with this pain,
 This endless…fucking endless hurting!
CHORUS: (*Aside.*) Some folk may find this stuff diverting,
 This beating of the breast, this swearing.
 I simply find myself not caring
 Either way for his dilemma.
JESSOP: A pounding here, down here a tremor!
 Sweating palms and shredded cheeks!
 I haven't slept a wink for weeks!
 My wife's all baby-struck, not talking!
 Life is piss, mate!
CHORUS: (*Rising.*) 'Fraid I'm walking.
 Had enough…so…if you please!
JESSOP: (*Rising.*) Can't see the wood for fucking trees!
CHORUS: Thank you, sir. I hope things…
JESSOP: Fuck!
 Consumer-prey! A sitting duck!
CHORUS: I hope you sort your…
JESSOP: Fry in hell!
 You evil little twat!
CHORUS: Farewell.
 (*JESSOP is ushered out.*)
 Don't think me hard of heart. I'm not.
 It's just I do this quite a lot:
 The doctor must preserve himself,
 To better tend his patients' health.

Scene Eighteen

FISHER, alone. She is dressed for the night and is applying red lipstick.

FISHER: It is the witching hour again,
When fear pervades the hearts of men
And darkness fills their troubled minds:
They draw the curtains, fix the blinds,
Stay huddled in and tucked up tight,
They cower and quake before the night.
Yet others, who cannot withstand
This emptiness, who need a hand,
So fortify themselves with drink,
Seek strength in numbers, so they think,
And scream and laugh and dance and kiss,
In arrogance, in cowardice,
These venture out and hurl abuse
Into the dawn... But me, I choose
To use this mess for my own ends.
I stand alone and need no friends,
Yet what I do need, what I lack,
What forces me to this attack:
Relentless infertility,
My husband's inability
To do the one thing that he's good for,
That function that the male has stood for
Ever since the dawn of time:
Most women's do. Not fucking mine!
And still my heart yearns for that man
Who was the key in this girl's plan...
The sweetest of relationships.
But no...along comes Itchy Hips
And wham! She takes him easily,
She snaffles him away from me,
Frog-marches him straight up the aisle,
And then, in hardly any while,
She drops his sprog. Yours truly's left
The nursemaid, nanny, sad, bereft.
My girlhood dreams are ripped apart:

I strive to mend my broken heart
And settle for a man who's rich.
But now, I'm set. One broody bitch,
Hellbent on sniffing for a mate:
The clock ticks on. It's getting late.

Scene Nineteen

The pub. Usual sounds. The CHORUS as barman. LIDDLE and JESSOP drink sadly at the bar. JESSOP is very drunk, chin on chest.

JESSOP: So fuck me! Fuck her! Fucking hell!
    And fuck the fucking kid as well!
    Fuck the Bank of England, fuck it!
    Here's my purple pecker, suck it!
    Fuck the fucking politicians!
    All fucking English…fucked…traditions!
    Fuck the fucking House of Lords,
    Those pompous cunts! They're fucking frauds!
    Ah, fuck the world! Those royal fuckers!
    We fund those leeches. Fucking suckers!
    They wallow in our income tax,
    With butchered beasts across their backs,
    The fucking royal, fucked-up fops,
    They stole our land! They stole our crops!
    And left us homeless, fucking shits!
    Then shipped us off to death with Fritz,
    Those fat-arsed fucks! They're fucking smug!
    They're peacocks strutting! I'm a slug!
    I'm worthless, broken, bolloxed, skint!
    I'll torch the fucking Royal Mint!
    I'll burn those bastards in their beds!
    I'll suck their brains from out their heads!
    Complacent, loud-mouthed turds, they stuff
    Their guts with…
CHORUS: That's enough!
    It's not the first time you've made clear
    Your tendency to violence here.

You seem to want to dish out punches,
Whilst punters chew their ploughman's lunches.
JESSOP: I'm sorry. Fuck it. Sorry. Here.
I'll keep me gob shut with more beer.
(*JESSOP drinks, watched by LIDDLE. A silence.*)
LIDDLE: (*Still full of child-like innocence and wonder.*)
Losing?
JESSOP: (*Drunkenly looking up.*) Uh?
LIDDLE: Seems you are losing?
(*A silence. JESSOP's head drops again.*)
You have a family?
JESSOP: (*Drunkenly looking up.*) Uh?
LIDDLE: You mentioned...
JESSOP: (*Head dropping, with scorn.*) Family...
(*A silence.*)
LIDDLE: We could pass the time?
JESSOP: (*Drunkenly looking up.*) Uh?
LIDDLE: You and I. We could pass the time?
JESSOP: (*Muttering.*) Fucked it...
LIDDLE: I'm sorry?
JESSOP: (*Head dropping.*) Fuck it...fucking fuck fuck fuck...
(*A silence.*)
LIDDLE: Solitude is...a more difficult adversary than...
It is arduous, tortuous to... A burden more onerous
than... (*Pause.*) We could exchange stories?
JESSOP: (*Drunkenly looking up.*) Uh?
LIDDLE: The stories of our lives. (*A pause.*) Where did you
come from? How did you come to be here? Like this?
We could go back in time. Look at your choices.
Unweave the whole affair. (*A pause.*) Or have you become
too...enmeshed? Too entangled?
(*A silence.*)
We could become...how shall I put it?... friends.
JESSOP: (*Drunkenly looking up.*) Uh?
LIDDLE: (*Taking out wallet and producing notes.*) I have it
now, look. Old ladies, old men, young wives loaded
down with shopping. And the cars, all the cars... I could
buy you a drink. Or would that likewise be theft?
JESSOP: (*To his chest.*) Fuck...you!

LIDDLE: Perhaps we... (*He breaks off.*) I could tell you about my child. He is young. I feel love. A love but... I have no recognition. We need to be recognised, do we not? To have someone's face light up when we enter a room. That is...that is what one might call...might call...home. Home. I have a child. There... there... could be a recognition there...
(*A silence.*)
What is it that...that causes this?

JESSOP: (*Drunkenly looking up.*) Uh?

LIDDLE: Why have we come to this? How is it...?
(*The sound of canned laughter, as before. They freeze. It fades.*)
(*To himself.*) Yes. Yes. One might call that home. Home.
(*MORRIS now enters, dialling his mobile, and approaches the bar.*)

CHORUS: Awright, my son? Awright? Awright?
The usual, is it?

MORRIS: Course. Despite
The fact that drink's my scourge.

CHORUS: It's coming up.

MORRIS: (*To LIDDLE, miming coke-snorting.*) You got the
                                   urge
Again, old son? Just wait one sec. (*Dials again.*)
For fuck's sake...who's this total wreck?
(*Lifts JESSOP's head.*) Jesus Christ...I might have known.
He's lost the plot. This fucking phone!
I'm calling for the last half hour.
She never answers. Fucking power's
Alright. Can't work this out.
(*Takes drink.*) Cheers. It's like a fucking drought
Inside my throat. Come on, you bitch,
And answer it! It's fucking rich!
She moans at me for... (*Into phone.*) This is Stu
And you're not in. So...where are you?
I'll see you soon. (*To LIDDLE.*) That's women, eh?
A nightmare. Now, you want to play?
So follow me and let's depart:
Soft powder for the head and heart.
(*MORRIS and LIDDLE exit. LIDDLE taking out wallet as he goes.*)

CHORUS: (*Chirpy, to the comatose JESSOP.*)
 Cheer up, cheer up, cheer up, cheer up
 It might never 'appen, might never 'appen.
 Cheer up, cheer up, cheer up, cheer up
 It might never 'appen, might never 'appen…
 (*He repeats this, whilst donning reversed baseball cap and
 shades. This refrain is slowly drowned out by loud thumping
 techno music and strobe lights etc, the set-up for.*)

Scene Twenty

*A club. FISHER, dressed as before, is dancing alone. The music is
loud and frenzied. The CHORUS, as The DJ is dancing like a tool.
After a while, wiping his nose and evidently freshly coked-up,
LIDDLE enters. He looks a bit nonplussed at first but then FISHER
sees him. She dances over to him. He now remains still, whilst she
dances provocatively around him. The CHORUS behind them both,
flapping about wildly. Soon, FISHER's intentions become fairly
explicit and the atmosphere becomes charged with the hostility of
sexual attraction.*

Scene Twenty-One

*Morning. MORRIS is in bed. He is not alone, though we can't see
his partner. He wakes.*

MORRIS: With all the stealth that I could muster,
 (And so's my breath would not disgust her
 I even brushed my tarnished teeth)
 I tiptoed in and underneath
 I swear I sensed a sleeping figure,
 Breathing gently, without vigour.
 And so in darkness that was pitch,
 I disrobed myself of every stitch,
 Stumbling on just three occasions,
 Suffering only mild abrasions,
 Then quietly slithered in beside
 Me lady love, me 'virgin' bride.
 Me paw goes out to cop a feel,

(Gently so's she wouldn't squeal)
… Sometimes she's only feigning sleep
When I into the darkness creep,
And slap my naked bulk beside her…
(She often wants me deep inside her)
But, au contraire, last night I find
Our wedded bliss is much maligned:
I'm lying in an empty bunk…
Unshagged, bitter, bored and drunk.

FISHER: (*Sitting up.*) Oh my God… What time is it?
    If it's past nine I'm in the shit.
    (*Up and dressing.*) I promised Vic I'd help her out.

MORRIS: Jesus Christ, you're getting stout!

FISHER: Shut your gob and pass me tights!

MORRIS: And where the fuck were you last night?

FISHER: Just out!

MORRIS: Just out?

FISHER: You're catching on.

MORRIS: Well, I weren't back till half past one.

FISHER: I'm sorry, Stu, is there some law
    Which says I must be home before
    You choose to roll in from the boozer?

MORRIS: (*Aside.*) There's not but still I must accuse her.

FISHER: Pass that shirt!

MORRIS: I want to know
    Your alibi before you go.

FISHER: That's tough!

MORRIS: Because I start to worry.
    It's cruel out there.

FISHER: I have to hurry.
    I'll look a state but never mind.

MORRIS: Laura, would you be so kind
    And tell me why you were not back
    Where you belong in this here sack?

FISHER: I have no need to justify
    Myself to you and therefore I
    Shall leave you stewing in your juice
    Of jealousy.

MORRIS: Look, let's call a truce.
    And tell me you were round at Lee's.

FISHER: I might have been.
MORRIS: Oh, Laura… please!!
FISHER: I'm going.
MORRIS: So… you do admit
    That's where you were?
FISHER: You hypocrite!
    One evening in our whole liaison…
    (Your cheek is absolutely brazen)…
    One evening and I come home late,
    And what d'you do? Interrogate
    The arse off me!
MORRIS: The truth is out!
FISHER: Dickhead!
MORRIS: Darling, when you shout
    Your eyes ignite like fairy lights.
FISHER: And I'll stop out as many nights
    As necessary.
MORRIS: I don't care
    If you stay at Vic's. It's fair
    Enough.
FISHER: I never said I was.
MORRIS: In future let me know because
    The world has grown so reprobate,
    So vile, so cold…
FISHER: I'm running late.
    I'll see you soon. Enjoy the game.
    (*FISHER exits.*)
MORRIS: She still can set my heart aflame
    And I concede that my desire
    For her ferments and fans this fire.
    Yet still I seek young flesh elsewhere:
    Willing maids with golden hair,
    With buttocks pert and silky thighs,
    With childish laugh and 'Fuck Me' eyes.
    But now I have four hours to kill
    Before the pub with Joe and Bill,
    So back to slumbers I revert
    To dream of breast and tongue and skirt.

Scene Twenty-Two

SMITH at a table, stuffing envelopes quickly. The pram stands to one side of her. She seems to be in a state of panic. LIDDLE's voice floats through her head.

SMITH: (*Stuffing.*) ever asked yourself the question why...
    beyond the mere bestial stirrings of the loins...
    we think you'll agree...think you'll agree...
    beyond the need for conversation...
    we all need a little reassurance in this world...
    I could look into your face forever...
    we're here to make things better...better.
    I could look into your face forever...
    we're here to make things better...
    I offer you myself...
    sure you'll agree...
    I have nothing...
    we're sure you'll agree.
    I am nothing...
    why not consider our new...our new...
    something beyond rationality
    there's nothing to lose...
    and the confines of cold logic...
    there's really nothing to lose...
    no need to compare personalities...
    we're sure you'll agree...
    let us be brave...
    we're sure you'll agree...
    and leap into the unknown...
    there's nothing to lose...
    my kisses will be worshipful...
    unbeatable value, we're sure you'll agree...
    so confident are we...
    we're sure you'll agree...
    and you can't say fairer...
    we're sure you'll agree...
    you can't say fairer than that...
    have you ever wondered why...

is it because we have the lowest…
is it because…
we're sure you'll agree…
we're here to make things better better…
we're here to make things better…
(*JESSOP enters, with an armful of envelopes/brochures etc.*
He has mobile. He sits next to his wife and stuffs.)
JESSOP: How long we got?
SMITH: Till half past ten.
     They're coming round.
JESSOP: If not, what then?
SMITH: 'If not, what then?' We don't get paid!
     They'll sack us!
JESSOP: Fuck, I'm so afraid.
     I've just been threatened by this bloke!
     This loan-shark geezer…
SMITH: This a joke?
JESSOP: He says he'll do me less I pay!
     He's just rung off.
SMITH: What loan?
JESSOP: Today!
     I need five hundred fucking quick,
     Oh, Jesus…
SMITH: Christ, you make me sick
     Just stuff these bastards! You're too slow.
     Where's Laura?
JESSOP: Knew she wouldn't show.
     (*Enter FISHER.*)
FISHER: I'm here. I'm sorry. No excuse.
     I overslept. (*Stuffs.*)
JESSOP: Look, what's the use?
     It's not enough. It's peanuts, this.
     It's nothing.
FISHER: The antithesis
     Of calmness, you.
JESSOP: You talk of calm!?
FISHER: Your voice a squeal of spite, alarm.
     You need to…
JESSOP: I need thirteen grand
     Like yesterday!!

FISHER: I understand…

JESSOP: You don't, you can't…you're loaded, wealthy
    Your bank account is stuffed, it's healthy.
    You sold yourself!

FISHER: Now, that's not funny.

JESSOP: We wed for love! You married money!
    (*The sound of the baby screaming from the pram.*)
    (*To pram.*) You took the words right out my gob,
    And why can't he go find a job,
    The idle, whining lump of meat?
    Look, why don't we accept defeat
    And bow our heads before the axe?
    We've fucked it!

SMITH: Jesus Christ!

FISHER: Relax!
    (*SMITH exits with the pram. A long silence as JESSOP and
    FISHER stare at each other. Slowly, JESSOP crumples into
    bitter tears.*)
    Your tears burn hot. They sizzle on the skin.
    Like liquid fire they…

JESSOP: Help me out!
    I'm plagued by dread and shame and doubt!
    I'm desperate!

FISHER: (*After a pause.*) Here's one idea.
    A way to dissipate your fear,
    Perhaps. Perhaps. It's up to you…

JESSOP: Please, anything!

FISHER: Here's what we'll do…
    (*A silence.*)
    I'll give you for your pains five grand.
    I'll bail you…

JESSOP: I don't understand!
    You'd save me from this death, this hell,
    This purgatory?

FISHER: You can repel
    All creditors, the institution
    Slavering for…

JESSOP: (*Rising triumphant.*) Destitution,
    Kiss my arse! Oh, Laura! Thanks!

I love you! Christ! You bastard banks,
You satisfied? Your pound of flesh
Is cut, it's sliced, it's bleeding, fresh.
The worm has turned! Your such a mate,
An angel!

FISHER: Don't exaggerate,
I beg you!

JESSOP: Laura, thanks, my friend...
You've saved my skin. That you could lend
Me hope...

FISHER: Now listen, Lee.
There's one thing you must do for me.

JESSOP: For you?

FISHER: I'm sure you can't have thought
I'd rescue you for fun? They taught
You nothing then, your kinsmen kind,
About the ways of man?

JESSOP: Don't wind
Me up! My life's on hold!
I'm shaking here.

FISHER: You said I sold
Myself when I...

JESSOP: A jest!
Stu's a knock-out! No, you're blessed
With him. He's...

FISHER: Now, take heed.
Let's to the point. (*A pause.*) I long to breed.
(*A silence.*)

JESSOP: You've lost me.

FISHER: Stuart, I affirm,
Is not well-stocked with decent sperm.

JESSOP: So, what am I... You're joking? Yes?

FISHER: Who's laughing?

JESSOP: I can't acquiesce!
He'd kill me!

FISHER: How? He'd never know.
It's business, Lee.

JESSOP: You'd better go.

FISHER: Your envelopes, though. They need stuffing.
So... stuff away!

JESSOP: Come on, you're bluffing!
     Five grand to…get you in the club?
FISHER: It's easy cash?
JESSOP: Beelzebub
     Is roasting me in dev'lish flames,
     He now turns up the heat. Reclaims
     My soul and drinks my blood,
     Which bursts its veins, a crimson flood
     Of pain, of terror, trepidation.
FISHER: A cost-effective impregnation
     Solves your worries in a flash.
JESSOP: You can't buy love with Satan's cash!
     I love my wife, you broker, whore…
     (*SMITH rushes back in with now silent pram.*)
SMITH: Lee, what the fuck you talking for?
     (*Sits and stuffs.*) Our backs are firmly 'gainst the wall
     So stuff we must until we fall!
     (*They all stuff on.*)

Scene Twenty-Three

*Football stadium. Sounds of fans singing, chanting etc. LIDDLE,
MORRIS and the CHORUS as The Lad are seated, football scarves
on. LIDDLE looks bored and miserable and evidently wishes he
were somewhere else.*

MORRIS: Where the fuck are this lot, Bill? Are they for the
                                             drop?
CHORUS: So stroll on, fucking Jimmy Hill! They're
                                   second from the top!
     It's that lad, Seven. He's the threat.
MORRIS: That little bastard there?
     He hasn't touched the ball as yet.
CHORUS: Got continental flair.
     He's lethal, mate. With both his pegs.
MORRIS: He's only five foot two!
     Why don't we bite his bastard legs?
CHORUS: That's typical of you.
     Football, Stu, 's a game of skill. A bond twixt ball and man.

MORRIS: This is the Third Division, Bill. We're not AC Milan.

CHORUS: Even so I have to state…

(*MORRIS and The CHORUS spring to their feet.*)

BOTH: Just play the fucker square!

CHORUS: My God, that's on a fucking plate!

MORRIS: Oi, ref! That isn't fair!!

Off the meat-head, that's for sure! And do it double-quick!

CHORUS: Old Psycho was clean through to score!!

MORRIS: Oi, ref! Where's your white stick?

CHORUS: Your insults, Stu, are novel. Ho! Ho! Ho! They
make me laugh.

To your inventiveness I grovel.

MORRIS: So he wants an early bath!

CHORUS: The yellow card is being waved. Your anger has
been heard.

But Psycho should have knocked it in.

MORRIS: That cunt should be transferred.

Time, I think, to light a fag… Ain't that your mobile phone?

CHORUS: And when that's lit I'll have a drag.

MORRIS: You never buy your own.

CHORUS: Don't be heartless. Times is 'ard. I fought you'd
understand.

MORRIS: That comment I shall disregard. You're earning
eighty grand.

CHORUS: I got responsibilities: a car to run, a spouse…

MORRIS: And two gold-digging mistresses.

CHORUS: …the mortgage on the house.

(*Change to a bedroom. FISHER is preparing herself for love.*

FISHER: Within this frame an impulse drives

Me on and bids me sin

And I have joined that list of wives

With emptinesses in their lives

Who'll let a lover in.

But not through wanton lust have I

Sought out excitement wild,

It's just I dream that come July

I'll sing a heartfelt lullaby

To my own darling child.

The world at large don't censure me

For filling woman's needs,
But treat me with your sympathy:
I wither in a poverty
Of Stuart's hopeless seeds.
(JESSOP, in his usual state of panic, enters.)
JESSOP: This feels so strange. I'm not so sure
    That I can do it.
FISHER: Lee, you swore.
JESSOP: I love my wife.
FISHER: And I love you.
JESSOP: Laura, please!
FISHER: You know I do.
JESSOP: All our lives we've been best mates
    And this mad scheme just aggravates
    The set-up.
FISHER: Lee, now we agreed.
JESSOP: Our deal was never guaranteed.
FISHER: Five thousand pounds for you and her
    To be a mild adulterer,
    Until such time as I conceive.
    You need the cash.
JESSOP: I don't believe
    I'm doing this.
FISHER: It's not so bad.
JESSOP: It's ill thought-out. Fuck that, it's mad!
    I shake with rage and fear and doubt!
FISHER: Relax!
JESSOP: He'll whip your liver out
    And suck the blood from your sick heart.
    And me he'll murder!
FISHER: Lee, don't start.
    The deal is this, it's not complex:
    You're getting paid for having sex.
JESSOP: I'm therefore just a common slut.
FISHER: Well, aren't we all?
JESSOP: Oh, Jesus!
FISHER: But
    The difference is you're helping me
    To find my dream.

JESSOP: Philanthropy
    Has never really been my bag.
FISHER: Five minutes.
JESSOP: Here's another snag:
    Should I then get you up the stick...
FISHER: I've worked out the arithmetic.
    I mate with Stuart all the time:
    The child will just be his and mine.
JESSOP: You sure?
FISHER: I'm sure. He won't suspect.
JESSOP: I doubt, though, I will stay erect.
    I'm feeling odd.
FISHER: I'm really flattered.
JESSOP: It might just help if I was battered.
FISHER: Charming.
JESSOP: It's because it's you.
    I've known you since the age of two.
    It'll be like shagging my own blood.
FISHER: Well, fear not, Lee...my rampant stud.
    For I shall wear this grisly mask,
    Facilitate your happy task,
    So you can, if you like, pretend
    That you're not doing your best friend.
    (*She puts on Thatcher Mask. A long silence.*)
JESSOP: My God, the devil lives and breathes.
FISHER: She and I as thick as thieves.
JESSOP: That nose, those horns, your sparkling eyes...
FISHER: You've half an hour to fertilise
    Me, Lee, before your friend's return,
    So let us...
JESSOP: How your eyeballs burn!
    My soul is stricken with a dread,
    The blood is boiling in my head,
    I cannot tear away my gaze
    From you. My darling, let me praise
    Your slender form, your fragile neck,
    Your shoulders, bosom. Let me check
    The velvet smoothness of your skin,
    My own satanic heroine.

FISHER: For fuck's sake, Lee, get in the sack!

JESSOP: Then let me take you from the back.

    Like beasts on heat, we'll hack and pound,

    I crave those buttocks pert and round,

    Your hair flows down in streams of fire,

    I'm now ablaze with lewd desire.

FISHER: (*Aside.*) My God, I tell you if I'd known

    That I could win a chaperone

    So easily in this disguise...

JESSOP: It radiates from your red eyes.

FISHER: ...I'd have worn this years ago.

JESSOP: Let's cultivate an embryo!

FISHER: I pray to God with all my worth

    To cast Your eyes now down to earth

    And bless this sad ejaculation,

    Then replicate Your own creation!

    (*Back to the football. The three men are seated. Chanting etc.*)

MORRIS: (*On phone.*) This line's not good... Alright there,

                Mick...Some violence on the cards?

    (*To the CHORUS.*) What's happening?

CHORUS: Direct free-kick from all of twenty yards.

MORRIS: He just won't play the fucking game. He has, he's

                      got a nerve.

CHORUS: He's taking it...Oh, what's his name?

MORRIS: (*To CHORUS.*) Bound to try a swerve.

CHORUS: Go on, my son, and have a crack and blast it

                    through that wall!

MORRIS: (*On phone.*) He can't afford to pay me back?!

CHORUS: Weave magic on that ball.

    (*Long silence. MORRIS and CHORUS spring to their feet*

    as goal is scored.)

      Oh yes!

CHORUS: Oh yes!

MORRIS: Oh fucking yes!

CHORUS: Who stuck the fucker in?

MORRIS: Releasing all my built-up stress!

CHORUS: And now we're down to win.

MORRIS: I love you, mate. You know that's true. One-nil!

CHORUS: One-nil!
MORRIS: One-nil!
CHORUS: And Stuart, son… I love you too.
MORRIS: So…hold me tightly, Bill.
CHORUS: The joy!
MORRIS: The hope!
CHORUS: The love I feel!
MORRIS: We're winners through and through.
CHORUS: Such bliss as this just must be real.
MORRIS: The only love that's true.

(*Back to the bedroom. FISHER and JESSOP in bed. She still with mask on.*)

JESSOP: My discontentment knows no bounds.
    I'm riddled with this gnawing guilt
    That eats away my soul, dumbfounds
    Me.
FISHER: Lee, the milk has now been spilt.
    So no use crying. Get a grip.
    It's finished.
JESSOP: My relationship
    Which was in tatters now lies dead.
    My life is crashing round my head.
    I feel like shit.
FISHER: Lee, look at me. (*He does so.*)
    We're still good friends…
JESSOP: Adultery
    Is one thing that I can't abide.
    The mouth of hell has opened wide
    And sucks me in.
FISHER: Five thousand pounds.
JESSOP: My discontentment knows no bounds.

(*Back to the football. The men are seated. Then they spring to their feet.*)

MORRIS: Oh no!
CHORUS: Oh no!
MORRIS: Oh fucking no!
CHORUS: He's like a bird in flight!
    It's over, Ref, so fucking blow!!
MORRIS: Bill, a corner on the right.
    Jesus Christ!

CHORUS: Who's on the ball?
MORRIS: That Seven! Shit!
CHORUS: Hold on!!
    God, you're right. He is quite small.
MORRIS: Well, clear it then, my son!!
    Sliced it!
CHORUS: Fuck!!
MORRIS: I sense a threat.
CHORUS: He'll never miss from there…
BOTH: No!!!!
CHORUS: The bastard's in the net.
MORRIS: If only life were fair.
    We let him walk the fucker in.
CHORUS: This pain requires more booze.
MORRIS: One minute you're about to win.
CHORUS: The next you're bound to lose.

Scene Twenty-Four

SMITH, alone, shaking with terror.

SMITH: Ten minutes since the doorbell went,
    A flabby man with face all bent
    Looked past my head and through the hall
    And said:
CHORUS: (*Appearing.*) Nice pictures on the wall.
SMITH: He said:
CHORUS: Nice carpet, newly-fitted.
SMITH: Then over me his dark eyes flitted:
CHORUS: Lovely dress so crisp and new,
    Nice earrings, love, a nice hairdo.
SMITH: Stunned, I asked what he required.
    He said:
CHORUS: Your car's to be admired.
    A lovely little German model.
SMITH: Then I watched him start to waddle
    Round the back, I followed him.
CHORUS: And look…
SMITH: He said.
CHORUS: Nice hedges, trim.
    Ooh, roses too. A lovely garden.

SMITH: I felt my heart begin to harden,
   So asked him firmly to get lost.
   He said:
CHORUS: How much did that thing cost?
SMITH: And pointed at Lee's hover mower.
CHORUS: A proper little Percy Thrower…
   Ain't he?
SMITH: I was growing scared
   And so, in abject fear, I dared
   To warn him that I'd start to scream.
   He said:
CHORUS: My love, I would not dream
   Of wasting more of your good time.
   I'm certain that you won't waste mine,
   So kindly pay me what you owe
   And I shall thank you, smile, then go.
SMITH: So I explained our situation.
   He said:
CHORUS: Your struggles with inflation
   Are really not my deep concern.
   Why won't you people ever learn
   That one must pay back what one borrows?
   There are no limitless tomorrows.
   I want it NOW, you understand?
SMITH: And then he raised a pockmarked hand
   And curled it up into a fist:
CHORUS: These knuckles, love, have often kissed
   The fleshy noses of defaulters,
   Two bony little face assaulters.
SMITH: Tears of fear burst through my eyes
   And then he said, to my surprise:
CHORUS: Your infant's skin…so young and fresh,
   Such dainty little baby flesh,
   I think you'd rather it remained
   Unblemished, rosy and unstained.
   I have no qualms 'bout hurting nippers
   Then going home to pipe and slippers
   So cross my palm with silver, gold.
   Your sorry life has just been sold.

SMITH: I turned to run, he grabbed my wrist
    And said:
CHORUS: My love, I do insist
    That I don't leave here empty-handed.
    Please try your best to understand it.
SMITH: He took my watch, my wedding ring,
    Then:
CHORUS: I'll be back but then I'll bring
    Some helpers, love. Your husband's dead.
    But have a lovely day.
SMITH: …he said.

Scene Twenty-Five

The bedroom. The same as before.

FISHER: My sweetheart, look me in the eyes.
JESSOP: I've tried. I can't.
FISHER: Then this disguise
    Must go back on… (*Puts on mask.*) Now listen, Lee:
    This attitude's no good to me,
    We made a deal.
JESSOP: I sold my soul.
    I lost all sense of self-control.
FISHER: You didn't mind a spot of matin'
    When you thought that I was Satan…
JESSOP: You tempt me with five thousand quid…
FISHER: I claim my right to have a kid.
    That's all.
JESSOP: I love my darling Vic!
FISHER: This bullshit, sweetheart, makes me sick.
    When I conceive…
JESSOP: Before…just now
    I fell in love…I don't know how.
FISHER: You serious?
JESSOP: No. Not with you.
FISHER: Tell me then. I need a clue.
JESSOP: At the table. With my wife.
    I looked at her and saw my life.
    Her loving eyes burned through my sin,

Her soul was seeping through my skin.
I felt a love I haven't felt
Since when…

FISHER: You're making my heart melt.

JESSOP: We kissed. It was a marriage vow
Renewed. A trust. And, look, somehow
I'm lying here in bed with you.

FISHER: It's strange what cash can make you do.

JESSOP: I really can't do this again.

FISHER: God save us from these hollow men!

JESSOP: Betrayal of the one I love.

FISHER: So tell me what you're guilty of?
You've seen a way to earn some cash…

JESSOP: My throat I'll cut, these wrists I'll slash.
Betrayal of a trusted friend…

FISHER: Why must you, sweetheart, still pretend
That you and he are bosom mates?

JESSOP: We are.

FISHER: That really irritates
Me.

JESSOP: Well… I've known him for so long
It strikes me as a little wrong
To bang his wife.

FISHER: You have a drink,
You watch the game. You really think
That constitutes a friendship?

JESSOP: Yes.

FISHER: It's we who are good friends. Confess
That you now bare your soul to me,
And not to him or Vic. Agree
That I'm the one who loves you most.
This love is real and not the ghost
Of former days.

JESSOP: I have to go.

FISHER: We've just made love, Lee.

JESSOP: Yeah?

FISHER: You know
That that was more than just a fuck.
I love you, Lee.

MORRIS: (*Off.*) Does Lady Luck
    Not ever shine her light on me?
    Defeated by four goals to three.
JESSOP: Why has he come home so soon?
    Oh, fuck!
FISHER: I'll keep him out the room.
JESSOP: If he sees me in here, we're dead.
FISHER: Push your clothes beneath the bed.
JESSOP: That's where I'll hide. But keep him out.
MORRIS: (*Off.*) I'm back...so where are you?
FISHER: Don't shout!
MORRIS: (*Off.*) Upstairs?
FISHER: Pass that!
JESSOP: I can't squeeze in.
FISHER: Come on!
MORRIS: (*Off.*) We lost!
FISHER: My violin
    Is broken, Stu. You'll make me cry.
MORRIS: (*Off.*) Laura, can you tell me why
    Three times you take the lead and still
    You fucking lose?
JESSOP: My sock!
    (*JESSOP tries to recover his sock for the rest of the scene.*)
FISHER: Was Bill
    With you?
MORRIS: (*Entering.*) Of course. (*A silence.*) In bed?
FISHER: I've not been feeling well.
MORRIS: You said.
    (*A silence.*)
    What's with the mask?
FISHER: It's just some fun.
MORRIS: Well, take it off. (*She does.*)
    (*A silence.*)
FISHER: Look, HoneyBun.
MORRIS: Don't HoneyBun me!
FISHER: Why so mad?
MORRIS: You know the reason.
FISHER: Cos I had
    One evening by my self, alone
    Away from you!!?

MORRIS: You know I'm prone
  To jealousy, so why d'you do it?
FISHER: (*Up and dressing.*) For fuck's sake, Stuart. We've
                                been through it!
  Go run a bath…
MORRIS: Just answer me!!
  I've checked your story out with Lee!
  He says you weren't round his last night!
  So where the fuck…
FISHER: That's not quite right.
MORRIS: What isn't?
FISHER: Lee was at the game?
MORRIS: Of course he was.
FISHER: Now that's a shame.
  He can't have been!
MORRIS: What did you say?
FISHER: Cos I've been with the twat all day!
  (*MORRIS suddenly hits her.*
  The sound of canned laughter hovers in the air. They freeze. It
  fades.)
  (*Holding mouth, quiet.*) We stuffed some brochures. What
                           d'you think?
  Remember?
MORRIS: Yeah. (*A pause.*) I need a drink.

Scene Twenty-Six

*LIDDLE alone. Walkman on. Football scarf on. Booze in his blood
and in his hands, the picture of misery. Thumping techno music ac-
companies the image. He stares ahead for some considerable time
until:*

Scene Twenty-Seven

*SMITH and JESSOP on a sofa, their faces flickering. Tracksuits.
They are open-mouthed, listless, glazed. Their pain mounts in step
with what they are watching. Each ball breaks their hearts further.
Suitcases and boxes by their feet. The pram. The booming and
celebratory voice of The CHORUS is heard, now as The Celebrity.*

CHORUS: And the first ball tonight is... (*Two hideous synthesiser blasts.*)...Number Thirty-two!! (*Whooping and cheering.*) And the second ball tonight is... (*Two hideous synthesiser blasts, a note higher.*)... Number Seventeen. That's one, seven!! (*Whooping and cheering.*) And the third ball tonight is... (*Two hideous synthesiser blasts, a note higher.*)...Number Forty-one!! (*Whooping and cheering.*) And the fourth ball tonight is... (*Two hideous synthesiser blasts. A note higher.*)...Number Five!! (*Whooping and cheering.*) And the fifth ball tonight is... (*Two hideous synthesiser blasts. A note higher.*)...Number Twenty-nine!! (*Whooping and cheering.*) And the sixth ball tonight is...(*Two hideous synthesiser blasts. A note higher.*)...Number Thirty-three!! (*Whooping and cheering.*) And the bonus ball tonight is... (*Two hideous synthesiser blasts.*)... Number Eleven!! (*Whooping and cheering growing to violence.*)

Scene Twenty-Eight

FISHER and MORRIS on a sofa. Flickering faces. FISHER wears shades.

FISHER: Will you shut up?
MORRIS: Well... have an 'eart.
     My favourite show's about to start.
FISHER: That stimulating snooker quiz?
     It's dreadful.
MORRIS: Laura, it's the biz.
FISHER: I'm watching this.
MORRIS: It's total crap!
FISHER: Just fuck off, there's a pleasant chap.
MORRIS: (*Aside.*) Hell, I say, it knows no rage
     Like Laura let loose from her cage.
FISHER: And why don't you just mend the vid
     Then all we'd have to do...
MORRIS: I did.
FISHER: You didn't.
MORRIS: Yeah, it broke again.
CHORUS: (*Camp, fake.*) And now, ladies and gentlemen...
     The moment you've been waiting for...

Let's see how our contestants score:
Two gerbils play against one duck.
Let's sound the bell and wish them luck!
(*His fake laughter builds underneath the following.*)
FISHER: Last week they had this tortoise on
    All dressed up as Napoleon
    That was his name: he had that hat...
    Oh, what they called?
MORRIS: Who is this twat?
FISHER: They put him in this yellow maze
    With lettuce hidden...
MORRIS: Saturdays
    Are meant for those who work to rest.
FISHER: Well, I work too.
MORRIS: I'm unimpressed
    With this daft mincer and his rats.
FISHER: They're gerbils.
MORRIS: Rodent acrobats!?
FISHER: Aren't they sweet?
MORRIS: That duck's a cheat.
    He pecked one.
FISHER: He's got funny feet,
    All webbed...
MORRIS: You see that hamster leap?
FISHER: They're gerbils!
MORRIS: Look, that duck's asleep...
    He flapped his wing and quacked a bit
    Then had a nap.
FISHER: He's just unfit.
MORRIS: Go on...
FISHER: So sweet!
MORRIS: And bite his beak!
    You're nearly through...
FISHER: This pig last week
    He had to eat his weight in...
MORRIS: Quiet!
    That's it, my son.
FISHER: Go on then! Try it!

(They now begin to laugh. It starts slowly at first and then builds into something more hysterical, more out of control.)
CHORUS: Congratulations! How d'you feel?
 Your duck faced up to her ordeal...
 And as for you, you must be thrilled
 To own these sweethearts. I just willed
 Them on to beat our champ...
 But never mind. This little scamp
 Got bored, my darling, half-way through...
 You'd had enough, love, hadn't you?
 You don't leave with an empty plate:
 This gerbil cage is quite ornate,
 So, darlings, here's your new abode.
 Now let's meet Loppy-Legs the Toad...

Scene Twenty-Nine

LIDDLE alone, exactly as before, only now he is seemingly unconscious. The music pumps violently across the stage for some time and then:

Scene Thirty

A few months later. FISHER (still in shades) and SMITH are laying a table for a fondue. The former, full of bustling celebration; the latter, despondent and dazed, still in tracksuit.

FISHER: ...I think as Bed and Breakfasts go,
 You've done quite well. I mean, I know
 That now Lee's unemployed
 You're struggling. *(Aside.)* They once enjoyed
 Their lives so much. *(To her.)* But see, I feel
 That things will change. It's not ideal,
 I know, to scrounge the Welfare State
 And bleed it dry. You hibernate
 Amidst the wreckage of your lives...
 (If you could kindly pass those knives...
 Good silver, see?)... and there you rot.
 I know it's hard. But worry not,

My darling Vic, because I sense
Your cares may soon... Look, no offence
But should you need a lend of clothes
Then please feel free to... Thank you, those.
...then please feel free to borrow mine,
My darling. Yes? At any time.
And you're still table-dancing, yes?
For that bit extra? They undress
You with their blood-shot stares
In smoky clubs? It makes the hairs
Stand up upon my neck
To think of it! Now, let me check
That's everything. A nice fondue!
(*As she is passed something.*) Thank you, love. That's good of you.
Tonight we all must celebrate.
SMITH: What's happened then?
FISHER: Now, just you wait!
   Wine-glasses there. No, there I think.
   And don't you mind about the drink!
   We've plenty here. I know the score.
   It's hard I... What you crying for?
   Please, darling. Don't. No, please don't cry.
   Downstairs we've got a huge supply!
   We thought you might not... Take a seat.
   (*Aside.*) Revenge is oh so bittersweet!
   There we go now. Dry those tears
   And put your feet up. (*Aside.*) It appears
   That something's pissed on her parade,
   The poor, poor girl. (*To her.*) Look, I'm afraid
   That since you are my special guest...
   I hope you won't feel underdressed...
   I just must quickly change my frock!
   I'll look in on the baby!
   (*FISHER exits.*)
SMITH: (*Through tears.*) Mock
   Me then if mock is what you must.
   No, I shall not be beaten by this shame.
   Success can spring from failure, strength from pain:
   It's time to fly. Yes, face this world alone.

The two of us! Yes, man-free we shall go.
The fire from his sweet cradle warm my life!
Without the load accrued in my delusion,
I'll fight a path through anger and confusion.
(*FISHER enters triumphantly, outlandishly dressed for celebration.*)

FISHER: Stroll on, you scrawny catwalk queens
And fan my brow! Those magazines,
They're printed straight from Satan's arse!
This woman's real! I'll take a glass
And drink I shall to my sweet self! (*Drinks.*)
I'm radiant with hope and health!
(*MORRIS now enters, supporting a paralytic JESSOP. He helps him to a chair, where he slumps, chin on chest until further notice.*)

MORRIS: You'll never guess… This bastard's pissed!
He wonders why he got dismissed.
He's slashed away his severance pay,
Sinks deeper in the swamp each day!

FISHER: Just leave him!

MORRIS: Plus he's run up debts
With nasty bastards.

FISHER: (*To SMITH.*) He forgets
His duties. Yes, his obligations.
It's such a shame!

MORRIS: Inebriation's
Not the word for…

FISHER: Leave him be!
Tonight belongs to you and me.

MORRIS: So…what's the deal then?

FISHER: Here's some wine.

MORRIS: (*Drinking.*) You look like fucking Frankenstein!

FISHER: Do fucking not!

MORRIS: Has she been crying?

SMITH: I'm fine.

FISHER: She's fine.

MORRIS: (*Inspecting pot.*) What's all this frying?
This oil's all sizzling. What's the score?
What are we celebrating for?

FISHER: It's…

MORRIS: Which sweet beast was hacked to pieces?
Were baa-lambs butchered from their fleeces?
Was Daisy's brain electrified
Before the saw gnawed through her side?

FISHER: For Christ's sake, Stu! Don't eat it raw!
You'll…

MORRIS: What the fuck's this party for?
(*A doorbell sounds. They all look at each other.*)
I did neglect, I think, to mention:
I asked a pal round.

FISHER: The convention,
Stuart…

MORRIS: Lovely chap.
Has only one slight handicap:
He hardly speaks. I'll fetch him, wait.
(*MORRIS exits.*)

FISHER: 'Look, Laura…meet my new best mate!'
Every week, a different loafer,
They waste their lives upon my sofa.
A mate to drink with, one for sport!
Some sex-starved chump in every port!
(*About JESSOP.*) And this sad crony's out of date…
(*MORRIS enters with a bewildered LIDDLE.*)

MORRIS: Look, Laura…meet my new best mate!
(*There is a stunned silence as LIDDLE and the two women stare at one another.*)
(*Oblivious.*) My wife, Laura. This is Vic.
And our friend Lee's a smidgeon sick.
(*Aside to LIDDLE.*) Wants caging in a fucking zoo.
And this is Joseph.

FISHER/SMITH: How d'you do.
(*MORRIS fetches an extra chair and they all sit. LIDDLE in the centre, the two couples on either side. There is a long silence. The atmosphere darkens. SMITH from time to time lifts up her husband's drooping head. The tension grows. Suddenly naturalism descends.*)

MORRIS: Have you met before or…?

FISHER: (*To SMITH.*) He's sleeping soundly upstairs, by the way.

SMITH: Right.

FISHER: Stuck my head round the door.

SMITH: Thanks.

(*They do not speak.*)

MORRIS: Drink? (*He pours wine for everyone.*)

SMITH: Thanks.

FISHER: Thanks.

(*They do not speak. The tension builds.*)

MORRIS: So…

FISHER: So…

MORRIS: What's this all about then?

(*They do not speak for some time.*)

LIDDLE: (*Rising.*) Would you please…would you please excuse me?

MORRIS: Upstairs. First on your right.

(*LIDDLE exits. SMITH looks on anxiously. A silence.*)

(*Aside to FISHER, grabbing wrist.*) So what's your fucking problem then?

(*No answer.*)

I'll ask you, shall I, once again?
I warned you…don't embarrass me
In front of friends…for slavery
Or punishments beyond compare
Shall be your lot! So, if you dare
To treat our guest with such disdain,
If you cold-shoulder him again,
Then you'll regret your day of birth,
That you saw light of day on earth,
That your sweet mother pushed you out!
That you from her foul womb did sprout!
That you could taste, touch, smell, see, feel!
Yes, I shall frame some cruel ordeal
And you shall suffer, suffer, oh!

FISHER: You're hurting me! Let fucking go!

(*He does. LIDDLE re-enters, somewhat unsteadily, as if he has just discovered a great truth. A silence.*)

MORRIS: (*To LIDDLE.*) Awright?

LIDDLE: (*Slowly, deliberately, with innocence and wonder.*) It seems as if…a moment of clarity. Perhaps…complexity. The act, the act shimmered with complexity. And this was a form of clarity in itself. Recognition and…love? Yes, love… But was it beyond love? The ultimate proof of it I… Feeling as if… My hand is shaking, my heart… There is a release of… The death of self?… Yes? And time…it stopped. For those seconds of… The sun hovered where it hung and…all…motion…ceased. It is love. Yes, love. (*He weeps.*) There is…love. Love…the word is…

(*Suddenly, SMITH leaps from her chair and rushes out.*)

FISHER: (*Transfixed by LIDDLE, dazed. Quiet.*) Pregnant. (*Canned laughter now fades in slowly and builds to the end of scene. It is mixed with applause and demonic whooping and cheering etc.*)

MORRIS: What?

FISHER: (*Louder, victorious.*) Preg-nant!

(*JESSOP drunkenly looks up. MORRIS goes into shock. A long, despairing scream echoes around the stage. A world shattered. A silence. The canned laughter kicks in loud. SMITH enters, distraught, desolate. She staggers forward and sinks to her knees.*)

SMITH: An innocent child you…an innocent child… What?… (*A laugh.*) What did…? (*A sob.*) No more of… (*Takes knife from the table.*) Not alone then… Never alone. (*A long silence as she chooses. She swiftly cuts her own throat. Falls.*

The following scenes of violence must be enacted in all seriousness, despite the increasing cartoon-like qualities of these characters. The laughter and applause – increasing gradually in volume and intensity – will provide the backdrop to the carnage. MORRIS stands. He takes a fondue fork and suddenly thrusts it into FISHER's belly. She screams. He does it again. Clutching herself, she takes a fork and stabs him in the groin. He stumbles. He takes her head and pushes it into the fondue pot, holding it there. She screams. He pulls her out. She gasps for breath, in agony. He pushes her head back into the pot and holds it there. She struggles wildly for a time and then her arms go limp. He sinks, clutching his groin. He falls. JESSOP drunkenly surveys the carnage. The sound of a door being kicked off its hinges. JESSOP looks up. A shot is fired. He is hit in the chest. As he dies, banknotes begin to flutter to the ground. The lights fade and the canned laughter gradually increases in volume. JESSOP crawls about in his spotlight, clutching at the money like some crazed TV gameshow contestant, stuffing the notes into his shirt. He falls. The laughter increases and slowly LIDDLE's face is all that is lit. The CHORUS steps forward, once again as The Prison Officer, and places a hood over LIDDLE's head. The shadow of the bars appear. A door slams.)

CHORUS: So…

LIDDLE: So.

CHORUS: Here we are.

LIDDLE: The end of the road.

CHORUS: The start of it.

LIDDLE: I shall miss you.

CHORUS: And I you.

(*The sound of a trap-door opening and the lash of a rope. The laughter dies away and darkness falls. A light comes slowly up on the face of The CHORUS. He steps forward.*)

Epilogue

The State decreed that this must be,
(Such vulnerable morality)
…that corpses should bedeck the stage
So's not to churn up public rage.
So we, mere servants, humble folk,
Providers of the laugh, the joke,
Are forced to bring them to their knees,
Since entertainers aim to please.
Now you must leave this grisly sight
And bravely face the coming night,
But…just before the first one stands,
Please pardon us…and clap your hands.

FIVE VISIONS OF THE FAITHFUL

The Invention of Morality

FLACK, *a security guard with wings*
SQUITS, *a security guard without*

What The Butterflies Said

CAROLINE, *a mother and wife*
LIZZIE, *an imaginative child*
THOMAS, *a doctor and lover*
GODFREY, *a lepidopterist*

I Am The Knife

PRIEST, *an alcoholic*
SCREW, *a sadist with a fine sense of dress*
INMATE, *an enemy of the state*
WOMAN, *his wife*
GIRL, *his daughter*
HANGMAN, *a hooded fellow*

The Art of Being Alone

MARY, *a beggarwoman*
SUITMAN, *an office worker*
STUDENTBOY, *a world-changer*
STUDENTGIRL, *a compassionate academic*
TATTOOLAD, *a dispossessed youth*

A Lesson in Arbitration

PILATE, *the Roman governor of Judaea*
REBECCA, *a servant*
COMEDIAN, *a man of the people*
TERRORIST, *a man of the people*

Five Visions of the Faithful was first performed at The White Bear Theatre, London on 10 October 2000, with the following cast:

THE INVENTION OF MORALITY

FLACK, *a security guard with wings,* Peter Kenvyn
SQUITS, *a security guard without,* Nigel Barrett

WHAT THE BUTTERFLIES SAID

CAROLINE, *a mother and lover,* Joan Walker
LIZZIE, *an imaginative child,* Rosie Morris
THOMAS, *an enthusiastic scientist,* Nigel Barrett
GODFREY, *a lepidopterist,* Terry Edwards

I AM THE KNIFE

PRIEST, *an alcoholic,* Ian Lindsay
SCREW, *a sadist with a fine sense of dress,* Bill Stewart
INMATE, *an enemy of the state,* Peter Kenvyn
WOMAN, *his wife,* Illona Linthwaite
GIRL, *his daughter,* Rosie Morris
HANGMAN, *a hooded fellow,* Costa Milton

THE ART OF BEING ALONE

MARY, *a beggarwoman,* Illona Linthwaite
SUITMAN, *an office worker,* Peter Kenvyn
STUDENTBOY, *a world-changer,* Costa Milton
STUDENTGIRL, *a compassionate academic,* Sheena Irving
TATTOOLAD, *a dispossessed youth,* Nigel Barrett

A LESSON IN ARBITRATION

REBECCA, *a servant,* Natasha Joseph
PILATE, *the Roman governor of Judaea,* George Pensotti
COMEDIAN, *a man of the people,* Costa Milton
TERRORIST, *a man of the people,* Nigel Barrett

Director, Peter Craze
Designer, Philip Witcomb
Lighting Designer, Stuart Billinghurst
Composer, David Schweitzer
Assistant Director, Yael Shavit

The Invention of Morality

Two security guards, FLACK and SQUITS, are seated staring out front at a screen we don't see. FLACK has been educated and speaks accordingly, while SQUITS, it would appear, has not been similarly blessed. SQUITS has a tabloid on his knee. They are both bored out of their minds.

FLACK: Tell you what…

SQUITS: 'ere we go!

FLACK: I had much higher hopes for myself than all this.

SQUITS: (*Aggressive.*) I know!!

FLACK: It's absolutely killing me!

SQUITS: Then ask for a transfer!

FLACK: What…and get shoved into some other shit-hole with some other sub-moronic arse?

SQUITS: Listen…don't push it.

FLACK: It's an absolute nightmare, a disgrace!

SQUITS: Just watch the screen!

FLACK: I've been watching this screen for as long as I can remember. Watch the screen, he says! You watch the screen!

SQUITS: I am fuckin' watching it!

FLACK: (*Standing.*) People like you make me sick. Inmates to a man! Willingly shackled to the teats of the State. There's no…wriggle in you, no fight. Look at yourself… sitting there. Getting fatter. Duller. Suckling away with your eyes gummed shut. Drinking it all in. Yesterday's cream dribbling down your double chins.

SQUITS: Si' down!

FLACK: Why should I?

SQUITS: They'll see you.

FLACK: Oh, but I really don't care!

SQUITS: They'll dock yer.

FLACK: There is more to life, sir, than the accumulation of wealth!

SQUITS: Change the fuckin' record.

FLACK: We sit here watching these monkeys galumphing about…we watch them all day, all night. And yet some fuckers there (*Points upwards to camera.*) and some other fuckers there (*Points upwards to second camera.*) are doing the same to us! And some other fuckers are watching those fuckers! And some other fuckers are watching those fuckers that are watching those fuckers that are watching us fuckers. And some other fuckers…

SQUITS: Alright!

FLACK: Only question is… Who's watching the cunt at the top of the tree?

SQUITS: The only thing more borin' than having to watch this fuckin' screen all day, is havin' to listen to you goin' on about how borin' it is havin' to watch this fuckin' screen all day.

FLACK: This kind of existence is easy for the likes of you. The electrical potential within your brain is of a strictly limited capacity. (*Tapping head.*) Whereas I, sir, I have ions of sodium and potassium firing through my nerve membranes up here. Synapses crackling away. There's an imagination here, an intelligence, churning about, writhing about like a snake. Dreaming of its own freedom. The prisoner who's forgotten what blue skies look like is a willing prisoner indeed. Give him his daily bowl of gruel and something to wank over and he's as happy as a pig in the proverbial poke!

SQUITS: (*Indicating screen.*) I got all the blue skies I need right here!

FLACK: (*Dramatically.*) But some of us…some of us were born for a higher station. Some of us were born with the desire to stretch out our wings. Get out there. Feel the sun on our faces, feel its rays tan our white flesh. Some of us aren't scared to die. Some of us…some of us are simply larger than life!!

(*A long, bored silence. They go back to the screen. After a while FLACK indicates SQUITS' paper.*)

Bung it over.

SQUITS: Buy your own!

FLACK: Come on!

SQUITS: You take the piss out of me for buyin' it but you always wanna ogle the tits.

FLACK: But I am very partial to a nice pair of bosoms.

SQUITS: So am I!

FLACK: Oh, come on! Don't be such a…

SQUITS: Buy your own!

FLACK: Why, when I can look at yours?

SQUITS: Pay me 'alf then!

FLACK: (*Turning away.*) You, sir, are a Scrooge!
(*A long silence as SQUITS stares at the screen listlessly and FLACK gazes out into the audience, deranged with boredom.*)
(*Upper crust.*) To be honest with you, Squits old chap…
I sometimes wish I'd joined the bally army.

SQUITS: Why don't you then? Get you out of my fuckin'
'air for a few years.

FLACK: See a little of the world. Sail the high seas.

SQUITS: Sounds more like the navy, dunnit?

FLACK: Risk my life defending the faith. Defending some
faceless stranger upstairs who has next to no regard for
me and who, if I were to meet any form of frightening,
lonely death in a foreign land, would simply roll over,
scratch his broad buttocks and go back to counting his
plundered gold.

SQUITS: Will you stop talkin' now?

FLACK: What, so you can concentrate on your work?

SQUITS: Somethin' almost happened then.

FLACK: (*After a pause.*) How can something 'almost
happen'? Either something happens or it doesn't.

SQUITS: I got a definite sense of something just then.

FLACK: A twig move in the wind, did it? Bit of sand
whipped up, perhaps?

SQUITS: More like an earthquake. (*Excited.*) A volcano.

FLACK: Okay…so a volcano is sometimes worth a look.
Generally. I quite enjoy a little molten lava. But…tell me
something new, I beg you! Give me an asteroid impact.
Give me a tidal wave. Give me a bit of death, some
suffering. Give me some drama!

SQUITS: Volcanoes can be very nasty.

FLACK: Ooh, nasty, nasty!

SQUITS: It's a carnival of death out there!

FLACK: But where's the drama? For drama, you need to grant your hero the right to make his own decisions.

SQUITS: If I want another fuckin' lecture…

FLACK: (*Ignoring him.*) More or less. You can't just programme him to do what you tell him. You must give the fellow the ability to wonder what it's all about. Then, you see, you have a story. Then you have your conflicts of interest, you have all sorts of wonders. At the moment these beasts want merely to stuff themselves stupid, hack away at as many sweating arses as they can find and then grab a little shut eye. Is this compulsive viewing? I think not, sir. No sensibility, no erotica. Just a reluctant proffering of the rear end, a couple of frantic thrusts and thanks very much, there's another hairy bastard in a matter of months. Does nothing for me.

SQUITS: (*Muttering.*) Pseudo intellectuals.

FLACK: I'd rather be dead, to be honest.

SQUITS: Well, someone pissed on your bonfire on that score then, didn't they?

FLACK: Come on…let's have a look at those knockers.

SQUITS: Fuck off!

FLACK: God, do we have to go through this charade every time?

SQUITS: (*Throwing paper over.*) Takin' the piss.

FLACK: (*Opening it.*) Good lord!

SQUITS: (*Grinning.*) Udders like you've never seen, mate.

FLACK: They're tampering with the images, surely? How can she be standing upright? Breasts like that and a vertical posture have got to be mutually exclusive!?

SQUITS: Let's 'ave it!

FLACK: Patience, sir!

SQUITS: I want it back in one piece.

FLACK: She's forcing that grin, isn't she? More like a grimace, I would say. Must have a spine of wrought iron.

SQUITS: Come on…!

FLACK: Not taking your eyes off the screen, are you?

SQUITS: Flack!

FLACK: 'At least one pair of eyes to be fixed on the screen at all times. The penalties for non-compliance…'

SQUITS: *You* fix your eyes on the screen for a change!
I want my tits back!

FLACK: I am, sir, fixing my eyes on these nipples.

SQUITS: Let's 'ave ya, let's 'ave ya!

FLACK: I bet you cut out and keep all these tits. Plaster
them all round your cell. You wake up on your left side:
tits. You wake up on your right side: tits. You wake up
staring at the ceiling and there's tits, tits, tits. No
imagination at all. You need to be swimming in a sea of
tits before you even feel a stirring. (*Throws it back.*)

SQUITS: (*Catching it.*) Cunt.

FLACK: (*After a sigh and a silence.*) I can't go on with this.
I really can't. (*Walks to edge of stage.*) One would have
thought that having no fear of death would be a positive
advantage in some places. Free you from servitude,
shouldn't it? Wipe my arse for me, says the man with the
knife. Go fuck yourself, says the man without the knife.
If you don't wipe my arse, says the man with the knife,
I'll puncture your heart with this. Do your worst, says
the knifeless man. Living in a world ruled by cunts like
you is worse than death. Alright, says Mr Knife, you
asked for it. And don't call me a cunt. Go on, says No
Knife, offering up the softest part of his breast. Sink your
sleek blade into my flesh. Deliver me. (*A pause.*) Only
here, one is caught by the testicles. There is nowhere to
go. Courage in the face of slavery makes very little
difference here. (*Pause.*) God, how I need a woman!

SQUITS: Buy your own!

FLACK: I mean a real woman! Something substantial.
Something to be inside of. Something to lose myself in.
Something to...
(*Suddenly something starts flashing on the screen. In his
surprise, SQUITS falls backwards off his chair. FLACK
turns.*)

SQUITS: Meemo! It says Meemo.

FLACK: Memo, fool. Memo.

SQUITS: Meemo, meemo!

TANNOY: *Attention all security, attention all security. As
you may be aware, the Management have been involved in a*

115

SERIES OF IMPORTANT MEETINGS OVER RECENT WEEKS, THE SUBJECT MATTER OF WHICH HAS BEEN A STRICTLY-GUARDED SECRET. NOW, AFTER LENGTHY DELIBERATION, A DECISION HAS BEEN MADE WHICH WILL HAVE FAR-REACHING IMPLICATIONS FOR EVERYBODY WITHIN THE ORGANISATION. PLEASE PAY CLOSE ATTENTION TO THE FORTHCOMING MESSAGE.

(*FLACK and SQUITS stare at each other in silence.*)

SQUITS: What...I mean, what...?

FLACK: Sssh!!

SQUITS: A voice...a...

FLACK: A voice, yes...

SQUITS: It spoke, Flack, it spoke...

FLACK: It fulfils its essence...

SQUITS: To us...to us...

FLACK: To everyone...

(*A silence.*)

SQUITS: Flack...

FLACK: Please!

SQUITS: Flack...

FLACK: Quiet!!

(*A silence as they wait.*)

SQUITS: Shittin' meself...

FLACK: (*Turning sharply.*) Ssshh!!

(*Another silence.*)

Come on, then...come on.

(*They wait on for an inordinate time.*)

SQUITS: Pissin' about...

FLACK: Look, one more word from you and...

SQUITS: What?

FLACK: One more...

SQUITS: (*Menacing.*) Then what, ya fuck, what...?

FLACK: Just...

SQUITS: (*Taking hat off.*) I'll tear you apart, ya cunt...

FLACK: Not now, not now...

SQUITS: You talk down to me, you...

FLACK: Squits, come on...

SQUITS: You piece of shit and arsehole cunt!!

FLACK: Your hat!!

SQUITS: What?

FLACK: Your hat…

SQUITS: (*Replacing it.*) I'll 'ave ya, I'll 'ave ya!

FLACK: Later. Soon.

SQUITS: I just wanna… I'm hungry for smackin' some…

FLACK: Not now…

SQUITS: I'm bustin' for violence! I'm…shakin' like a…

FLACK: Squits!!

(*A silence.*)

SQUITS: I need a wank.

FLACK: Well, have a wank!!

SQUITS: I'll 'ave ta, I'll 'ave ta!!

FLACK: Just please stop talking!!

(*SQUITS turns to go.*)

SQUITS: When I get back…you're mine.

TANNOY: *It has come to our attention that there is a growing discontent amongst the collective and that the movements of the beast perhaps make less than compelling viewing. Consequently, it has been proposed that certain changes are to be made in order to render him slightly more interesting and observable in the field.*

(*FLACK sits.*)

The Management are currently seeking volunteers from within the collective to embark on a mission. The purpose of this mission being to inject, into as many creatures as possible, a serum. This serum will stimulate self-awareness and an appetite for wonder. It should spread through the population in the usual manner. In time this will, We hope, provide us all with some much-deserved entertainment. Please note…we seek volunteers who are already in pairs.

(*FLACK looks at SQUITS.*)

In the world alone you would suffer too greatly. It must also be understood that, in order to improve the leisure time of your fellows at home, these volunteers will be giving up their immortality. This is a mission from which there can be no return. This is termed, We believe, self-sacrifice. Any volunteers to make themselves known as soon as possible. Thank you.

(*A long, stunned silence.*)

FLACK: (*Rising.*) My immortal soul.

SQUITS: What?

FLACK: My immortal soul!!

SQUITS: What!!?

FLACK: We do it!

SQUITS: Fuck you!!

FLACK: This is our chance!

SQUITS: I'm not dyin' for no fuckin'...

FLACK: We can make history, Squits... Get out there... get out there and finally...

SQUITS: Not a chance, mate...

FLACK: What do you want to do for all eternity? Stare at a screen all day, wank in your pit all night? This is your chance to blaze a trail! Let others live in the prison! We can be...free!

SQUITS: I'm 'appy 'ere.

FLACK: 'Appy 'ere? 'Appy 'ere? How can you be 'appy 'ere?'

SQUITS: Alright, I'm not 'appy especially...but I'm still breathin', in't I?

FLACK: (*On knees.*) I'm begging you. I'm down on my knees. Let's give the beast a chance...let's...

SQUITS: Fuck you! You are askin' me to die!!

FLACK: Listen...

SQUITS: (*Turning.*) Flack, read my lips: I do not want to fuckin' die! (*Pause.*) End of story.

FLACK: End of story?

SQUITS: End of fuckin' story.

(*FLACK releases his legs. A long silence.*)

FLACK: Cunt.

SQUITS: You're the cunt.

FLACK: (*Springing to his feet, grabbing SQUITS' collar savagely.*) Hear me out, you cud-chewing reprobate, you piss-swilling shit-for-brains... This is my destiny. This is my chance...I have to go... I need the death of it... I can offer you nothing, nothing but your own freedom, nothing but your own agony... Don't...don't just dismiss it with your ill-mannered pig-instinct... Think, if you can. Think, if you dare. This...this is the only decision you will ever have to make. (*Pause.*) Let us fly, Squits. Please! Let us fly!!

(*A long, tense silence as SQUITS cogitates. He then viciously head-butts FLACK who drops like a stone. SQUITS regards the fallen angel, thinking whether or not to add insult to injury. He is panting with the desire for violence. He turns, goes to his chair and picks up the tabloid. He opens it, folds it back. Looks again at FLACK. He leaves.*)

What The Butterflies Said

The song of birds, the hum of insects. It is a glorious summer's day. Lincolnshire, England. 1860. We are on the top of a grassy hill and a young girl of six or seven years (LIZZIE) is playing with her dolls while, some distance apart, her mother (CAROLINE) sits on a blanket and, from a hamper, lays out a small picnic. A large wooden case lies at one side. Both mother and daughter are dressed unostentatiously.

LIZZIE: (*Addressing audience.*) The framework of bones being the same in the hand of a man, wing of a bat, fin of the porpoise, and leg of the horse – the same number of vertebrae forming the neck of the giraffe and of the elephant – and innumerable other such facts, at once explain themselves on the theory of descent with slow and slight successive modifications. (*With dolls.*) Oh, poor soldier...a deep and painful wound in the chest. Lie still and let Nurse Elizabeth tend to your needs. (*She plays on.*)

CAROLINE: (*Calling over.*) Do be careful, dear, not to muddy your dress.

LIZZIE: (*To audience.*) The similarity of pattern in the wing and leg of a bat, though used for such different purposes – in the jaws and legs of a crab – in the petals, stamens, and pistils of a flower, is likewise intelligible on the view of the gradual modification of parts or organs, which were alike in the early progenitor of each class. (*With dolls.*) Now, soldier...I shall try to remove the shrapnel but you will have to be brave. You will have to be ever such a brave darling soldier.

CAROLINE: (*Calling over.*) You are happy, dear, aren't you? You are happy in your childhood?

LIZZIE: Terribly so, Mother.

CAROLINE: And what a lovely day!

LIZZIE: It is the greatest of days! (*With dolls.*) Thank you, Nurse Elizabeth. You have saved my life. I will always love you for that. And I will always love *you* for your bravery and your strength of character. You have helped to keep the Russians at bay and your nation is deeply grateful.

THOMAS: (*Entering. Brighter, looser clothing.*) Isn't it a glorious day, Caroline? Isn't it simply a glorious day?

CAROLINE: It is.

THOMAS: We're on the top of the world up here, are we not? Lincolnshire laid out before us like a beautiful green carpet. And the Wash sparkling in the distance like a thousand diamonds!

CAROLINE: You are so poetical, Thomas.

THOMAS: A man of science can also be a man of the spirit, Caroline. I help the sick by day and I pore over Shakespeare by night! (*Calling to LIZZIE.*) And how are you this beautiful morning, my angel?

LIZZIE: Magical, Uncle Tom!

THOMAS: She grows more like her mother by the day. And if she ever becomes half so beautiful as you, then she will have suitors trailing her all the way from Lincolnshire to London! And no doubt all the way back again!

CAROLINE: You are in a merry mood.

THOMAS: I have everything in the world to be merry about, do I not? Summer has finally got into her glorious stride, I am about to have a feast fit for a king and I am spending the whole day with the three people I love most in the entire world! (*Breathing in deeply.*) Just smell the fragrance of that air!

CAROLINE: (*Smiling.*) You are quite mad, Tom. (*Pouring drink from a bottle.*) Have some lemonade.

THOMAS: (*Taking cup.*) Do you know…I don't think I have ever felt as blissfully happy, so utterly at peace with the world, as I do this day. (*Drinks.*)

CAROLINE: It certainly is quite perfect.

THOMAS: We are all young, we are all in the peak of health, we are all doing the things we always set out to do…I do, Caroline. I feel quite like a god at this moment!

CAROLINE: You mustn't say such things.

THOMAS: Only happier than a god. Happy that I am helping my fellow man, happy that I can use my meagre skills to ease his sufferings, happy that I am now earning a reasonable salary and happy that I now have my father finally off my back.

CAROLINE: You talk as if you are drunk, Thomas.

THOMAS: And so I am! Drunk with life! Drunk with life and happiness!

CAROLINE: You are such an extraordinary man. I find it hard to understand why you are unable to find a woman that suits you. You ought to marry. You cannot remain a bachelor forever.

THOMAS: Why not?

CAROLINE: All men need a woman to take care of them. What will you do when you are old and frail?

THOMAS: I shall dose myself with laudanum and put myself on a diet of wine and brandy!

CAROLINE: Oh, do at least try to be serious.

THOMAS: When the right woman happens to come along then no doubt...

CAROLINE: You are in the prime of your life, Thomas... and quite a catch.

THOMAS: (*After a pause, quiet.*) Why are you always so eager to marry me off, Caroline? I told you it should not happen again.

CAROLINE: (*Also quiet.*) It should not and it will not.

THOMAS: My desire for you, however, will never die. I still dream of you nightly.

CAROLINE: She will hear.

THOMAS: You chose my brother and he is a worthy man for you but swear to me you will never forget our passion. I treasure it, Caroline. We were alive, like animals. But you...

CAROLINE: She will hear!

THOMAS: (*Calling to LIZZIE.*) And how is the good Nurse Elizabeth this fine morning?

LIZZIE: She is caring for a badly-wounded soldier, Uncle.

THOMAS: Do you think he will survive?

LIZZIE: His wounds are merely physical injuries. Time and nature will see to them. He is likely, however, to die of a much more serious complaint!

THOMAS: What will cause him to die?

LIZZIE: He is sick with love, Uncle. He would suffer all the barbarity of five years on the battlefield for just one kiss from his beloved's lips.

THOMAS: Her imagination…

CAROLINE: I think she will become a great novelist one day.

THOMAS: She has a natural inclination for medicine, Caroline. She is forever bombarding me with questions about diseases, remedies, the latest developments in anaesthetics…

CAROLINE: Most young girls are fascinated with nursing, Thomas…

THOMAS: The country needs carers, Caroline. Not writers. We are crying out for dedicated professionals, who can help stem this relentless tide of suffering. We should be encouraging her to make something of herself. Women have surely more to offer society than housewifery and the odd piece of embroidery.

CAROLINE: Yes, but she is so young.

THOMAS: Imagination is a dangerous thing, Caroline. If permitted to expand unchecked, it can grow into a disease which brings enormous anguish to the victim. It serves no useful purpose whatsoever.

CAROLINE: I think you have a life planned out for her already…

THOMAS: The poor are restless and desperate, conditions are harsh, children are starving, death is everywhere. Those who are concerned for humanity owe it to themselves, to their country, to their very species…to do all in their power to ease this burden of misery which becomes ever heavier with each passing year. All hands should be placed firmly on deck, both male hands and female ones.

CAROLINE: You really are such an extraordinary man.

THOMAS: And we live in such relative comfort. Have you ever seen the face of a woman who has lost her child from a disease caused solely by the appalling conditions in which she lives? The agony, the pleading…the hopelessness.

CAROLINE: Please, Thomas…

THOMAS: Imagine your beautiful daughter there…imagine her face becoming a bed of sores, her skin turning white, her whole body racked with agony as it struggles to keep her wonderful girlish spirit alive. And then…nothing. Death. We must all fight this hideous devil of disease. The time for idle contemplation and futile flights of fancy is past.

CAROLINE: There is comfort, Thomas. Surely…Not nothing, not…nothing.

THOMAS: Well, that is the territory of people like Godfrey…

CAROLINE: But could we possibly talk about this another time? It is such a wonderful day and I should like us not to dwell on matters of such…morbidity…

THOMAS: (*Examining case again.*) And then one has only to look at the wing of a butterfly, hasn't one? The colours, the lines, the regularity of its form, its delicacy. The whole vista of colour, here in this case. Created by the glory of God and for the delectation of the human spirit! (*They both look at the case and seem moved by what they see.*)

LIZZIE: (*To audience.*) We ought not to marvel if all the contrivances in nature be not, as far as we can judge, absolutely perfect; and if some of them be abhorrent to our ideas of fitness. We need not marvel at the sting of the bee causing the bee's own death; at drones being produced in such vast numbers for one single act, and then being slaughtered by their sterile sisters; at the astonishing waste of pollen by our fir-trees…

THOMAS: The sheer flawlessness…

LIZZIE: (*Continuing.*) …at the instinctive hatred of the queen bee for her own fertile daughters…

CAROLINE: You have such…hands.
(*CAROLINE gently touches THOMAS's hand after which he lifts hers to his mouth and after a quick glance around, kisses it.*)

LIZZIE: The wonder indeed is, on the theory of natural selection, that more cases of the want of absolute perfection have not been observed.

CAROLINE: He is coming...

THOMAS: You are a witch.

CAROLINE: Promise me you will speak with him. Promise me you will help save him from his obsessions.

THOMAS: I will try...I will try...

CAROLINE: He listens to you...

THOMAS: I long to be naked...

(*GODFREY enters. A clergyman, he has a large satchel round his waist, carries a butterfly net and notebook. A pencil is behind one ear.*)

Quite a come down for you, Godfrey...a spot of human company for a change.

GODFREY: Isn't it a wonderful day?

(*CAROLINE and THOMAS are now eating chicken drumsticks.*)

THOMAS: And have you found any more for your collection?

GODFREY: They were too clever for me this morning, too clever by half. It was as if God Himself was helping them to escape my net!

THOMAS: Sorry to hear it!

GODFREY: There was, however, a speckled, copper-coloured creature which I've not seen before. Enormous size. It's just possible it is the female of some rare species...you understand they are clothed in much less alluring apparel than the males...

CAROLINE: Come and eat, Godfrey. You have been running about down there for hours.

GODFREY: (*Opening satchel.*) My jars and traps, however, have provided me with a few specimens to examine under the microscope when we...

CAROLINE: I beg you, Godfrey... Let us please indulge in some discourse other than beetles and butterflies.

THOMAS: You were such a serious, bookish boy, Godfrey. This seems something of a conversion.

LIZZIE: (*At his feet.*) What have you found, Father? What have you found?

THOMAS: How do you kill these beasts?

GODFREY: They fall through the soil at the top of the jar and then are quickly killed by a solution of ethyl acetate.

CAROLINE: It seems terribly cruel.

GODFREY: For your lunch, my dear, you are eating ham, chicken...

CAROLINE: This is our food, Godfrey...it is not to take home, to dissect, to pin onto display cases.

GODFREY: (*Removing beetle from jar and showing his daughter.*) This, my darling, is what is called a carrion beetle. Note the robust frame and the hard carapace. They have these wonderful antennae because they need to locate the decaying corpses of birds and mammals which is their main source of food.

CAROLINE: Please...

GODFREY: They are renowned for their habit of burying small carcasses...moles, birds, frogs, anything...and they play an important role in the decay of dead bodies. Everything, Lizzie, is woven into this cycle of birth, death and decay.

CAROLINE: Godfrey, please come and have your lunch...

GODFREY: They are lured to the smell of rotting flesh and the first individuals to arrive at a carcass battle against any other intruding beetles. Consequently there will be only one or two beetles on each carcass.

LIZZIE: They fight over dead animals, Father?

GODFREY: They do, and the males also fight furiously for the right to mate. They then bury the mole, the rat or whatever it is, by digging underneath the corpse with these strong jaws, look. They then skin the dead animal as it is dragged into the soil.

LIZZIE: Let me see, let me see!

GODFREY: If the carcasses legs become a problem, the beetles will simply amputate them.

THOMAS: (*Laughing.*) He is incorrigible!

CAROLINE: He does it simply to annoy me.

GODFREY: The female lays her eggs close by the rotting creature and she will then begin to feast off it.

CAROLINE: (*To THOMAS, gnawing at the chicken.*) He is spoiling that girl's sensibilities.

GODFREY: And when her little ones have hatched, they head for the odorous ball of flesh where they essentially beg for regurgitated food from their mother.

CAROLINE: Do come and eat, Lizzie

LIZZIE: I'm really not at all hungry, Mama!

CAROLINE: (*To THOMAS.*) Would you like some more lemonade, Thomas?

THOMAS: (*As she pours, mouth full.*) Thank you, thank you…

GODFREY: (*Replacing beetle in jar. Then quickly to LIZZIE as if to catch her off-guard.*) Adder?

LIZZIE: (*As quickly back, confidently. Excited.*) *Vipera berus*!

GODFREY: Grass snake?

LIZZIE: *Natrix natrix*!

GODFREY: Slow-worm?

LIZZIE: *Anguis fragilis*!

GODFREY: Common lizard?

LIZZIE: *Lacerta vivipara*!

GODFREY: Common frog?

LIZZIE: *Rana temporaria*!

GODFREY: Common toad?

LIZZIE: *Bufo bufo*!

GODFREY: Natterjack toad?

LIZZIE: (*After a think.*) *Bufo calamita*?

GODFREY: Great Crested newt?

LIZZIE: *Triturus cristatus*?

GODFREY: Common newt?

LIZZIE: *Triturus vulgaris*!!

GODFREY: (*Picking her up and whirling her round.*) Excellent! Excellent! We shall make a taxonomist of you yet! (*She covers his face with kisses in ecstasy.*)

THOMAS: Come on, old chap! Come and join us. You and I have been strangers to each other over the last few months.

GODFREY: (*Setting down his daughter, who returns to her dolls.*) You are the man with the mission these days. (*Going to others.*) The enemy of death and pain, I think.

THOMAS: (*Sitting.*) The avowed adversary.

GODFREY: (*Helping himself to food.*) I fear you are working too hard, Thomas.

THOMAS: How can one possibly ever work too hard? Humanity is on the brink of...

GODFREY: You talk of my conversion and yet it is you who has changed the more dramatically. What ever happened to the young, ale-swilling rake with an eye for the ladies and a contempt for the starched collar?

THOMAS: I have become a man, that is all. And if you must know...it is your example, the example of my younger brother that inspired me to the change.

GODFREY: You say we are living a disaster but the country has never enjoyed such prosperity. We are building our own Jerusalem in every continent of the globe.

THOMAS: Commercial prosperity perhaps, and for the elect, the few. But the poor die horribly in the meantime.

GODFREY: What can we do? It is the law of nature that some members of any given species...

CAROLINE: This is not any given species, Godfrey, this is your fellow man!

GODFREY: I no longer feel capable of easing their suffering. What can any words of mine do to bring comfort to the bereaved and the lonely? I truly believe that God does not care for us.

THOMAS: You seem to be forgetting the means by which you earn your living, the means by which you can provide this delicious food for your family and live in this...

GODFREY: I feel as if I am living a lie, I...

THOMAS: You are losing your faith?

GODFREY: (*After a pause.*) I don't know.

CAROLINE: Godfrey...I beg you to speak to somebody in the Church about this? It simply cannot go on. Even if you are less...ardent than once you were...even if you have the occasional doubt...surely there is no need to transmit your anxieties to the people?

GODFREY: Doesn't one have to be honest?

THOMAS: You are needed.

GODFREY: But you are a doctor, Thomas...You encounter the most hideous...

THOMAS: I do not think as deeply as you. I never have. I see pain and I treat pain. I see suffering and I do all in my power to ease it. I am happy to accept that there is a higher purpose behind it. We were only just now admiring the splendour of your collection here. The beauty of these insects here shout out the wonder of God's mind. How much louder is the cry of a human child. Your daughter...she is the essence of divinity. The pinnacle of His inventions.

GODFREY: (*Sadly.*) I know... And it saddens me, looking at her now at this moment, to think that one day she too must...

THOMAS: When we allow one child to die, one child to die from starvation in the slums of our country, then we are essentially killing a part of Him that created us.
(*Unseen, CAROLINE reaches over and squeezes THOMAS's hand.*)

GODFREY: I am so miserable with the thought of it all sometimes. It's as if the whole world was teetering under my feet. It can only be, perhaps, that God enjoys pain.

THOMAS: You are my brother, Godfrey, and you will always be dear to me but you are running the risk of making a fool of yourself. The country needs you, it needs what you provide. It is your duty to provide it.

GODFREY: The words stick in my throat, Thomas. Last week a man was crying all over me because his wife had died. Forty years of marriage, of tenderness, caring, love, fidelity, hard work...and then a cold white corpse at the end of it all. He seemed very angry with me. I could not...I could not say with confidence where she had gone to.

THOMAS: You have a beautiful wife, a beautiful daughter, a beautiful life. You can spend your free time doing something you love. You must tell the man...

GODFREY: I am overcome with...melancholy. Excuse me...(*Rises.*) I have some traps down by the pond and I should like to...

THOMAS: You have a duty to your family, Godfrey.

GODFREY: Please...excuse me. Thank you. Thank you both. I...will not be long. (*He leaves, tearful. They watch him go. A silence.*)

THOMAS: I fear for him.

(*Suddenly CAROLINE reaches out and puts her hand on THOMAS's groin. He moans. She takes her hand away. She is mad with desire.*)

CAROLINE: (*Quiet.*) In five minutes, come down to the stream. In five minutes.

THOMAS: Caroline…

CAROLINE: (*Slow, serious. In a whisper.*) I want you… inside me.

(*CAROLINE rises, eyes fixed on her husband. THOMAS's hand is in her skirts. She watches for a bit longer and then turns and goes in the opposite direction.*)

LIZZIE: (*To audience.*) The whole history of the world, as at present known, although of a length quite incomprehensible by us, will hereafter be recognised as a mere fragment of time, compared with the ages which have elapsed since the first creature, the progenitor of innumerable extinct and living descendants, was created.

THOMAS: Lizzie?

(*LIZZIE turns.*)

Why don't you follow your father down to the pond? He is looking for his toads again! You could help him, couldn't you?

(*LIZZIE rises and runs off after her father. THOMAS alone stares off after CAROLINE. He rises. He breathes in deeply, trying to remain calm. He paces. He looks off again. He picks up the case. Puts it down. He unbuttons his shirt slightly. Loosens his belt. Paces. Then, unseen by THOMAS, LIZZIE re-enters and picks up her two dolls. THOMAS goes off after CAROLINE.*)

LIZZIE: (*Two dolls raised above her head, in either hand.*) There is grandeur in this view of life, with its several powers, having been originally breathed into a few forms or into one; and that, whilst this planet has gone cycling on according to the fixed law of gravity, from so simple a beginning endless forms most beautiful and most wonderful have been, and are being, evolved.

I Am The Knife

A PRIEST alone in a dark room. He is sat at a table. On the table stands a bottle of spirits, two glasses and a bible. He holds a handkerchief over his mouth and nose throughout. The smell is evidently emanating from a bucket in the corner. Somewhere close by we can hear the sounds of a man being beaten up. The blows seem to fall at regular intervals. It is troubling him. He mops his brow, has a drink and opens the book. To distract himself, he reads at speed from the book.

PRIEST: Blessings are upon the head of the just, but violence covers the mouth of the wicked. The memory of the just is blessed, but the name of the wicked shall rot. The wise in heart shall receive commandments, but a prating fool shall fall. He that walks uprightly walks surely, but he that perverts his ways shall be known. He that winks with the eye causes sorrow, but a prating fool shall fall. The mouth of a righteous man is a well of life, but violence covers the mouth of the wicked. Hatred stirs up strifes, but love covers all sins. In the lips of him that has understanding wisdom is found, but a rod is for the back of him that is void of understanding.
(The sounds of violence cease. The PRIEST's eyes are closed and he sits in silence, head back, sweating. He takes another slug. Wipes his mouth. A door is unlocked. The SCREW enters, straightening his uniform. He is immaculately dressed. He stands to attention at one side. A silence.)
Nice?

SCREW: Very nice, sir.

PRIEST: Enjoy?

SCREW: Wouldn't say that, exactly, sir. But I think 'e's resigned to it now.

PRIEST: I rather meant, did *you* enjoy the process?

SCREW: Oh, yes. Very much. Thank you, sir. *(A pause.)* Flecks of blood on me nice, bleached collar, look.
(A pause.) Bleached me shirts last night, sir.

PRIEST: I see.

SCREW: And ironed them this mornin', sir. Nice new steam iron, sir.

131

PRIEST: Good stuff.

SCREW: Pressed me trousers, polished me shoes, lacquered me flowin' locks.

PRIEST: Flowing?

SCREW: Sprayed on the aftershave, slapped on the body lotion, clipped me nostril 'airs…

PRIEST: Yes, well…you're always very well turned out.

SCREW: Thank you, sir. Thank you. Nice to be appreciated.

PRIEST: You're very welcome.

SCREW: Nice for someone to take the time to pass comment, if I may say so, sir.

PRIEST: Well…cleanliness is next to…

SCREW: To godliness. Exactly, sir. That's what they say, ain't it? I mean, the clobber people are wearin' these days. On the streets, sir. It's shockin'. No sense of…no sense of…

PRIEST: Decorum?

SCREW: Decorum, sir. Thank you. No sense of decorum at all, sir. Anythin' goes, don't it? These days.

PRIEST: Well…

SCREW: Pornography, sir. If you don't mind my sayin' so. Out there. Pornography. Girls in low-cut dresses, wigglin' their 'ips. Bare shoulders. Bellies on display at all hours, sir. Shoulders out for all to see. It's provocation, if you ask me, sir. No wonder we're always full to burstin' in 'ere, sir.

PRIEST: It is the height of summer, officer.

SCREW: 'air flickin' about. All sorts of lengths. Calves, thighs, backs. And those brassieres, sir. They don't leave a great deal to the imagination, do they, sir?

PRIEST: As I say…

SCREW: I mean, I know it's not my place to voice an opinion. That's your particular field, ain't it? But all I *would* say is that unless some sense…sense of…

PRIEST: Decorum?

SCREW: Decorum. Thank you, sir. Unless some sense of decorum is returned to the streets, there is goin' to be trouble. That's all I can say on the matter, sir. They'll be

doin' it in the road, they'll be doin' it up alleyways,
they'll be doin' it in shop windows…before you can
say…

PRIEST: It wouldn't be at all possible to open a window,
would it? It's incredibly…close.

SCREW: Do you think so, sir?

PRIEST: I'm finding it rather hard to breathe actually.

SCREW: There ain't no windows down' ere, sir. We're a
good twenty foot below street level.

PRIEST: Of course.

SCREW: You're quite safe 'ere, sir.

PRIEST: Safe?

SCREW: You're not goin' to be infected down 'ere…by all
the sickness on the streets. Don't you worry yourself
about that, sir. The lepers in the pubs, in the offices, the
classrooms. They can't touch you down 'ere, sir.

PRIEST: Then perhaps it would be possible to remove the
bucket?

SCREW: The bucket, sir?

PRIEST: It's… I'm afraid it's making me feel rather sick.
The smell.

SCREW: The smell?

PRIEST: You can't…?

SCREW: There's no smell 'ere, sir. I run a clean and tidy
ship, sir. Get 'em scrubbin' and cleanin' and polishin' and
scourin'…

PRIEST: I see but…

SCREW: And washin', disinfectin'…

PRIEST: I appreciate that but…

SCREW: All is refined, purged and…decontaminated 'ere, sir.

PRIEST: The bucket does seem…it appears to be…how can
I put it?…rather full.

SCREW: 'e 'ad a bad night, sir. Tossin' and turnin' like a
thing possessed 'e was. And, if you will forgive me
crudeness just this once…shittin' not infrequently.

PRIEST: I see.

SCREW: Did a few 'angin's next door, see. 'angin' nights
generally make for sloppy mornin's. If you get me drift, sir.

PRIEST: Well...perhaps...

SCREW: And what this one doesn't know is...and I 'ope I can rely on you to keep this as our little secret...what 'e doesn't know is...that it's 'is turn this mornin'.

PRIEST: You're going to...?

SCREW: My idea, as it goes, sir. They obviously find 'angin' nights...'ow shall we say?...somewhat... disconcertin' and, as you've already noticed, it tends to churn their bowels up a bit. But they also know, when we've finished dispatchin' for the night and they realise that they're still breathin', as it were...they also know that they've got a bit of a stay of execution. 'angin' nights, as you probably know, bein' spaced out at monthly intervals. More or less, sir. But now, and 'ere's the clever bit...we're 'avin' an 'angin' mornin' this mornin' to follow 'ard on the 'eels of the 'angin' night we 'ad last night. Lull 'em into a false sense of security. More 'umane, in a manner of speakin', see. Since they don't 'ave thirty days and thirty nights of wonderin' and thinkin' and thinkin' and wonderin' and...

PRIEST: You do talk a lot, don't you?

SCREW: Talk, sir?

PRIEST: Yes, it's not an attribute one commonly associates with prison officers.

SCREW: (*After a pause.*) You've lost me, sir.

PRIEST: And I was wondering, actually...if you could tell me something?

SCREW: Anything, sir.

PRIEST: This daily round of beatings. Is it absolutely necessary? I mean, does it serve any purpose at all?

SCREW: Purpose, sir?

PRIEST: Yes...what exactly is to be gained from all this...violence?

SCREW: (*Nonplussed.*) Nothing, sir. (*After a think.*) Pleasure, sir?

PRIEST: Yes, but whose pleasure?

SCREW: (*Nonplussed again.*) Mine, sir.

PRIEST: (*Pouring.*) Drink?

SCREW: Never on duty, sir.

PRIEST: Fair enough.

SCREW: Nor off-duty, sir.

PRIEST: (*Drinks.*) Cheers.

SCREW: (*After watching him drain glass.*) Like a drink, do you, sir?

PRIEST: No.

SCREW: Make you feel better, sir?

PRIEST: Not really.

SCREW: My old man died of drink. Forever on the piss. (*After a pause.*) Choked on 'is own vomit. Thirty-nine years of age, sir. They cut 'im open...and they found that 'is liver 'ad shrunk to the size of a pickled gherkin. Like a blistered grey slug, it was. Apparently. (*After a reminisce.*) Course 'e 'ad a weakness for the ladies. I actually think it was the women what killed 'im. Rather than the wine. Quite particular, though, to all manner of intoxicatin' beverages 'e was, sir. But 'e needed it, see. Stoked 'im up. For the slags.

PRIEST: Listen...do you think I could see him soon? I have a number of other engagements this morning and...

SCREW: Just cleanin' 'im up for you, sir. Don't want 'im meetin' first your good self and then 'is Maker lookin' like a piece of butchered meat now, do we? Gotta show some respect. Bit of decorum, sir. As you so graciously phrased it.

PRIEST: And you're executing him this morn...?

SCREW: Keep it down, sir! Please! Don't wanna lose the old element of surprise, now do we?

PRIEST: I beg your pardon.

SCREW: But 'e'll crack, sir. This one, 'e reckons 'e's strong. Reckons 'e's not frit. Reckons 'e can go into it like simply walkin' into another room. I seen 'em so many times. The ones what seem the quietest, the clever ones...the writers, the readers...political and that... they're the ones what shits themselves, piss themselves... and cry like the newborn. When it comes to it, sir. You've only to 'ave a good look in that bucket.

PRIEST: Well, as I say, I do have rather a busy schedule today so...

SCREW: You don't want to sit around gossipin' with me all mornin'. I quite understand. You 'ave matters of a more...elevated nature to discuss.

PRIEST: Well...

SCREW: And you're bein' troubled by some form of smell, sir?

PRIEST: It's incredibly overpowering actually.

SCREW: You sure you never trod in somethin'? On the pavement.

PRIEST: My olfactory organs are in perfect working order, I can assure you, and the smell...

SCREW: All sorts of business on the streets these days. Never know what you might step in...

PRIEST: Is there no way you could...?

SCREW: My duties do not include sloppin' out, sir. I am what is known as a government administrator, a professional, and not...I 'ave to say...a toilet attendant. I am no slopster, sir.

PRIEST: I understand...

SCREW: (*Going to bucket and examining the contents.*) The last movements of a public enemy. Tells a sorry story, does this. Certainly don't say a lot for prison grub either. 'ardly a solid to be seen.

PRIEST: If you'd be so kind...

SCREW: You are aware that I'll 'ave to...

PRIEST: I've been doing this long enough to know the procedure...

SCREW: Just so as no monkey-business goes on.

PRIEST: I know the procedure, thank you.

SCREW: If you'll excuse me...(*Makes to leave. A pause.*) Been nice talkin' to you, sir. (*The door is unlocked. He leaves. Alone, the PRIEST begins to dab his brow again. He pours another drink. Fills the other glass. Drinks. He covers his mouth and nose again. He opens the bible. Flicks through it listlessly. Takes out a cigarette. Lights it. Smokes. He pours another glass. When not drinking or smoking, his face is covered by the handkerchief. The door is unlocked. The INMATE walks in, ankles and wrists shackled. His face is swollen and one eye is closed. He walks with pain but with dignity, head down. He is dressed in prison clothes. He starts when he sees the PRIEST. The PRIEST stands. He seems slightly in awe of the INMATE. The SCREW enters. The door is locked. He stands to one side. A silence.*)

PRIEST: Would you...care to...care to sit down?

INMATE: (*To SCREW.*) What's he doing here?

PRIEST: You hadn't had a visit for over six months. We thought it was time...

INMATE: Who thought it was time?

PRIEST: We did.

INMATE: I don't want you here. Please go.
(*A silence.*)

PRIEST: (*To SCREW.*) Listen...you couldn't make an exception, could you? As he is such a special case.

SCREW: Everyone's treated the same 'ere, sir. Equal society in 'ere, sir. (*To INMATE.*) Socialist utopia, innit?
(*A silence.*)

PRIEST: How are you...feeling?

INMATE: Is it not the height of bad manners to intrude uninvited into somebody else's private space and then to smoke cigarettes without asking?

PRIEST: Sorry...I...(*He puts out cigarette.*) You don't...?
(*A silence.*) A drink, perhaps? (*No answer.*) I'm afraid I'm a little prone to all manner of addictions.

INMATE: You have a cold?

PRIEST: No...it's just...it's just a little...

INMATE: Please...go.

SCREW: You are deemed in need of spiritual enlightenment and so spiritual enlightenment is what you must 'ave. Extend a little courtesy to your guest.

PRIEST: (*Sitting.*) Please...

INMATE: I prefer to stand.
(*A silence. The PRIEST finds it hard to talk with the SCREW present.*)

PRIEST: Is a man not to be allowed to make his confession in secret?

SCREW: I am the eyes of the State.

PRIEST: I know but this is a man who…

SCREW: I am the ears of the State.

PRIEST: Could you not at least take off his…?

INMATE: I neither wish to make a confession, nor do I wish to have my chains removed.

(A long, tense silence. The PRIEST drinks. He rises and approaches the SCREW. He takes a wallet out of his jacket and counts out some banknotes.)

SCREW: I'm moderately insulted, sir.

PRIEST: Please…Grant him a little humanity.

SCREW: 'umanity, sir?

PRIEST: Take it. Buy yourself a new ironing-board or…

SCREW: I 'ave a perfectly adequate ironin'-board already, sir.

(The PRIEST counts out some more money. A silence.)

You are aware that attemptin' to bribe…

PRIEST: This is a favour you'll be doing *me*. Not him. You heard what he said.

SCREW: *(After a pause.)* Five minutes. *(Takes money.)* This'll get you five minutes. *(He approaches the INMATE and is about to unlock his handcuffs.)*

INMATE: Please…leave me as I am.

SCREW: Suit yerself. *(He walks to door.)* I'll be watchin' you. Through the door.

PRIEST: I understand.

SCREW: I 'ope I can rely on you…

PRIEST: Of course. Thank you. *(The SCREW leaves. The door is locked. There is another long, tense silence.)* This is…this is something of an honour for me. *(No answer.)* It would have been nicer, though, to have met you in slightly happier circumstances. *(No answer.)* Are you sure you won't sit? *(No answer.)* You mind if I…*(Pours another drink. Drinks.)*

INMATE: You're an alcoholic?

PRIEST: *(After a pause.)* I am. *(A silence.)* Does that make me slightly more human in your eyes?

INMATE: I never had you down as a god.

PRIEST: No…well…a god I am certainly not. *(A silence.)* I don't think I've ever met anyone as famous as yourself… Makes me a little nervous, actually.

INMATE: Is the smell of my shit upsetting you?

PRIEST: I have to say…

INMATE: I have learned to regard it with equanimity.

PRIEST: I see…

INMATE: It's a part of myself. I will not be disgusted by myself.

PRIEST: Do you mind if I…? (*He reaches for his cigarette packet. He has run out of cigarettes and is forced to relight his previous half-smoked one. He puffs at it desperately.*) Is there nothing you want to say to me?

INMATE: No.

PRIEST: That saddens me.

INMATE: You feel I am missing out?

PRIEST: It often helps to unburden yourself of whatever…

INMATE: You whole existence has been an appalling waste of time.

PRIEST: (*After a pause.*) Perhaps. (*He drags on the butt.*) You are at peace with the world? You are ready to…?

INMATE: I am.

PRIEST: And you will not sign the…?

INMATE: No!!

PRIEST: You could walk under the sun again. As a free man. You could spend time with your family. Watch your daughter blossom into a woman.

INMATE: I have said my goodbyes.

PRIEST: But your wife…

INMATE: Outwardly she is my loyal supporter, inwardly she aches for compromise.

PRIEST: Surely…

INMATE: Women…they seek proof of our mettle, they spur us on to show ourselves worthy. It is for them that we steal, it for them that we murder, it is for them that we die.

PRIEST: Well…

INMATE: You have nothing to teach me, you offer no consolation for me.

PRIEST: It is only a signature. Swear to renounce all…

INMATE: Your cowardliness is an affront to my sight.

PRIEST: Yes.

INMATE: Your trembling, your shaking hands...

PRIEST: Yes.

INMATE: I do not have such a long time to live, Father, and so if you'll excuse me, I should like to be alone.

PRIEST: (*After a pause.*) I find it increasingly difficult to abide my own company.

INMATE: That is your cross.

PRIEST: I...I respect your desire for solitude but...you are what I would call a truly honourable man. You are somebody I have always...respected. There are so few people of integrity these days. We...to execute those who... It is an abhorrent waste, is it not?...To snuff out honourable minds. (*No answer.*) I...as I say...it is a great honour to...

INMATE: I am the knife that cuts through your complacency. I am the knife that slits open your over-stuffed belly and makes your self-satisfaction ooze from the wound. I am the knife that causes you pain but only through pain is there hope of a cure.

(*A silence. The PRIEST is in despair. He drinks.*)

PRIEST: I feel so wretched. I do not feel worthy of...

INMATE: Then go.

PRIEST: I think I must...

INMATE: Go and drink your vapid days away, dishing out your uncertain crumbs of comfort to the bewildered flock.

PRIEST: We all must survive. Somehow. Those born without talent must...

INMATE: Go.

PRIEST: If you would only sign...

INMATE: Get out.

(*The PRIEST stands weakly. He slowly approaches the INMATE.*)

PRIEST: I'm sorry to have wasted your time... If I might have the honour of...shaking your hand...

INMATE: Your breath reeks.

PRIEST: I apologise.

INMATE: Good luck to you.

(*They shake hands. A long silence as they stare at each other. The PRIEST seems to be holding onto the INMATE for dear life. They finally disengage, the PRIEST still staring deeply into the other man's eyes.*)

PRIEST: (*Suddenly, despairingly.*) But the beatings...! How do you take the beatings? Sleeping on the floor there? With only a bucket? Waiting for your death. How...how can you stand it?

(*A silence.*)

INMATE: Withstanding violence is the prisoner's daily grind. It is not so different on the streets, however. In the offices. They are at least fair here. I can count the punches. It's the honest face of clockwatching.

PRIEST: Surely you owe it to the people to stay alive? What you stand for must not simply be exterminated with you! Surely a small reconciliation...

INMATE: There is nothing more contemptible than the spectacle of the philosophy unadhered to. You tremble like a child in the face of passion. You will die alone, in a doss-house, forgotten.

(*After a silence, in which the PRIEST stares miserably at the ground, the door opens and the SCREW re-enters.*)

SCREW: Couple of sweet-smelling females come to see you.

INMATE: But I just want to be left alone!

SCREW: (*To PRIEST.*) You gotta admire 'im, 'aven't you, sir? Thinks 'is wants 'ave some bearin' on proceedings.

INMATE: Will you both just leave me...

SCREW: (*At door.*) This way, please.

(*After a time, two women appear. They are the INMATE's wife and daughter. The WOMAN is dressed as a bank clerk. The GIRL is in her school uniform. They both immediately cover their noses and mouths. The door is locked. A long silence.*)

INMATE: Did you have to bring them down here?

SCREW: I 'ave my instructions. (*He moves to his former position. Another silence. The WOMAN is weeping quietly.*)

PRIEST: (*To SCREW.*) Could we not leave them alone? For a few minutes?

SCREW: I'm sorry, sir?

PRIEST: If I...

SCREW: One official to be present at all times.

PRIEST: (Approaching SCREW, wallet out.) This is all I've got.

SCREW: *(Taking money.)* You'll 'ave to stay, though, sir. And I shall make sure you're properly fucked over if you let me down. *(Goes to door.)* Two minutes. *(The door is unlocked. The SCREW leaves. Key in door. A long, long silence.)*

PRIEST: Listen…I'll stand over here. *(Walks into dark corner and turns his back.)* You'll not know I'm here. Please… don't waste any time.

(A silence.)

GIRL: Father? *(No answer.)* Father?

INMATE: Will you ask her to stop crying?

GIRL: I've missed you. We both have.

INMATE: Why did you come?

GIRL: They telephoned us. This morning.

INMATE: Why is she dressed like that? *(To WOMAN.)* Why are you dressed like that?

GIRL: When they took you…she had to work. To pay for my schooling.

INMATE: *(Laughing.)* She has her name on a badge and she is paying for your schooling.

GIRL: She works at the bank.

(A silence.)

INMATE: *(Moved.)* I hoped I should…never see you again. I thought I'd written…

GIRL: They asked us to come.

(A silence. The GIRL is struggling to overcome her nausea.)

INMATE: Let's not draw this out. Go. Please. I'm sorry.

GIRL: They are beating you?

INMATE: Yes.

GIRL: That man outside. Does he beat you?

INMATE: Yes.

(A silence.)

GIRL: Do you wish to be alone with Mother?

INMATE: No.

GIRL: She wishes it.

INMATE: I have cut you both out of my mind. You are both dead to me. Please go. I cannot bear to look at you.

GIRL: Please sign, Father.

INMATE: You talk like a machine.

GIRL: Please.

INMATE: Go.

> (*The GIRL shoots a look at the WOMAN and then walks to the door. She knocks on it. The SCREW unlocks it.*)

GIRL: I need some air. (*She leaves. The door is locked. A silence.*)

INMATE: The bank?

WOMAN: I love you so much.

INMATE: With a badge on your breast?

WOMAN: You are determined to die?

INMATE: I am.

WOMAN: Do you wish to…make love to a woman for one last time?

INMATE: I am separate. I can't explain.

WOMAN: (*Moves towards him.*) Please…

INMATE: There is a priest in the room.

WOMAN: (*Removing her shoes.*) I love you.

INMATE: There's an eye in the door. And I am chained.

WOMAN: (*Peeling off tights.*) Your daughter loves you.

INMATE: (*After a pause, understanding.*) No!

WOMAN: You are my husband. You are her father. You are loved.

INMATE: No!! (*He shuffles desperately over to the door.*) No!! Not with him!! Christ, no!

WOMAN: Quickly!!

INMATE: No!! (*He falls. A silence. He curls up on the floor in terrible anguish. She approaches him and stands over him.*) Please…go. It's over. (*They do not speak. The terrible silence is broken by the scream of the SCREW somewhere off. After a while the door is unlocked and the GIRL enters.*)

GIRL: We have to go. I'm sorry. He was…

WOMAN: (*To INMATE.*) I am your wife.

GIRL: We have one minute.

WOMAN: (*Kneeling to him.*) We have to go. I love you. I am not as good as you. Your life has touched mine. You will always be the love of my life. I will never forget you. My heart is breaking.

GIRL: (*Kneeling also.*) Your influence will remain with me always. You are a light in my darkness. I will work hard. I love you more than you will ever know. My heart is breaking. (*They both kiss him, one on each cheek. The WOMAN begins to weep. She holds him tightly and covers him with kisses.*)

WOMAN: Say something...please!

INMATE: (*After a pause.*) I have nothing further to add. (*There is a terrible silence. The door is then opened and the SCREW enters.*)

SCREW: Ladies...could we...?

(*They slowly rise, the WOMAN weeping more heavily and they both have a long last look at the man on the floor. He keeps his face away from them. Then they both rush out. The SCREW follows them. The PRIEST slowly emerges from the shadows. He walks over to the fallen INMATE. He helps the man to his feet. The INMATE's state of mind has been altered by the appearance of the women.*)

INMATE: Bankers and whores, bankers and whores. And the priests forever concerned. Concerned. Damn the empathisers, damn the concerned. And the bleeding hearts. Bankers and whores, bankers and whores... Don't touch me...don't you dare put your sympathetic arm around my shoulder. Your hideous pity, your concern. Death to all pity. Bankers and whores, bankers and whores... Ah, the women. God, all the women. The curve of her spine. I used to...I would...I would suck on her arsehole, vicar. (*He laughs.*) Yes, vicar. Suck on her flesh. Drink in her dirt. Bankers and whores, bankers and whores...And a badge on her breast, her name on her breast. I wrote poetry for that name. Sonnets for that name. And now...and now...her name on a badge, her name on a plastic badge... No! No! Bankers and whores, bankers and whores...Don't touch me, drunk! Lawyer! Take your foul breath out of my face. Go fuck a choirboy! (*Laughs.*) Go fuck a choirboy! Hide him under your cassock as you belch out your sermon. Bankers and whores, bankers and whores...(*Laughs.*) Don't be fooled, boys! Don't let them love you, boys! (*Laughs.*) Stay alone.

Always alone. Bankers and whores...bankers and whores... (*The PRIEST sits him down.*) Give me a drink... Fill me with shit, vicar. Fill me with shit. Make my body cry out! (*The PRIEST pours him a glass.*) Bankers and whores and bankers and whores...(*The PRIEST brings the glass to his lips and helps him drink.*) Bankers and... (*The INMATE spits the liquid into the PRIEST's face.*) Blinded the eyes of the world-changers! Deeply concerned, deeply concerned at the state of the world. Deeply concerned, deeply concerned. Bankers and whores, bankers and whores...

(*The PRIEST is holding his head, staring into his eyes, trying to calm him. Suddenly, the SCREW and a HANGMAN burst through into the cell. The HANGMAN quickly covers the INMATE's head with a hood. The INMATE screams. He struggles wildly. He is kicking out and flailing his arms viciously. The PRIEST instinctively helps the two men restrain the prisoner. It takes all the strength of the three to subdue him. The table and chairs are kicked over and they wrestle on the floor. During this:*)

INMATE: No! No! Please! Please! God, no! No! Please! Please! God, no! No! Please! Please! Please! No! No! No! Please! Please! Please!

(*He is eventually dragged off, leaving the PRIEST alone.*)
(*Off, weeping furiously.*) Please...Please!! Please!! No!! No!! Please!

(*Suddenly we hear the lash of a rope and then silence. Another long, terrible silence. The PRIEST's mouth is bleeding from the INMATE's kicking. He covers his face with his handkerchief again. He is shaking, sweating. Soon, the SCREW slowly walks back in. He looks at the mess. Shakes his head and smiles at the PRIEST.*)

SCREW: Thanks for that, sir. Caught you a nasty blow on the mouth there, didn't 'e? (*No answer.*) Like a trapped bloody animal, weren't 'e, sir? (*No answer.*) But a charmin' lady, 'is wife. And 'is young daughter there. Absolutely charmin'. Wouldn't you say so, sir? (*No answer.*) Wouldn't you say so?

The Art of Being Alone

An old woman, Irish, dressed as The Virgin Mary, is sat outside a bank, beside a cash-dispensing machine. She has been badly beaten, her hair is matted with blood and she is filthy. She has a small bunch of daffodils in her hand. A polythene bag by her side. It is raining slightly.

MARY: Spitting. Another day of spit. Tourists taking their morning coffee. Drudges scuttling for the tube, newspapers raised up, keeping the water off their fat necks. (*A long silence. She spits out something she's been chewing.*) It was raining on the day I was rodgered by the Holy Spirit. Pissing down. All day, all night. Heard the water dribbling through me knackered guttering for the duration. (*We hear the sound of car-horns in a gridlock. She listens and nods her head in time with the monotonous dirge.*) Sometimes, when I really lose myself in it, I can put myself into something like a trance. I hallucinate. See all sorts of things. Beautiful colours, shapes. Visions. Visions of the future. (*She listens, her head bobbing up and down. She suddenly calls off.*) Oi, you!! Put yer teeth away!!… yeah, you! Snarling like that…I can see yer gums!! (*The horns continue. She listens and bobs, eyes closed.*) No use fighting. Got to go with the flow. (*It continues then suddenly stops. A pause.*) The snake of metal, red, white and blue, slithers forward for a couple of yards and then… (*Her eyes quickly follow someone walking.*) A daffodil for you, my friend? To go with your beautiful smile! Spring is in the air and the time for regeneration is here!! (*No success. She mutters.*) Wanker. (*Pause.*) They're all wankers. And the ones who shower their pity and guilt over me. The bigger wankers, they. The furrowed brow, the There-but-for-the-Grace-of-God tilt of the head, the look of concern. I will suck out your pity and turn to gold. I'll drink down your guilt and I'll pickle my brains. For I am Mary, the Mother of God. (*A pause as she pulls her cloak more tightly around herself. She examines her flowers. She removes something from the petals of one.*) Cannot sell these to my customers when they are overrun with all manner of insects. Need to develop a reputation for quality. (*Throws insect away.*) Go and shit in somebody else's corner! (*She inspects other flowers.*) Swiped this lot from outside the police station. Growing in such a lovely little row, they were. All lined up. Heads facing the morning sun. Before the clouds came and pissed out their drops. Adding a touch of natural gracefulness to the chipped grey concrete, they were. There is a beauty in that, is there not? The police plant the bulbs, the flowers grow in the sun, I take the flowers, I sell them as guilt, I drink all me profits and then they put me in their van. I wake up in their cells and then snuffle along their lawn again, eyeing the talent. (*Pause.*) Ah, maybe not. (*The cars resume their demonic bleating. She again bobs her head like a shaman. It stops. She faces the sky and opens her mouth.*) I drink in the rain. Accept it with gratitude…the blessings of the Father. (*Pause.*) Ah, the night I was taken…The night of all nights. I shall never forget, I still hold that memory close to me and wear it like a cloak. Such aggression, such determination, such an honour. To be the chosen. To be deemed as worthy. I can die happy now, see, having had one night of feeling so special. Some go to their graves without ever feeling so special. Not even for an hour.

(*SUITMAN enters, with an umbrella, and approaches the machine. He fumbles in his trousers, pulls out his wallet. Takes out his card. Inserts it in the wall. Eyes MARY with contempt.*)

MARY: Haven't seen your grizzled face feeding from this particular pump before? (*No answer.*) Care for a flower to brighten your day?

SUITMAN: What is mine is mine.

MARY: Well…

SUITMAN: I do not wish you to address me in any way. I do not wish to be aware of your existence. Indeed, your whole existence is an impertinence.

MARY: A fiver and you can beat me.

SUITMAN: I can beat you for free.

MARY: But…

SUITMAN: I can stamp on your feet, I can spit in your
    face, I can elbow your ribs…

MARY: I am Mary, Mother of God…

SUITMAN: I have come to this spot for what's rightfully
    mine. I'll hold up my notes and I'll force you to smell
    what comes hot off the press. Virginal notes.

MARY: The Mother of God!

SUITMAN: (*Money withdrawn.*) The Queen smiles up at me
    from each and every one. A half-smile, an intelligent
    smile, a knowing smile, a smile of approval, a smile of
    approbation. Oh, modest, modest tiara!

MARY: Beat me!!

SUITMAN: (*Smelling notes.*) Ah, the stink of the ink! You
    flood me with comfort and I am not ashamed. Not
    ashamed.

MARY: I am homeless and hungry and you can beat me!

SUITMAN: (*Turning on her suddenly, pointing.*) You have no
    power over me. None whatsoever. (*The gridlocked cars once
    more resume their rhythmic honkings. Both MARY and
    SUITMAN bob their heads quite instinctively. After a while,
    it stops.*) If you were now to embark upon a long and
    distressing cardiac arrest right in front of my eyes, then I
    would simply place my sweet-smelling notes in my
    wallet and then walk off into yet another day of
    adventure.

MARY: I am human and you may punch me in the face!

SUITMAN: I care little for humanity. The species is
    doomed. I reject the lie that we have a duty to care.
    I do not care. I do not care about you.

MARY: Any change then? Any coins…?

SUITMAN: (*Laughing.*) Your feigned dignity evaporates and
    now you would scrabble on the ground for unwanted
    coppers. You sneer at the monied, you scoff at the caged,
    you taunt us with your imagined freedom and yet, like a
    rat in the sewer, you gnaw your own flesh and you fight
    for the scraps. Good day to you. (*Leaving.*) Incidentally…
    I shall be taking a shower with a seventeen-year-old girl
    tonight. (*Stops and turns.*) Kindly die soon. (*Leaves.*)

MARY: (*Looking up, sighing.*) Sometimes, after a day spent
scrutinising the heavens in search of a sign, sometimes I
get...how shall we say?...despondent. But He will
come...He will send down one of His boys and I will
once more know a love that's divine. And still falls the
rain. The tears of the Lord. He weeps for our sins.
(*Reaches into bag and pulls out a can of strong lager.*) The
profits of half an hour's immortality. Yesterday afternoon.
Outside Marks and Spencers. Charity wanes in this land.
Perhaps there is hope after all. (*Opens can.*) When He
came He came with such power that the earth shuddered
and God wept. (*Drinks.*) I was ragged and raw but in such
a state of hollowness, in such rapture that...I was
uncontrollable with grief and happiness. I think of that
feeling constantly. As I say, it keeps me warm at night.
(*Drinks.*) There goes a woman with a regular infant in a
push-chair. Have to say I find the misery on her face
rather...gratifying. (*Drinks.*) Faceless bitches, churning
out the same unremarkable bundles of whining snot and
turd. (*Calls.*) Daffodil, darling? You look like you need a
bit of colour in yer day!! Ga...look at her, putting her
head down, wheeling it away as quick as she can. Got to
get Daddy's pies from the supermarket. Got to get him
his peas.
(*The STUDENTBOY enters.*)
Ah, this looks like...what...a half of bitter maybes in the
warm, in the Horse and Hounds...for lunch. Maybe an
ounce of tobacco. You can smell it in the air, his
sympathy. Strong as manure.
(*The STUDENTBOY goes to dispenser.*)
Spare any change for the mother of Christ? Spare a little
kindness for an ageing virgin?
SBOY: You are the mother of Christ?
MARY: I am she.
SBOY: And you are down on your luck?
MARY: I depend solely on the good nature of ordinary
citizens like you.
SBOY: When we have overthrown the government and
radically restructured the way in which society conducts

itself, there will be no need for ugly old women to live on the streets.

MARY: Not so old, if I may say.

SBOY: You're as old as the hills.

MARY: And you're not too old to take a good hiding from those you should be respecting.

SBOY: I respect nobody. I respect nothing but the Truth.

MARY: I am the Truth so respect me.

SBOY: And yet, as a Christian revolutionary, I do not seek to erase all religion from politics. My religion is your religion and your religion is my religion and their religion is her religion and his religion is…

MARY: Just give me some of your fuckin' money!

SBOY: I seek total transformation yet I still believe wholeheartedly in the Supreme Being.

MARY: The Supreme Being left me with child!

(*The STUDENTGIRL enters.*)

SBOY: (*Noticing her and striking a pose.*) He has seen reigning on the earth tyranny, crime, and imposture. He sees at this moment the youth of a whole nation, grappling with all the oppressions of the human race, and is it not He whose immortal hand, engraving on the heart of man the code of justice and equality, has written there the death sentence of tyrants? Is it not He who, from the beginning of time, decreed for all the ages and for all peoples liberty, good faith, and justice?

SGIRL: (*Approaching.*) You talk like a revolutionary and yet here you are stuffing your pockets with money, money stolen from the people, money robbed by those who annexed the land, who dispossessed the poor and who now offer out titbits to a disgruntled nation so as to buffer insurrection.

SBOY: (*Yet more histrionic.*) Man, whoever thou mayest be, thou canst still conceive high thoughts for thyself. Thou canst bind thy fleeting life to God, and to immortality. Let nature seize again all her splendour, and wisdom all her empire! The Supreme Being has not been annihilated…

SGIRL: You speak of the Supreme Being and yet here, by your very feet, sits an ugly old woman who has been forced, by the tyrants you profess to despise, to beg for alms on the cold, wet pavement.

MARY: I am the mother of the Saviour.

SBOY: (*Aside, to MARY.*) I find it difficult to engage with girls emotionally and so I must strut about like this in a desperate attempt to persuade them to have sexual intercourse with me.

SGIRL: Stand aside and allow me to withdraw money, some of which I will give to the poor, some of which I will give to the needy, some of which I will give to the hungry, the meek, the unfortunate, the humble, the dispossessed, the...

MARY: (*To SBOY.*) Stand aside for her!

SBOY: (*Doing so.*) Here. (*Gives MARY some change.*) Buy yourself a tea-cake on a rainy day.

MARY: I will not insult you with gratitude.

SBOY: The humble I loathe. The humble, the meek...why do they warrant our concern?

SGIRL: By showing yourself as tender-hearted, you stand more chance of seeing me naked.

SBOY: I see, I see...

MARY: They crucified my baby! I watched them hoist him up! Imagine that, you herd of apprentices, you tribe of round-rimmed specs and patched-up clothes. You wear your thoughtfulness like a sticker on your coat...but imagine the torment of a mother as she watches her boy being nailed to a tree.

SGIRL: My God! What crime had he committed?

MARY: The crime of opposition, the crime of seeking change, the crime of telling the truth.

SGIRL: Your heart must be breaking. Here. (*Gives her note.*)

MARY: And I bore it alone. His father would not stand by me.

SGIRL: (*To SBOY with contempt.*) The predictable spinelessness of the male!

SBOY: Not all men are like that. Let me convince you of my decency, let me tell you how much I love my mother, let me do voluntary work, let me write heartfelt doggerel in your honour, let me rail against environmental degradation, anything! Just let me finger your flesh!

SGIRL: I would have you perform various tests in order for you to prove your worth to me. I would have you demean your embryonic masculinity, emasculate your individuality, lie to the heart of your soul, before I grant you your request.

SBOY: If I give this old hag half of my...

SGIRL: Tokenism!

SBOY: How well you use your God-given power!
(*The car horns now restart and, as before, all three nod instinctively and moronically to the sound. It ceases.*)

SGIRL Do you have an umbrella?

SBOY: No but...

SGIRL: Go buy me an umbrella and I will possibly grant you a stroke of my skin.

SBOY: A night in the dark? An American film?

SGIRL: Somehow enjoying the mediocrity, the tastelessness, the insult of the message...

SBOY: Unseen in the gloom, perhaps skin touching skin?

SGIRL: Only when, by accident, our hands reach for the popcorn at the same time.

SBOY: And then when I have convinced you of my responsible nature, when I have fought back the tide of passion in my blood, when at length you are assured that I am what you want...?

SGIRL: Then there is always a chance...

SBOY: And that chance, however remote, is good enough for me... (*He rushes off.*)

MARY: Ga...it sickens my soul...the young. To be admired for no reason. To be desired as an impulse.

SGIRL: How would you have me desired?

MARY: For the contents of your mind. For the sum of your experiences, when life's stripped you down.

SGIRL: Lust is so...ugly. So debasing. What of me, myself? What of my sweet characteristics? I want a man to bow down and bring offerings for me, to yearn to die for me, to drink in my personality like a parched tramp in the desert.

MARY: It's belly on belly he wants! It's calves wrapped round thigh. It's toes in the air, tongues down the throat, fingers in scalp and moaning and moaning and moaning...

SGIRL: He will ask me my life-story. He will listen to me.

MARY: He will stare at your chest, getting high on your scent.

SGIRL: He will nod in consent, he will make many connections…

MARY: He will nail down a smile but be stirring within.

SGIRL: He will be all…acquiescence.

MARY: He will be chewing his cheeks.

SGIRL: Oh, how I long to be adored!

MARY: You will never be adored as I was adored.

SGIRL: (*After a pause.*) What makes you so sure?

MARY: The dead of the night, water plashing on the roof, a chill wind blowing through the gaps in the sill. A touch of moonlight slanting across the room, the clock ticking. Blankets sodden with rain, a sleep beckoning, fuelled by quality malt. A wind outside making the leaves crackle, the branches creak. Cigarette smoke hanging deliciously in the claggy air of the room. And then, like a velvet whisper, he spoke to me as if in a dream…I want you, Mary. I want you. And then…on a sudden…I was gripped by a bone-crushing passion. We were in a frenzy of desire, the world was obliterated, we were lost in the moment. He held me by the throat, he squeezed out my breath like a lemon, the pips of my soul burst through the air. Death's cold embrace and then…and then…it was day. And then it was day. And he was gone. But his love left me altered. His love left me moved…

(*The TATTOO LAD now enters. He is very scruffy and heavily-tattooed on his forearms and face. He has an outlandish hairstyle and a lethal pair of boots. He stares at the women.*)

MARY: What you want?

TLAD: (*Sullen, Irish.*) Mam.

MARY: You find your own spot.

TLAD: (*Head down.*) I need me mam.

MARY: Well, you can fuck right off.

SGIRL: This is your son?

MARY: Will you look at the state of him?

SGIRL: You have more than one?

MARY: He's me one and only…

SGIRL: (*After a pause.*) You said they nailed him to a tree!

MARY: And so they did.

TLAD: Need a cuddle.

SGIRL: You said he was a criminal of the opposition.

MARY: And indeed he was.

TLAD: Need a hug and such…

SGIRL You said they crucified him!

MARY: Yes, and now he's back to life. If you can call it that.

TLAD: Need me mam…need me mam…

MARY: You're on your own. Away with ye!

SGIRL: You poor boy…

TLAD: Cuddles, cuddles…

MARY: Look what he's been reduced to. Used to have a bit of fire in his belly. Used to be a champion of freedom. Used to laugh at the destruction he caused, used to smile at the pain of his making…

TLAD: Mammy, Mammy…

MARY: But now…they've sucked all the manhood out of him, they've snapped his spine for him.

SGIRL: It makes me weep to look at him.

MARY: I know how you feel. (*They stare at him. He shuffles over, chin on chest.*) They had such a high regard for him once upon a time. The hope for the future. Was going to lead his people to The Promised Land…

(*The TATTOOLAD begins to cry like a child.*)

Life's too big for him, too unkind. It's not remorse at his murders even. Just an inability to wipe his own arse.

SGIRL: He has killed?

MARY: (*Snorts.*) Has he ever? Bathed his hands in babies' blood, burnt folk alive.

SGIRL: He seems so…unhappy.

MARY: Don't fall for his tears. I'm his own ma and I'm not convinced.

SGIRL: You must go to him!

MARY: No such thing as must.

SGIRL: He seems so alone. So tender. So…in need of comfort, consolation. (*Approaches cautiously.*) Hello? Boy?

MARY: (*To herself.*) Seen it all before…

SGIRL: (*Offering money.*) Perhaps you could…?

MARY: Never accepts money. He's just after love. Thinks he's been deprived.

TLAD: Mammy. I want me Mammy.

SGIRL: (*Puts a hand on his arm.*) Please...don't cry.

MARY: Used to scoff at the tears of others, he did. Used to do callous impersonations of grieving mothers. Go on, lad! Do your Bereaved Parent routine! (*To SGIRL.*) Well worth a look.

SGIRL: Let me be your...your mammy.

MARY: Jaysus!

> (*The TATTOOLAD walks off slowly. He stops, turns and looks again at the STUDENTGIRL, trying to stifle his sobs. The car horns chime in as before. They all bob their heads mechanically. The sounds cease. A silence. He now beckons the STUDENTGIRL with a head movement.*)

He wants you to go to his squat. He wants you to go with him.

SGIRL: To his squat?

MARY: A place of soiled underwear and festering sinks, of tins of food and cans of beer, of filthy sheets and dripping walls.

SGIRL: He wants *me*?

MARY: Seen it all before...

> (*The TATTOOLAD leaves.*)

SGIRL: His suffering has torn at my heart.

MARY: He'll weep you to sleep with his head on your lap.

SGIRL: I must go to him...I must share my advantages with that unfortunate boy. (*She follows him off.*)

MARY: People like that always have folk following them round. But...if he coulda been half the man his father was. Half the man. (*Drinks.*) Clouds coming in darker now. Could be time to move on.

> (*The STUDENTBOY comes rushing on with an umbrella. He stops in his tracks.*)

She's gone. And, you know what...I suspect she'll be killed. But you never know.

SBOY: Gone?

MARY: Time to move on, lad. Time to move on.

> (*They stay where they are. It rains on.*)

A Lesson in Arbitration

A room in a government building. REBECCA, an attractive young woman with a studious air, is seated at a large, plush desk and is examining some documents. Stools. Somewhere off we can hear the furious baying of a large mob.

REBECCA: (*Writing.*)...The exposition of the self-evident to be made a crime punishable by death. All superficialities...all insincere salutations, the double cheek-pecking, the limpness of the handshake, to be... (*Sudden thought.*) Those who would play the jester to kings to be sacrificed on the altar of truth. All remarks aimed at inveigling the rank and file to be unequivocally outlawed. (*Looks up.*) Oh, my people, my people, I legislate, my people, in order to liberate. Do not judge me too severely, I... (*Sudden thought, writing.*) All citizens, at an age to be prescribed, to spend a year in solitary confinement with only...with only books for company... Ah! (*Throws pen down. Leans back.*) Where to go from here? Oblivion, perhaps. Oblivion. At such a tender age. But when you've climbed as far as... (*Sudden thought, writing.*) The unambitious to be forcibly...to be forcibly... Not so easy, not so easy... The unambitious to be... What do we do with the unambitious? Praise them for their... (*A loud shout from the mob.*) These people, if only they would still their incessant... I can't hear myself... (*To crowd.*) Shut up, shut up, you... Oh, it is so difficult to wade through it all when...when...I hate people perhaps? Is that the problem? Do I detest the species?... No, it is not hatred. Merely disappointment. It falls so far from my high expectations. Yes, it disappoints. Furiously. (*She leans back and inhales, exhales.*) Always loved this chair, the smell of the leather, the unbridled luxury. The way it yields to my quite, quite...exquisite arse.
(*PILATE, an edgy and cowed man of middle age enters. REBECCA springs to her feet.*)
PILATE: (*Despairingly.*) Oh, Rebecca...
REBECCA: Aggressive?

PILATE: I stand before a seething multitude, deaf to reason. A hundred thousand gaping mouths, a hundred thousand skyward fists. I am shaking...

REBECCA: (*Approaching him. We see her ankles are chained.*) Won't you sit...?

PILATE: These are your people, Rebecca.

REBECCA: We share a nationality, nothing more.

PILATE: I feel...I feel a sickly creature. I am always so unwell. Oh, God, just to look at you.

REBECCA: You like what you see?

PILATE: We must have those chains lengthened.

REBECCA: I walk with ease. Look. (*She demonstrates like a fashion model. He watches her hungrily.*)

PILATE: No more, no more...

REBECCA: (*Walking more.*) Barely restricted at all...

PILATE: (*Watching her.*) My wife... Rebecca, you know that my wife doesn't under...

REBECCA: (*Heard this before.*) You married too young.

PILATE: It is her doing that I am here. I could still be in Rome. A tiny fish, an anonymous minnow in the massive ocean. Not this floundering whale in this festering swamp. Please stop...

REBECCA: (*Walking still.*) I enjoy tormenting you.

PILATE: You...I...the way your... You have these thighs...this movement so fluid, so...I...you...

REBECCA: And you would grant me my freedom for one touch of... (*He advances. She moves away.*) As lust slowly sucks the control from your eyes.

PILATE: Please...

REBECCA: (*At desk, taking papers.*) I have studied the two profiles and...

PILATE: You are always...reinventing yourself. Never the same two days in a row...

REBECCA: ...I think we need to tread very carefully this year. One can tell from the noise...

PILATE: ...but she, like white lard on her stool, that look...

REBECCA: ...that this will be a sensitive decision...

PILATE: ...that look of tired affection and contempt... She binds me with kindness, I...

REBECCA: ...whichever way we go.

PILATE: ...and fat, so fat these days...always had this...
always had this tendency...

REBECCA: The point, of course, being...how much do we
allow the wants of the pack...

PILATE: ...to plumpness...even in her youth...even in her
salad days but now...she...

REBECCA: ...to inform our judgement.

PILATE: ...and she grips hold of me in bed...White and
cold and wet. So wet.

REBECCA: Do we...do we give them what they want, do
we stay popular by bowing to their demands, staying as
we do...one step ahead of their desires?

PILATE: Claggy. Yes, a great blubbery squid, a... I lie there
in the dark and she...

REBECCA: Or should we be guided by our own
principles? (*She laughs.*)

PILATE: ...she burrows her face into my neck she...the lips
ever wetter, ever colder, seeking...

REBECCA: Both men are, or were, the people's people...

PILATE: ...and she holds onto me and I lie there awake
and I dream and I need and I want... And I just...

REBECCA: ...whatever that means...

PILATE: ...but I will not bend from my...must not stray
from my...the children, you see...I need their
respect...that is all that I have...

REBECCA: Personally, I don't care at all...

PILATE: But she...the contentment oozes from her pores
like a poisonous sweat... A thump to the face could not
dislodge it...she'd merely smile, wipe the blood...

REBECCA: ...either way...

PILATE: ...wipe the blood with the back of her hand and
pity me, pity me, oh... The pressures of work, the torture
of office but no...

REBECCA: ...and they were formerly loved and by some
they still are...

PILATE: ...just the joy of causing her pain and I... Rome,
Rome...if only...

REBECCA: ...but if it's blood that they want then it's blood
they shall have...

PILATE: In Rome...

REBECCA: ...but I find, though the details are sketchy in parts, their parents, their upbringing, grinding poverty in both, though...

PILATE: In Rome...

REBECCA: ...one sought a trade, of sorts, and the other to live off the labour of others...

PILATE: In Rome they are not like you...in Rome I could find peace...

PILATE: ...I could...

REBECCA: One a laughter-maker, the other a widow-maker but both...

PILATE: ...go to my grave in a passionless daze...

REBECCA: I suppose...deem themselves truth-seekers, deem themselves...

PILATE: ...walk to my death in the grip of a sleep.

REBECCA: ...truly evolved, ahead of their time, et cetera, et cetera... Square pegs and such... Which is why they are here.

PILATE: (*Sadly sitting at desk.*) In the grip of a deep, deep sleep.

REBECCA: (*More assertive, business-like.*) We have a list here, as long as my arm...of victims of one...relatives, friends, creditors...three soldiers' wives...even their children have demanded his death. The other...a comedian to some, a ranting entertainer, end of the world stuff...followers, yes but...well, they both have followers... As you saw there have been fights leading up to this, between the two factions...and, well, I think you have to decide what our priorities are. Do we want discipline or do we want variety, complexity... It's a difficult question. Bread in their bellies or sleepless nights and perhaps...But the people are fickle... Personally, I don't care at all.

PILATE: Rebecca...

REBECCA: They believe, you see, that it is God who visits all this agony upon them, that their unending misery is due to his displeasure. They therefore do not entirely blame we empire-builders, they...

PILATE: Rebecca...

REBECCA: Would it be impudent of me to suggest, sir, that your mind is not totally focused on the task in hand?

PILATE: (*Decisively.*) I do not wish to make another decision for as long as I live.

(*A silence. He stares at her longingly, she sifts through the paperwork.*)

(*Tired. Miserable.*) A comedian, you said?

REBECCA: So he describes himself.

PILATE: Is he...funny?

REBECCA: I never laugh.

PILATE: You must have done once, surely?

REBECCA: The louder a man laughs, the more he signals how unendurable he finds his own life. I have always thought this.

PILATE: But does this man have any...what is the word...talent?

REBECCA: A few everyday observations, it seems. The odd impersonation. They say he captures your own mannerisms rather well.

PILATE: I see.

REBECCA: This man, sir, presents himself as a hero of the people. Says a man has the right to say what he likes. Yet now, to survive, to pay the rent and to keep his numerous women content, he is forced to use his dubious gifts for mimicry to draw attention to his uncle's avocado stall.

PILATE: A comedian and a...a murderer, you say?

REBECCA: Family were drunks. Father a killer, mother a whore. Rumour has it that, as a child, he witnessed his father decapitate a beloved sister.

PILATE: And how many has he...?

REBECCA: At least a score, we think but...

PILATE: I cannot bear to look at you.

REBECCA: Some only alleged.

PILATE: I torture myself by keeping you here...

REBECCA: Soldiers...

PILATE: He kills soldiers?

REBECCA: A couple of lawyers...

PILATE: Then we should honour him!

REBECCA: He certainly has blood on his hands. (*A pause.*) You are staring, sir.

PILATE: You are a delicious-looking young woman.

REBECCA: And yet you shall never taste me.

PILATE: (*With a sigh.*) Life is cruel.

REBECCA: A true Italian gentleman. An imperialist with breeding.

PILATE: I would love to… You make me, you know you make me hard.

REBECCA: You could always force me, sir… Many of your colleagues have shown fewer scruples than you.

PILATE: (*Head in hands.*) Please, God…
(*The shout of "Crucify him!, Crucify him!" is heard outside, angry.*)
(*Standing.*) Rebecca, I…I cannot stand it. Will you be…?
(*Pause.*) I will never force you and you won't consent so… (*Sinks back to chair and weeps. Chants increasing.*)
I so…want to…to…

REBECCA: You cry every day now.

PILATE: (*Through tears.*) And…you…you never once place a sympa…sympathetic hand on my sh…shoulder.

REBECCA: (*Laughing.*) Is that what you'd like me to do?

PILATE: I want you to…want you to…want to… Not because…

REBECCA: You would have to command me…

PILATE: I would never, as many do, go to a…visit a…

REBECCA: Your self-esteem!

PILATE: (*Despairing.*) I am so…unhappy.

REBECCA: You are such a…gallant, so bred for your work.

PILATE: You are…my daughter is… I look at my daughter and…sometimes I…(*Weeps.*)

REBECCA: So many men, sir. So many men I have been with…not one with your delicacy, not one with your…grammar school bashfulness…

PILATE: I want to…

REBECCA: …and they hacked at me, spat at me…like I was a chop…

PILATE: You are so…

REBECCA: Nostrils flaring, eyes scrunched shut, grimacing, grimacing…

PILATE: Listen…

REBECCA: …tearing my hair and slapping my face…

PILATE: Reb…

REBECCA: …they butchered me, buggered me, tore me in two and they…

PILATE: (*Standing.*) But I love you!!

(*A long silence but for the furious chanting outside. He slowly sits again. After a silence, waving his hand.*)

You are free to go.

(*Another long silence.*)

REBECCA: Go?

PILATE: I will…will have a guard unshackle you.

REBECCA: Go?

PILATE: You have served me well and I…

REBECCA: And so you reward me by casting me out onto the streets?

PILATE: Your…liberty, your…birthright…

REBECCA: You…you…you…mewling administrator, you…!!

PILATE: Please don't shout at me…

REBECCA: Haul me to Rome rather, throw me to the bears rather, let my beautiful belly be torn for the pleasure…

PILATE: I offer you your…

REBECCA: You offer me nothing!

PILATE: I only want to…

REBECCA: You offer me street! You offer me crowd, you offer me…heat and dirt and dust, you offer me…

PILATE: (*Standing.*) Enough! (*He walks towards her.*) I…I am sick of you shouting at me. Remember your…remember your place. I… I… (*A silence.*) They will riot. Whichever way we…

REBECCA: Let them…

PILATE: Blood will flow…the shops will…

REBECCA: Ah, the shops, the shops…Why do we care so much for the shops?

PILATE: There will be murders, Rebecca. I cannot take any more murders...

REBECCA: Let them murder, let them rape, let them disembowel. What care we?

PILATE: They frighten me... (*For a time, staring at each other, they listen to the escalating sound of the crowd outside. The noise is now becoming worrying.*) Bring them in... (*REBECCA leaves.*) Look at that...oh, look at that arse... that arse is my curse, is my...the thighs, oh the firmness of those calves, the curve of her...the hips and the... That arse is a curse, a curse... How I long to... Enough, enough...But I would like to... No, I need to control my... to flip her over and...ram her against that wall, like a beast, like a beast. I am a beast, oh... (*Pacing.*) The ache in my breast will never be soothed...and she...she would not cure it, just add more fuel to the fire...If she would only take me...in her mouth, that mouth that she has... Oh, my God. It's me that they crucify, me that they... hound. They bow as I walk and they offer me gifts but they'd spit on my corpse and they'd tread down the dirt on my cold, lonely grave.
(*A few loud, individual cries of 'Crucify him!!' from outside.*) It's me that they mean, it's me that they want, it's me, yes it's me, yes it's me...
(*REBECCA now strolls in, pulling a long chain behind her. Presently, the TERRORIST and the COMEDIAN, both in neck chains with hands tied behind their backs appear in tow. They are only very partially clothed. They both wear crowns made of thorns and have been beaten. REBECCA indicates where they are to stand. They both stare ahead.*)
So which of you is the...the comedian? (*No answer.*) And which of you seeks the destruction of the Empire? (*No answer. To the COMEDIAN.*) Are you scared to die? (*No answer. To the TERRORIST.*) Are you? (*No answer.*) Look at them. They are mere boys. This is...I can't do this. (*To REBECCA, pathetically.*) Help me.

REBECCA: (*To the COMEDIAN.*) You look at me with hatred. Why? (*No answer.*) You are full of pride, sir. Do you imagine people will remember you when you are dead? (*No answer.*) You think your legacy will live on after you? (*No answer.*) You crave immortality? (*No answer.*) Your ridiculous human pride craves immortality but only the gods will live forever. (*No answer. She slowly runs a finger down the COMEDIAN's chest. She trails her finger through his blood.*) They say you are a man who adores women? (*She brings her finger to her mouth.*) And whom women adore? (*She puts her finger in her mouth and tastes the blood.*)

COMEDIAN: (*Quiet.*) You are a traitor to your people.

REBECCA: And what have *you* ever done for the 'people'?

COMEDIAN: (*Quiet.*) And the cynical whore of the cynical Empire.

(*REBECCA laughs.*)

PILATE: These are brave words. Under the...circumstances.

REBECCA: (*To the TERRORIST.*) And you? Do you not regret the actions which have brought you here?

(*No answer.*)

COMEDIAN: He is afraid.

PILATE: (*To the TERRORIST.*) Are you? (*No answer. They all listen to the violent noise outside. REBECCA nods towards PILATE.*)

(*Rapidly.*) Very soon...in a matter of moments...one of you will be walking free from here and...and the other will be...will be condemned...to die... (*A cough.*) We will...they will be taking one of you...shortly...we will take one of you...from here...and...to the courtyard... and you will be scourged...you will be scourged with a whip made from birch. With...with each blow you will lose a strip of your flesh. You will be beaten and spat upon and...and...as is the case with the military these days it appears...urinated upon. (*Clears throat. They stare at the prisoners.*) You will then...you will then...be made to carry the timber, the cross-beam...through the streets...your...your enemies will be free to deride you...your friends to despair for you I... (*A pause.*) On reaching...on reaching the place of execution... (*A cough.*) ...you will be pushed to the ground, on your back and you will he stripped naked, completely naked...you will

be totally, totally exposed...The crowds pushing round for a...for a view...I...your arms outstretched will be... will be bound with rope to the...to the beam. (*Coughs.*) Iron nails will then...will then...long iron nails will be hammered through both of your wrists...and... and into the timber the...(*Pause.*) You will then be hoisted up and the beam will be fastened to a vertical...vertical stake. Your feet will be nailed to a...a support peg in the...in the stake...Through the instep and the...the sole... (*Pause.*) Your face will then be smeared with honey to... to...to attract...insects and...(*Coughs.*)
(*A long, long silence.*)

REBECCA: (*Suddenly, to the COMEDIAN.*) You! Tell me a joke. (*No answer.*) I require...a joke. (*He does not speak.*) I want to laugh. I want you to make me laugh. I want momentarily to lose control of my intelligence. Therefore a joke, if you please. (*No answer.*) I want to be entertained so...entertain me!! (*No answer. Quiet.*) Tell me, how did the comedian overthrow Rome? How did the comedian overthrow Rome? (*No answer.*) Comedian? You enjoy entertaining the easily-pleased? (*No answer.*) You relish your status as the King of Comedy?

COMEDIAN: Those are your words.

REBECCA: It is a living, is it?

COMEDIAN: A living. Yes.

REBECCA: A master of satire?

COMEDIAN: You have betrayed your...

REBECCA: A lampooner of all authority?

COMEDIAN: ...your country.

REBECCA: You are a great lampooner, yes?

COMEDIAN: Freedom...

REBECCA: You lampoon?

COMEDIAN: ...of speech...

REBECCA: The bloated merchant enjoys your lampoonery...

COMEDIAN: What do you know of...

REBECCA: He enjoys your wit and so he gives you a discount...

COMEDIAN: What do you know of what I do?

REBECCA: ...as he goes and tells his friends in the square...

COMEDIAN: You who bow and scrape.

REBECCA: So the merchant...

COMEDIAN: You lie!

REBECCA: So the chuckling merchant...

COMEDIAN: You are lying!

REBECCA: If you'd only let me speak...

COMEDIAN: There is no merchant I...

REBECCA: So the chuckling, gurgling merchant and his belly...his ever-expanding belly...

COMEDIAN: *You* condemn *me*!

REBECCA: ...is the master...

COMEDIAN: ...for my courage...

REBECCA: ...he remains the master...

COMEDIAN: ...in speaking out!?

REBECCA: ...and he calls for more...

COMEDIAN: In speaking out, I say!

REBECCA: ...snaps his finger for more and you return with yet another voice...

COMEDIAN: It is humour!

REBECCA: ...with yet another hat...

COMEDIAN: Only humour!

REBECCA: ...and so your belly grows like his!

COMEDIAN: It is humour!

REBECCA: And it is harmless!!

(*They do not speak. Still the violence outside increases.*)

PILATE: You can imitate me?

REBECCA: He can.

PILATE: I would...would like to see it.

COMEDIAN: I am not...

REBECCA: The Governor would like to see it!!

(*They do not speak. A violent cry is heard above the din.*)

PILATE: I said, boy, that I would like to see your impersonation.

COMEDIAN: It will not please you.

(*Just the noise outside for a time.*)

PILATE: I am waiting.

COMEDIAN: Do I have a choice?

REBECCA: We are waiting. Demonstrate your talent to us.

COMEDIAN: But…

REBECCA: And you may yet live.

(*After a nervous hesitation, the COMEDIAN slowly transforms himself into PILATE. He is as if addressing a large, hostile crowd and he is thoroughly convincing.*)

COMEDIAN: I…stand before you…before you now. A quite…quite miserable man. Fate has decreed…I say that F…Fate has decreed that I should be your governor, that I should be the man who is charged with maintaining peace, maintaining order. I…as I say…I am a man weighed down by the bur…burdens of office and I want it to be known…known that I seek only to please. I want people, even if it seems trite, to lead…to lead…contented and useful lives and…if I use violence upon you then know that…it is always with a heavy heart and that…it is for the good of civilisation…that I…that I…that I do it. I am your friend…

PILATE: Enough! (*REBECCA is laughing.*) Enough!!

REBECCA: It is good!

PILATE: No! It is not!! (*The COMEDIAN is himself again. A long silence.*) He will pay for that with his life.

COMEDIAN: I will…?

PILATE: The decision is made.

REBECCA: Wait!

PILATE: No. I have made my…

REBECCA: He is harmless.

PILATE: You find him amusing?

REBECCA: It is a harmless entertainment.

PILATE: You think that that jerking and juddering… that pathetic creature was me?

REBECCA: No!

PILATE: And yet you look at him with such desire!

REBECCA: No!

PILATE: I can see your hideous desire when you look at this man!

REBECCA: No!

PILATE: Your life too, girl, your life is mine if I choose!

REBECCA: Listen…

PILATE: I have you all in my hands. All of you!!

REBECCA: Please, sir.

PILATE: And you, you *will* be freed.

REBECCA: No!

PILATE: This afternoon!

REBECCA: I beg you!

PILATE: Your own people can deal with you as they see fit.

REBECCA: I have aimed only to serve, to please...

PILATE: Your desire to please is no longer pleasing!!

REBECCA: The freedom you offer is not freedom, it's...

PILATE: I am not addressing you!! (*The violence outside continues to escalate. PILATE's fury is now in danger of spinning out of control. To the TERRORIST.*) You! You have killed? (*No answer.*) Answer or die!

REBECCA: Sir!

PILATE: I too have killed of course yet never face to face.

REBECCA: Please!

PILATE: Quiet! (*A pause.*) Thousands have died on my orders but tell me...what is it like to actually...? Did they beg for their lives, these lawyers you strangled? Did their eyeballs bulge from their sockets? Did they call for their wives, their mothers, their daughters?! (*No answer.*) You think... You think that because I am old and I am fat and I am ugly that I... Will nobody beg for their lives? Will nobody go down on their knees and beg for their lives? Kiss my foot, lick the sand off my toes and I may spare you yet!? Will you? Will you? What have we done to you all that you are all so indifferent to your own extinction? That is it! Yes, in the heart of every one of you is this unspoken desire for oblivion! (*Nobody speaks.*) The first one of you to...

(*The COMEDIAN suddenly throws himself to the ground at PILATE's feet.*)

COMEDIAN: Merciful Governor, I entreat you...

(*PILATE suddenly pulls out a dagger and holds it across the TERRORIST's throat.*)

PILATE: You! Beg! Beg me! Beg! Beg! Beg! There is fear in you, I can feel it! So beg me, man ! Beg! Do you not know who I am? Do you not know what I am capable of? Do you not understand what I am saying to you? Speak, man! Only words, only articulation will save you now!

(*During all this the TERRORIST has been fighting back his tears but now slowly and painfully they begin breaking out. The others watch him.*)

He weeps for his people. For his forgotten land.

(*The TERRORIST's pain now floods out, slowly, silently. The violence outside increases: screams, shouts, then the splintering of wood and falling masonry. The lights change and choral music fades in. It builds to a deafening crescendo and then blackout and silence.*)

SILENCE AND VIOLENCE

Characters

HOLLOWAY
an aristocrat

GIESBACH
an artist

WINDERMERE
a patriot

The first production of *Silence and Violence* was scheduled for a London theatre in the autumn of 2001. The venue was not confirmed at the time of going to press. The cast was as follows:

HOLLOWAY, Sheena Irving

GIESBACH, Mark Huckett

WINDERMERE, Costa Milton

Director, Nick Claxton

Designer, Helen Shore

Assistant Director, Yael Shavit

Lighting Designer, Jae Forrester

Costume Designer, Mayou Trikerioti

Part I

An artist's studio, chaotic with both finished and unfinished sculptures (of naked women) and canvasses all around. Easels. Screams of rage from an angry (female) crowd outside. A wind howls. GIESBACH lies, possibly dead, on the floor. He has been badly beaten, is bleeding heavily and his threadbare clothes are in tatters. A crystal decanter full of water stands elegantly, despite the surrounding debris, on a table. There is also a coat-stand, a stool and a chaise-longue. The screams continue for a time. HOLLOWAY enters. She is beautiful and exquisitely-dressed in expensive fur coat, hat, gloves, high heels etc. There is some evidence of snow on her clothing. She is immaculate, aristocratic. She gingerly steps over all the palettes and paint pots on the floor.

HOLLOWAY: There are of course three clear reasons why this has happened. Permit me to detail them. Firstly: your name. Giesbach. From where does that originate? Certainly not these shores. It brands you, as all names do, and I do think under the current climate that it might have been prudent to have changed it to something less…conspicuous. Though I do sympathise. One's name, it speaks volumes of one's parentage, one's history, et cetera et cetera and so to alter it merely to avoid persecution, well… But you chose not to. And I admire you for that.

(She walks to a sculpture of a naked woman. She inspects it.)

Secondly: your profession, if one is to describe all this…this self-indulgence of yours with generosity. For a profession can surely only be defined as such when the customer is satisfied, when his demands have been met. Perhaps you don't agree? And what you are doing here is… She has large breasts, this woman. You like large breasts, do you? Oh, it is so thoroughly predictable, isn't it? You think she is attractive? She has a smooth, flat belly, I grant you, but this is supposed to designate… what? Does this quality of the abdomen mean that the horrors of childbirth have not yet shredded her stomach muscles or that she is perhaps as yet unplucked and therefore more desirable to the male sense of...shall we say...ownership? Her flesh unsullied by the sweaty palms of others? But I digress. All this...it marks you out as an eccentric, as someone who is not particularly concerned with the good of the collective. For what does all this contribute to the happiness of your fellows? You barricade yourself away from the problems of the age, away from the light of the sun, and you produce all these adolescent images. As you can tell from the commotion outside your window, it is not always greatly appreciated.

(*A window is smashed.*)

I think that you have always intrigued the womenfolk of the town. Your refusal to participate ignites our sense of curiosity. I wonder, sir, what your opinion is of *my* stomach? You'll notice that I am tightly corsetted – a necessary inconvenience of course, for it is essential that a woman like me gives out to the world of men that the belly is in perfect proportion to the hips. And the hips relate exactly to the bust. You rate my hips? Well, let me promenade for you. (*She does so, self-admiringly.*) I think you will agree that my movement, despite these evident restrictions, remains both graceful and coyly alluring. I am not sure, sir, that you are paying close enough attention. Let me... (*She continues to walk up and down the room. As she does so, she looks at the sculpture again.*) Might I enquire which woman of the town sat for you when you chiselled out this, let me be courteous, this fantasy, this impossibility in stone?

(*No answer.*)

I always assumed, since the artist advertises himself as a truth-seeker, that reality ought to be reflected in his creations, but it appears from all this that you chiefly concern yourself with some utterly laughable ideal of the female. These women here are your pornography, are they not? No, these thighs are too perfect, too smooth and – but she is so cold, so cold to the touch. Quite... cold.

(*She looks around the room. We hear only the occasional shout from outside.*)
You were asked to commemorate the event of my recent marriage with a large portrait in oil, to freeze in time my youth, my happiness and the coming of age of my handsome new husband. The fee was generous, the deadline achievable and yet you declined. Why? The day, as is commonly agreed, was quite perfect. I have never looked so beautiful. Ravishing, the papers said. Do you read the papers? Do you know what is happening in the world? Do you understand what it is like to fall in love, marry and then watch as your beautiful young soulmate leads his nation into war? Did you see him that day? When the soldiers amassed in the square? Did you see him? He was so…
(*She breaks off with emotion. A pause. She quickly recovers.*)
It would of course be unnatural if other men did not hate him. His excellence, I am sure, is an affront to some. I will admit that he has a tendency to turn up his nose, as if he were some hero from antiquity but humility can be coached into him. Before, you understand, he was all potential. His unlimited possibilities chafing at the bit, imprisoned by the inactivity of peace. The civilian life dulling his unexpressed savagery, his noble instinct for conquest. He was confident, yes. And perhaps a little arrogant. But his patriotism, what you would sneer at as blind nationalism, and his pride, a much misunderstood virtue, yes virtue…this is merely a conviction that, when evil finally threatens as it has now threatened…yes, you do the neck and shoulders well. I'll concede that. (*She admires the sculpture.*) And, of course, reason the third: it is your pitiful cowardice which has brought the rage of all these lonely women down upon your head. Their husbands, their fathers, their sons, are at this very moment marching towards bowel-churning dangers whilst you, the artist, stubbornly refuse to bear arms. You know that, had I not intervened and used my influence as I did, that they would have torn you to pieces?

(*No answer. An isolated shout from outside. The mob is evidently dispersing.*)
Why do you not love your country? It has given you everything. Everything. (*She turns to him. There is still no sign of life.*) Oh, listen, we all want unconditional love. I understand your misery, your isolation. I do. But you won't get it. I am loved, adored even, but I know that a large reason for this is that naked, bar these dishonest creations of yours, I come as close to perfection as a man might expect. And I am, sir, a quite spectacular fuck. Relentlessly inventive. A genius beneath the sheets. And for this I am loved. It is trade, of course, but trade is good. Trade is...organic. You, I imagine...

GIESBACH: (*Weakly.*) I do not...hate trade.

HOLLOWAY: Ah! A dialogue! Finally. I was, and this happens rarely I can assure you, I was beginning to tire of the sound of my own... (*Picking up a canvas.*) Now, this is an interesting item. I recognise this woman. She is the wife, is she not, of the Governor? And how much were you paid for this? Why would you turn down our commission and yet here you...? Somehow I recognise her, though again you have brutalised the truth. In the flesh she is not remotely so...so captivating as this. I think well of her but really, you have made a purity of her ugliness, drawn some unlikely beauty from the despair, the tedium that is her life. So you are, like the rest of us, prepared to lie for money? I understand. But, as far as I am concerned...do I use the first person singular too often? Tell me. Do I? You think I am self-obsessed?

(*No answer.*)
Say.
(*No answer.*)
Why have you filled out her bosom in this way? There is a joke in circulation, I am sure you must have heard it, the subject of which is her unfortunate flatchestedness. And yet you, you have transformed her boyishness, her dryness, her brittle demeanour into warmth, sensuality and the breasts, the breasts of... She has quite beautiful

breasts. Breasts to soothe the soul and pacify the… No, this has upset me. Why should this humourless bitch, this power-obsessed fake be looked upon by future generations as curvaceous, taut-limbed and utterly fuckable when in truth she is large-mouthed, ill-proportioned and… God, it is well known that her husband has a weakness for the whores, has a tendency, despite his prominent position, to crawl the kerbs in search of cunt and he… Sorry, let me pause for a while for suddenly I am overcome with the injustice of it all.

GIESBACH: (*Weakly.*) Water.

HOLLOWAY: Sorry?

GIESBACH: There is water.

HOLLOWAY: Water?

GIESBACH: Please.

HOLLOWAY: Do you not have a servant?

GIESBACH: No. I…

HOLLOWAY: Yet you keep your water in such exquisite crystal?

GIESBACH: Please.

HOLLOWAY: And you wish me to assist you?

GIESBACH: Water.

HOLLOWAY: Yes, you keep saying.

GIESBACH: I am weak.

HOLLOWAY: I have already told you how I used my position, my rank, to keep the rabble off you.

GIESBACH: Why did you…?

HOLLOWAY: (*Laughing.*) Now, that I do not know.

GIESBACH: I don't thank you for it.

HOLLOWAY: But I am your saviour!

GIESBACH: You should have let them kill me.

HOLLOWAY: (*Laughing.*) Oh, but you are so adolescent!

GIESBACH: Please!

HOLLOWAY: Where is your servant?

GIESBACH: I have said already that…

HOLLOWAY: (*Calling off.*) Hello! Hello!

GIESBACH: What are you…?

HOLLOWAY: (*Calling off.*) Your master needs you!

GIESBACH: Just…need…the water.

HOLLOWAY: (*Calling off.*) Your master needs the water!

GIESBACH: I have no servant.

HOLLOWAY: (*Calling off.*) I would advise you to come quickly! (*To GIESBACH.*) I can assure you, sir, that if my own domestic was as casual as this then she would find herself flung upon the mercies of the state before she could say…before she could say…

GIESBACH: Let me save you from completing your metaphor and implore you once again to…

HOLLOWAY: (*Calling off.*) I say! I say!

GIESBACH: All I want from you, now that I find myself unhappily alive, is that you provide me with…

HOLLOWAY: You need to be aware that if you indulge the working classes for a moment they will soon make you suffer for it. You evidently know little of the ways of the world, which is hardly surprising since you have spent so many years skulking in this shed of yours, with only your infantile contempt for humanity to keep you warm and your hatred for those who endeavour to seek pleasure from existence and your affected revulsion at…

GIESBACH: You attack me but all I want is a glass of…

HOLLOWAY: (*Laughing.*) Oh, I am not attacking you. You are too sensitive.

GIESBACH: Please understand. I am very weak. Losing blood.

HOLLOWAY: (*Calling off.*) Your master is losing a lot of blood!

GIESBACH: It seems…

HOLLOWAY: Yes?

GIESBACH: It seems that I am once again alone in the world.

HOLLOWAY: Yes?

GIESBACH: And that I must rely upon nobody but myself. I will now attempt to stand. Unaided. (*He slowly and painfully attempts to stand. He is too weak and slumps back to the floor.*)

HOLLOWAY: Alone then you are nothing?

GIESBACH: Nothing.

HOLLOWAY: Do you see? (*No answer.*) Those whom you condemn are hardly likely to rush to your aid when you descend, as is happening now, into a pitiful helplessness. No, one mustn't deride one's fellow man for one never knows when one may need his help.

GIESBACH: You talk too much.

HOLLOWAY: I'm sorry?

GIESBACH: I said you...

HOLLOWAY: I heard what you said. (*A pause.*) Are you criticising me?

GIESBACH: Just...just passing comment.

HOLLOWAY: You think me garrulous?

GIESBACH: You are evidently missing your husband.

HOLLOWAY: How you presume, sir!

GIESBACH: There is only one true way to pacify a prattling woman.

HOLLOWAY: May I take it then that you are insulting me?

GIESBACH: Or perhaps he is not a man who relishes the sound of a woman's voice? Perhaps he rarely allows you to finish a...?

HOLLOWAY: Did you hear what I said?

GIESBACH: (*Pulling a bloody tooth from his mouth.*) I thought this only happened in dreams.

HOLLOWAY: I will admit that I am the kind of woman who flourishes more in the company of men than in that of women. And the former *are* rather thin on the ground at present. And perhaps I am a touch competitive. That accusation has been levelled at me before. Who of us is without their faults? But prattling? No. I take great care with my speech. Yes, I choose my words...very carefully. (*GIESBACH spits out another tooth.*) Very carefully.

GIESBACH: (*Dabbing his bleeding mouth.*) And you are certain that your words are worth listening to?

HOLLOWAY: (*Picking up portrait again.*) Listen, I shall come to the point. I should like to sit for you.

GIESBACH: I think my arm is broken.

HOLLOWAY: Very much. I should.

GIESBACH: I feel sick with the pain.

HOLLOWAY: I assumed, and oh how you have been masquerading as a man of integrity all these years, as a man who has an irrational hatred for the aristocracy, despite all we do for the people of this town... Yes, I assumed that your refusal to paint our wedding portrait was because you revile those of us who dare to live in comfort, but as it appears you are only too happy to whore your meagre talents out to the Governor and his scrawny, weedy-hipped little boywife...

GIESBACH: That is not the Governor's wife.

HOLLOWAY: No?

GIESBACH: No.

HOLLOWAY: Of course it is.

GIESBACH: It is no-one.

HOLLOWAY: Of course it is.

GIESBACH: No-one.

HOLLOWAY: You mean to tell me...

GIESBACH: An invention. Yes.

HOLLOWAY: And so how do you survive?

GIESBACH: It's a mystery.

HOLLOWAY: Your imagination feeds you, does it? And who buys all these women?

GIESBACH: I never sell my work.

HOLLOWAY: And so you subsist on thin air?

GIESBACH: Among other things.

HOLLOWAY: So the cliché of the starving artist is true in your case?

GIESBACH: I have an arrangement with the Grand Hotel.

HOLLOWAY: I see.

GIESBACH: The kitchen porters save me their slops. Or they did. Before all this began.

HOLLOWAY: 'All this' will be your country's finest hour.

GIESBACH: Now I must wait until they arrest me.

HOLLOWAY: And arrest you they surely shall.

GIESBACH: I have heard they do a nice meat pie in the jail.

HOLLOWAY: And then they will hang you.

GIESBACH: And so my hunger will end.

(*A female cry of 'Giesbach!' outside.*)

HOLLOWAY: (*Removing her coat and revealing a stunning evening dress.*) It is clearly no longer safe for you here.

GIESBACH: It is the place of my birth and I intend...

HOLLOWAY: Your servant will, I presume, hang up my coat?

GIESBACH: Before I lost consciousness I could have sworn I saw you in the crowd...

HOLLOWAY: As I said, I am your saviour.

GIESBACH: You spat.

HOLLOWAY: Spat? Me? Please!

GIESBACH: You put the boot in.

HOLLOWAY: No.

GIESBACH: When I was down.

HOLLOWAY: Explain then why I...

GIESBACH: I'm sure it was you. The heel of your shoe skewering my thigh.

HOLLOWAY: You are mistaken.

GIESBACH: Possibly.

(*GIESBACH once again tries to stand. This time, though it is a great effort, he is successful. His right arm is completely useless.*)

HOLLOWAY: Congratulations.

(*He walks slowly to the table and pours himself a glass of water.*)

Your clothes are ruined.

GIESBACH: Yes.

(*He drinks. There is a silence as she watches him. She is still holding her coat.*)

HOLLOWAY: One assumes from this delay in taking my coat that you rarely entertain? You lead a solitary existence? I, on the other hand, am at my best when I have an audience. You will hang my coat for me presently? (*No answer.*) Or perhaps your domestic will take it for me? There is a coat-stand over there. And here there is a coat. One coat-stand. One coat. I see a connection. Don't you? Do you like this coat? Sixteen seal cubs were bludgeoned to a pulp to produce it. Sixteen, I say! Sixteen animals, left raw, skinless and bleeding on the snow just to keep a woman like me a little warmer in winter. Yes, this coat is derived from the icy wastes of the Arctic. Specially tailored to drape around my physique at a not inconsiderable expense. My husband is a man who loves to bestow offerings. Before his promotion to captain, this coat was a month's salary. For the act of giving only becomes a virtue when a sacrifice is involved. Would you agree? When the gift causes the giver just a little inconvenience? (*No answer.*) Yes, I had resisted him until this coat. Not even a kiss had I allowed him. But this…this was such a sincere expression of his devotion to me that no sooner was it on my back then I had decided to reveal my nakedness to him, to let him… Look, I will hang the coat myself. (*She does so. A silence as he watches her. With her back to him.*) And so…what do you intend to do now?

GIESBACH: Now?

HOLLOWAY: Now that you have survived the rage, the indignation of your community?

GIESBACH: I shall wait.

HOLLOWAY: Wait?

GIESBACH: Wait for the law to run its course.

HOLLOWAY: You are a respecter of the law, are you?

GIESBACH: I have no quarrel with the law.

HOLLOWAY: Then why will you not fight?

GIESBACH: Because I have no quarrel with anyone.

HOLLOWAY: But you disagree with the war?

GIESBACH: I am too weak to talk politics.

HOLLOWAY: You want me to go?

GIESBACH: I need to rest.

HOLLOWAY: Do you mind if I take off my hat?
   (*She carefully unties her hat and then takes it off.*)
   My milliner has talent, would you not say? It is a great service he provides. I have always thought that the wearing of hats is a mark of true courage. That is of course… (*she places the hat on the stand.*) …unless one is bald. (*She takes the clips from her hair and then shakes her long and healthy-looking mane free.*) Do bald women appeal to you, Giesbach? Admittedly baldness is an affliction more common in men but it has been… This painting

here…what does it mean? (*No answer.*) These colours, they represent what exactly? Tell me, do people actually pay you for this?

GIESBACH: (*Using just his left arm, he is bandaging his wounds with rags from his ripped shirt.*) I told you, my work never leaves the building.

HOLLOWAY: These colours. These violent maroons, these sensuous ochres, this soothing turquoise…what is the point of it all? Tell me, what does it all signify?

GIESBACH: They are just colours.

HOLLOWAY: I think I prefer your portraits.

(*Distant shell-fire starts up.*)

Listen!

(*They listen to the cannons and the explosions.*)

Can you feel it? The ground is vibrating.

(*Silence but for the guns.*)

My poor, poor boy!

(*She steps out of her high-heel shoes as the explosions continue.*)

GIESBACH: It has finally begun then.

HOLLOWAY: (*After a pause.*) How dare you be so flippant?!

GIESBACH: Again, just a comment.

HOLLOWAY: How dare you 'comment'? You who value your squalid little life so highly that the thought of protecting the vulnerable, the women, the children, the doddering cripples, the thought of it makes your bones creak with fear, it makes the flesh quiver on your bones! And yet you 'comment', like some chin-scratching critic, like some sneering journalist: 'It has finally begun then'! Does the world need your self-evident assertions? Does the world, whom you deny even the dubious pleasure of looking upon all this juvenilia here, does the world need your 'It has finally begun then' and your 'I have no quarrel with anyone'!?

GIESBACH: I have upset you.

HOLLOWAY: Yes! You have upset me! Quite. You have! Let me now remove my gloves. (*She delicately begins to remove both her elbow-length gloves.*) Would you like to make a 'comment' on my hands, my fingers? I think you'll agree they are amongst my finest features.

GIESBACH: You have good hands.

HOLLOWAY: Good?

GIESBACH: Your hands are good. Yes.

HOLLOWAY: That is all?

GIESBACH: Well...

HOLLOWAY: No other adjective springs to mind?

GIESBACH: 'Good' does the job.

HOLLOWAY: 'Good'? 'Good'?

GIESBACH: It works for me.

HOLLOWAY: You are not a man who loves language then?

GIESBACH: I work with images.

HOLLOWAY: And so 'good' is all I shall get?

GIESBACH: If, however, I were to transform this momentary flesh of yours, these knuckles, this wrist, these long and slender fingers, if I were to transform them into stone, or paint, then I could create a permanence that...

HOLLOWAY: No, you are wrong... (*She hangs up her gloves.*) Would you like to know how much money has been lavished on these hands? The ointments, the creams, the moisturisers...?

GIESBACH: Your hands are good.

HOLLOWAY: So you keep saying.

GIESBACH: But the living flesh is imperfect.

HOLLOWAY: Not mine!

GIESBACH: Even yours. Here is a tooth.

HOLLOWAY: There is nothing imperfect about these hands.

GIESBACH: They are good...

HOLLOWAY: A tooth?

GIESBACH: ...but they are impure.

HOLLOWAY: I always imagined the artist shunned the moral directive?

GIESBACH: I know what your hands are capable of. (*More distant cannons.*)

HOLLOWAY: Let me see the tooth. (*He passes her the tooth.*) An incisor, no?

GIESBACH: Correct.

HOLLOWAY: That is unfortunate.

GIESBACH: Yes.

HOLLOWAY: For the incisor has evolved for the purpose of biting into flesh.

GIESBACH: Yes.

HOLLOWAY: My teeth, like my hands, are elegant, enchanting. They are a study in symmetry, a lesson in dental distinction. Would you not say?

GIESBACH: You have good teeth.

HOLLOWAY: That word again!

GIESBACH: They are...good.

HOLLOWAY: My smile is, I am told, wonderfully seductive. Confident yet quite...quite...enigmatic.

GIESBACH: I have not yet seen you smile.

HOLLOWAY: No?

GIESBACH: Laugh, yes. But not yet a smile.

HOLLOWAY: Then I shall smile for you now. (*She smiles.*) Do you think you could paint that smile?

GIESBACH: It seemed forced.

HOLLOWAY: Forced?

GIESBACH: As if years of despair might be eradicated by a mere contraction of the facial muscles.

HOLLOWAY: This... (*She smiles.*) is not a forced smile. It is a welcoming smile, a little suggestive yes, but welcoming, friendly.

GIESBACH: As you wish.

HOLLOWAY: And your tooth here. So alone, so...

GIESBACH: I shall learn to live without it.

HOLLOWAY: Giesbach, where is your wife?

GIESBACH: I'm not married.

HOLLOWAY: You have a girlfriend?

GIESBACH: No.

HOLLOWAY: Then perhaps you are an arsefucker?

GIESBACH: (*After a pause.*) No.

HOLLOWAY: Why did you hesitate?

GIESBACH: I found the phrase...peculiar.

HOLLOWAY: Peculiar?

GIESBACH: Coming, as it did, from the mouth of one so refined, it sounded somehow...jarring.

HOLLOWAY: It is an expression my husband likes to use.

GIESBACH: I see.

HOLLOWAY: But, seriously, all artists hate women, do they not?

GIESBACH: Not at all.

HOLLOWAY: I generalise, do I?

GIESBACH: Yes.

HOLLOWAY: Here. (*She hands back the tooth.*)

GIESBACH: Thank you.

HOLLOWAY: Put it under your pillow.

GIESBACH: And in the morning there will be a silver coin?

HOLLOWAY: You never know what you might find in the morning.

(*They stare at each other. More distant guns/explosions. She smiles.*)

GIESBACH: You smiled.

HOLLOWAY: Did I?

GIESBACH: Just then.

HOLLOWAY: I don't think so.

GIESBACH: The corners of your mouth curled slightly upwards. It was very...animal.

HOLLOWAY: I don't remember.

GIESBACH: The sound of murder pleases you?

HOLLOWAY: (*Absent-mindedly.*) It is such a long...long... way...off.

(*The explosions continue.*)

(*Unfastening her dress.*) It's rather warm in here, don't you think?

GIESBACH: I enjoy the cold.

HOLLOWAY: It is...close.

GIESBACH: I can see your breath in the air. (*Pause.*) Are you being ironic?

HOLLOWAY: Ironic?

GIESBACH: You are trying to make a joke?

HOLLOWAY: Do you think your servant would be kind enough to help me unfasten my dress?

GIESBACH: I'm afraid I have no heating system here. You will catch a chill.

HOLLOWAY: Are you concerned for my welfare, Giesbach?

GIESBACH: (*After a pause.*) No.

HOLLOWAY: But you don't want me to be ill.

GIESBACH: There is snow on the ground outside.

HOLLOWAY: I do not suffer from the cold.

GIESBACH: You have a gorgeous dress.

HOLLOWAY: So you *can* conjure up the odd adjective when it is my clothing you are commenting upon? 'Gorgeous' is hardly inventive, is it, but certainly it is an improvement on 'good'. Are you sure you're not a homosexual?

GIESBACH: Quite sure.

HOLLOWAY: As it is unusual for a man who is not to use a word like 'gorgeous' when describing a dress.

GIESBACH: I am neither a homosexual nor do I hate women.

HOLLOWAY: Now, I am used to having a helper in these circumstances. The buttons at the top and at the bottom are positioned, as you will note, just out of the reach of my slender fingers. You see I am in need of assistance?

GIESBACH: I am too weak to paint. My arm is…

HOLLOWAY: Too weak to paint, too weak to talk politics. You are hardly inspiring company for a woman on a winter afternoon! (*Calling off.*) Hello! Hello! I wonder if you might help me unbutton my dress! (*To GIESBACH.*) I am being polite, as I do try to be to other people's servants. At home, however, I have been known to have the occasional tantrum. And, yes, to throw items of crockery. (*No answer.*) I can recommend someone for you. This woman of yours must be instantly dismissed. My own maid has a twin sister: she is young and long-legged and I'm sure she will be a vast improvement on this sloppy and indolent wretch. Her breasts are not quite the monstrous ones you seem to prefer but then she is not yet fully-developed. She is only eighteen and is just learning the art of servility so will require only her food and lodging as wages. (*A pause.*) As no help is forthcoming, it seems I will have to rely upon your good nature. (*She turns her back to him and waits for his help.*) Yes, friends of mine warned me against hiring a maid so young and so fetching, as one or two of them have seen their own husbands succumb to temptation. You can imagine the distress of having the man who shares your bed impregnating the girl who makes it for you. But no. My husband is a man of integrity and I feel it is a public signal of my faith in him that I choose for a maid an attractive female of such tender years. You are slow, Giesbach. Very slow. I talk to my servants when my back is turned but do not like doing so to someone I regard, not as an equal exactly, but certainly…

GIESBACH: I am flattered.

HOLLOWAY: If you would allow me to finish my sentence!

GIESBACH: I felt if I didn't interrupt, you might have gone on till the end of time.

HOLLOWAY: Giesbach, for God's sake help me out of this dress!
(*He approaches her and, with his left hand only, slowly begins to unfasten the many buttons on the back of her dress.*)
You would find that your life would be a lot easier, not to say happier, if you dedicated more of your time to the service of others. It is how an enlightened society works. There is something healthy about it, isn't there? You are now helping me and this act of kindness, though it did have to be prompted, will be remembered. You help me to undress and I will help you in your work. Your art. You might find that if you use both hands…

GIESBACH: My right arm has been shattered by the rage of your friends.

HOLLOWAY: You know that the hospice recently opened on the east side of the square was built by money raised by my industry?

GIESBACH: I did know.

HOLLOWAY: So that those afflicted with incurable diseases may now die in comfort.

GIESBACH: The hospice bears your name.

HOLLOWAY: And that my family invested thousands to open the new wing of the hospital?

GIESBACH: It bears your name.

HOLLOWAY: And we also converted the scrubland on the south of the river into an exquisitely-landscaped park replete with a wide variety of flowers and plants and a playground for the children and also ducks and swans in the Japanese-style pond, not to mention the…

GIESBACH: The park bears your name.

HOLLOWAY: And that we supplied over six hundred antique books to the library?

GIESBACH: The library is now the…

HOLLOWAY: And that we paid for the preservation and restoration of several treasured paintings for the art gallery? Paintings that were going to have to leave the country because of the Government's lack of enthusiasm for…

GIESBACH: The gallery also now bears your name.

HOLLOWAY: My father inculcated into me from an early age that the only worthwhile life to lead was a life of public service.

GIESBACH: Your much-expressed desire to serve is quite unable to conceal your much greater desire to rule.

(*A silence. The explosions again. He stops unbuttoning her.*)

HOLLOWAY: Please continue.

GIESBACH: (*Continuing.*) It is odd that someone so contemptuous of the artist should be so generous when it comes to the preservation of three original paintings by a long-dead Dutchman.

HOLLOWAY: A civilised country should have at least one art gallery and an art gallery is of little value if no paintings hang on its walls.

(*He helps her out of her dress. She stands, shivering, in her corset and stockings.*)

GIESBACH: Where would you like me to put this?

HOLLOWAY: Now, do you think I will make a good model for you?

GIESBACH: If I tried to paint you now, I should have to paint you left-handed.

HOLLOWAY: Would you like me to remove the rest of my clothing?

GIESBACH: You seem suddenly nervous.

HOLLOWAY: Nervous? Certainly not.

GIESBACH: As if your confidence were being stripped away with your garments.

HOLLOWAY: It is just the cold. I shivered.

GIESBACH: Would your husband appreciate the fact that you wish to be an artist's model? I wonder how pleased he would be that his wife is so…

HOLLOWAY: It was his idea that we commission you.

GIESBACH: Yes, but I understood that particular portrait was to be of a rather different nature.

HOLLOWAY: I cannot breathe properly in this ridiculous contraption. (*She begins to untie her corset.*)

GIESBACH: The money you paid for this dress would…

HOLLOWAY: It was a gift. From a previous lover.

GIESBACH: He must have loved you very much.

HOLLOWAY: I think he did. You may hang it on the stand.
(*He walks to the coat-stand, folds the dress, and hangs it there.*)
As you don't accept payment for your work, perhaps you will allow me to arrange for a doctor to visit you? My regular physician is at the front but I know another. He is old and drunk and lecherous but I am certain that a shattered arm is not beyond his capabilities.

GIESBACH: Thank you.

HOLLOWAY: This is called exchange. You have something that I require and I have something that you require. Nobody is stealing, nobody is lying, nobody is hurt.

GIESBACH: The painting will not be good. My arm…

HOLLOWAY: And the poor do not suffer.

GIESBACH: …is broken.

HOLLOWAY: You will paint me using the arm you always…

GIESBACH: That will not be possible.

HOLLOWAY: The agony of its creation will surely add to its quality.

GIESBACH: I think my arm is…

HOLLOWAY: And I do wish to be complimented. In your representation.

GIESBACH: Complimented?

HOLLOWAY: As you enhanced reality for the Governor's wife...

GIESBACH: I told you that...

HOLLOWAY: ...so I would like you to enhance reality for me. (*She removes her corset.*) Here. (*She holds it out for him to take.*) Please. Don't stare.

GIESBACH: How am I to paint you if I cannot look at you?

HOLLOWAY: You are not painting me at this moment, are you?

GIESBACH: All of a sudden you have become beautifully vulnerable.

HOLLOWAY: I told you, it is the temperature.
(*He takes the corset and hangs it up.*)
Now, where would you like me to sit? Perhaps I should sit here. (*She walks to the chaise-longue and sits.*) How about this? And how should I pose? Like this? Or like this? Would you like me to be completely naked, Giesbach? Like your fantasies here? What would you like?

GIESBACH: You are the customer. You must do as you...

HOLLOWAY: Aha! So you do care for the customer!?

GIESBACH: You are the first to...

HOLLOWAY: Should I pose like this then? Or this?

GIESBACH: I would choose something more comfortable.

HOLLOWAY: Yes, I would be most grateful if you would overlook any irregularities of form I possess. I have one or two moles which I detest and I have also been told that the right breast is marginally larger than the left. I trust your loyalty to the facts might...

GIESBACH: I see no irregularities.

HOLLOWAY: You see...?

GIESBACH: No irregularities.

HOLLOWAY: Then begin.
(*She sits in an affected pose, with a fixed smile, trying to remain still. The cold of the room makes her shudder*

occasionally. He walks to where his sketchbook lies and picks it up. He takes a pencil from the floor. He sits on a stool. He watches her. The guns start up again and continue to sound until the end of the scene. He transfers the pencil from his left hand to his right.)

You are wincing, Giesbach. Something stirred inside me then. When you winced. Was I moved by your pain perhaps? Sorry, am I allowed to talk? Is that permitted? I do find it so difficult to be silent. To be silent and to sit still are two things at which I lack practice. So sitting for you will require more endeavour on my part than it will on yours. I expect. Let me regain my smile. *(She smiles.)* That was not it. There. Like so. Ah. But each time I talk I destroy the pose. It is not easy this, is it? You make your subjects suffer, Giesbach.

GIESBACH: We have only just begun.

HOLLOWAY: How much do you pay these women to suffer for you like this?

GIESBACH: I have already told you that I never use…

HOLLOWAY: I feel restless.

GIESBACH: Should we stop?

HOLLOWAY: No. No. I want this. I want this very badly.

GIESBACH: And I want to please you. Why I do not know.

HOLLOWAY: And that you are prepared to draw me with such a painful handicap, it is a great privilege.

(Slowly and painfully, GIESBACH tries to lift his right arm towards the sketchbook. He is in agony.)

Ah, that look on your face. But you do this for me. For me.

(Despite his pain, GIESBACH begins to sketch her. The explosions continue.)

How long do you think this will last, Giesbach?

GIESBACH: Normally I draw quite quickly but under the present…

HOLLOWAY: I meant the war, Giesbach. The war.

GIESBACH: But this is not a war.

HOLLOWAY: Not…a…war?

GIESBACH: The people your husband is killing are unarmed civilians. They are peasants merely.

HOLLOWAY: Of course this is a war! You evidently do not read the papers!

GIESBACH: I assumed that a war… (*He yells in pain.*) …was when two sides were fighting.

HOLLOWAY: Just so.

GIESBACH: So this is one-sided slaughter. It will continue until your husband and his friends grow tired of it. (*Silence but for the distant explosions. She shudders.*) You will freeze to death.

HOLLOWAY: I am an emancipated woman and I do not need looking after!

GIESBACH: I just don't want you to be cold.

HOLLOWAY: And I thought you were too weak to talk politics.

GIESBACH: And so I am. (*Silence but for the gun-fire and explosions. He continues.*)

HOLLOWAY: How is it progressing?

GIESBACH: Slowly.

HOLLOWAY: And are you in great pain?

GIESBACH: Yes.

HOLLOWAY: And I…I am very, very cold.

GIESBACH: Yes. (*Silence but for the gun-fire and explosions.*)

HOLLOWAY: Perhaps…perhaps you might bring me my coat? Just until I warm up a little?

GIESBACH: Of course.

(*He rises painfully and walks to the stand. He takes the coat. He approaches HOLLOWAY. She smiles up at him. He smiles at her. He opens it out, despite his pain. She stands, shyly, and turns. He wraps the fur around her shoulders. As he does so, she gently holds his arm. She turns towards him. They stare at each other for some time. After a while, they make a sudden movement towards each other.*

Blackout.

In the darkness, the deafening screams of numerous jet aircraft close by.)

Part II

The screams of the jet aircraft begin to fade and are replaced by the screams of celebration from an enormous crowd. The light returns. We are in a master bedroom. One end of an elegant four-poster bed is visible, with a well-tailored suit laid out on it. HOLLOWAY is discovered in a state of anxiety. She is sitting at her dressing table. She is wearing a night dress and is combing her hair. The cheering continues throughout.

HOLLOWAY: And so the artist swings tomorrow. The artist whom I fucked, the artist whose tongue covered every inch of my skin, whose neck I bit into, whose buttocks I clawed, whom I rode through the night, whose fractured fingers I sucked as I rode. Yes, the artist dies tomorrow. And my portrait scarcely underway. And he was painting me as such…such a beauty. No, I am not the first woman to fuck a man who is not her husband. So this feeling of despair cannot be unique to me. How many men see across the breakfast table a woman who aches to offer up herself to another? Her offspring might be tugging at her skirts, bouncing on her lap or hanging off her udders, but when the opportunity appears, she will welcome a stranger's flesh between her thighs with a snarl on her lips and with desperation in her eyes…

(WINDERMERE enters, in a state of high excitement. His military uniform is covered in blood and he carries an exquisitely-wrapped present, the size of a hat-box, under one arm. HOLLOWAY leaps to her feet.)

My darling! I'm so glad that you… What has happened to your…?

WINDERMERE: *(Who talks at great speed.)* Missed me?

HOLLOWAY: You know I…

WINDERMERE: Dreamed of you. Nightly. In HQ.

HOLLOWAY: Naturally.

WINDERMERE: Imagined intercourse.

HOLLOWAY: Yes.

WINDERMERE: With you. Too long without grind.

HOLLOWAY: We can soon put that...

WINDERMERE: These days. Army full of arsefuckers.

HOLLOWAY: What has happened to your clothes?

WINDERMERE: My boy. Carried equipment. Made tea. Polished medals. Polished my gun. Old gun. Faulty mechanism. Blew off his face. Standing right by me.

HOLLOWAY: You know you are on public...?

WINDERMERE: Face slid down wall. Still smiling as it slid. Had just cracked joke about Irish. Funny joke.

HOLLOWAY: The people want your words, darling. You are a...

WINDERMERE: Did you hear news?

HOLLOWAY: And I'm sorry I'm not dressed yet. Your arrival...

WINDERMERE: Governor been caught playing Hide the Sausage with whore.

HOLLOWAY: ...was announced scarcely...

WINDERMERE: Think he'll resign. They want me to take over.

HOLLOWAY: Really?

WINDERMERE: When fighting finito.

HOLLOWAY: I thought it was...?

WINDERMERE: Not till they beg us. Beg us for mercy. Should we kiss now?

HOLLOWAY: Yes. Yes, of course.

(*They kiss.*)

WINDERMERE: (*Proffering gift.*) For you.

HOLLOWAY: I know what this is.

WINDERMERE: Don't think so.

HOLLOWAY: It's a hat, hand-crafted by the peasants across the water. They are famous for their dress-making and their...

WINDERMERE: Not quite.

HOLLOWAY: But it is a hat, surely? You always buy me hats. We have had to build another room to accommodate them all. I'll open it after we've...

WINDERMERE: (*Putting box on the table.*) Seen outside house?

197

HOLLOWAY: Yes.

WINDERMERE: Flag-wavers on lawn. Children on gate, climbing on wall. Police getting edgy. Banners and such. 'Captain Windermere, your nation is proud.'

HOLLOWAY: And so is your wife.

WINDERMERE: Killed many thousands.

HOLLOWAY: Yes.

WINDERMERE: Hundreds of thousands.

HOLLOWAY: It's alright.

WINDERMERE: Women and children. Huddled in houses.

HOLLOWAY: That's the nature of…

WINDERMERE: Still love me then?

HOLLOWAY: Yes. Of course I…

WINDERMERE: Press playing game.

HOLLOWAY: We need to change your clothes…

WINDERMERE: Keeping herd diverted.

HOLLOWAY: …if you are to make this speech.

WINDERMERE: Not good with words.

HOLLOWAY: I know you're not.

WINDERMERE: Not good with language.

HOLLOWAY: No.

WINDERMERE: Man of action.

HOLLOWAY: You are.

WINDERMERE: Speech written for me.

HOLLOWAY: Of course.

WINDERMERE: Might stumble over complicated phrases.

HOLLOWAY: We can practice.

WINDERMERE: Be grateful. Have it learned. Took all day.

HOLLOWAY: Lift up your arms.

WINDERMERE: (*Doing so.*) Like to be Governor's wife then?

HOLLOWAY: (*Undressing him.*) Well…

WINDERMERE: Always on display?

HOLLOWAY: I think I should like…

WINDERMERE: Help me govern.

HOLLOWAY: I will do anything to help my…

WINDERMERE: Bit nervous.

HOLLOWAY: Of course you are.

WINDERMERE: Man of action.

HOLLOWAY: Yes.

WINDERMERE: Not words.

HOLLOWAY: That's why you are loved. You act. You are not afraid to...

WINDERMERE: Where is maidgirl?

HOLLOWAY: She had to leave.

WINDERMERE: Why? Good totty. Long legs. Nice little titbuds.

HOLLOWAY: She didn't agree with the invasion. She felt she could no longer remain in our...

WINDERMERE: Shame. Pert arse. Flat belly.

HOLLOWAY: We can easily...

WINDERMERE: Need grind.

HOLLOWAY: Later.

WINDERMERE: Need one now.

HOLLOWAY: You must first address your...

WINDERMERE: Some officers...strict secret this...some officers...away from bitches...turn arsefucker.

HOLLOWAY: You said.

WINDERMERE: Monotonous war.

HOLLOWAY: Really.

WINDERMERE: All maps in HQ. All bombs from air. Blowing up bridges. Targeting dumps. Rarely see whites, the whites of their eyes.

HOLLOWAY: Turn around.

WINDERMERE: Conscripts all bored. Train 'em up. Sit about playing blackjack. Watching rugby in mess. Game shows.

HOLLOWAY: (*Removing his jacket.*) How old was this boy, this...?

WINDERMERE: Flew a few sorties. Dropped some explosives.

HOLLOWAY: Good.

WINDERMERE: Interesting arsenal. But all done by computer. No sense of teamwork.

HOLLOWAY: That's a shame.

WINDERMERE: Like some male bonding.

HOLLOWAY: Listen, darling...

WINDERMERE: And so high up. Prefer hands get dirty. See man when I kill him.

HOLLOWAY: I can imagine.

WINDERMERE: But this...turn up, press that, launch missile, village disappear, go home, have beer, watch television.

HOLLOWAY: Well, the less dangerous it is the...

WINDERMERE: Ancestors, digging trenches, going over top, bayonets flashing, screaming, fear, terrible sounds, shells dropping, bullets fizzing, slicing bellies, hand to hand, man to man. Good clean fighting.

HOLLOWAY: Sit down.

WINDERMERE: (*Doing so.*) Inspected some wreckage. Mashed some civilians. Bit disagreeable. Limbs and lungs and broken heads. Clusters. Mark 40. Dropped very many. Toddlers get shredded.

HOLLOWAY: It is the nature of war that...

WINDERMERE: (*Waving hand.*) Make no mention. See boy's blood here? Sad really. One loss: my boy. Cleaning rifle never used. Souvenir rifle. Ancestor's rifle.

HOLLOWAY: (*Untying bootlaces.*) Let's just get these off for you.

WINDERMERE: Don't think, darling...don't think things will ever be same again.

HOLLOWAY: No.

WINDERMERE: (*Laughing.*) Noisy shower outside, eh!

HOLLOWAY: More than a shower, darling.

WINDERMERE: And Governor gone.

HOLLOWAY: It was clear that his career had reached its...

WINDERMERE: Think an arsefucker.

HOLLOWAY: Really?

WINDERMERE: Likes young boys. Early twenties. Rumps like marble.

HOLLOWAY: I don't believe it.

WINDERMERE: Be surprised.

HOLLOWAY: Not everyone in government is...

WINDERMERE: Backpatting arsefuckers. Full of bad piss.

HOLLOWAY: (*Removing boot.*) Well, darling, I would just like to say that it's nice to have you...

WINDERMERE: (*Nodding.*) Have to impart policy. To waiting crowd. New beginnings. Et cetera.

HOLLOWAY: Well, I'm certain...

WINDERMERE: Building new nation. Family values. Marriage. Hard work and...saving for future.

HOLLOWAY: Of course there...

WINDERMERE: Time ripe. Years of corruption. Economy slacking.

HOLLOWAY: You are the natural...

WINDERMERE: Sweet life.

HOLLOWAY: Yes.

WINDERMERE: Good-looking.

HOLLOWAY: Yes.

WINDERMERE: Good at job.

HOLLOWAY: Yes.

WINDERMERE: Got money.

HOLLOWAY: Yes.

WINDERMERE: Hero of people.

HOLLOWAY: Yes.

WINDERMERE: Fit woman.

HOLLOWAY: (*After a pause.*) Thank you.

WINDERMERE: Down in history books.

HOLLOWAY: You will...

WINDERMERE: Place assured.

HOLLOWAY: It is.

WINDERMERE: Father be proud.

HOLLOWAY: I know that he'd be...

WINDERMERE: His son success. (*He breaks off with a slight emotion.*)

HOLLOWAY: (*Quickly.*) It is no mean feat to win both the adoration of the masses and the respect of the intellectuals...

WINDERMERE: (*Recovering.*) Top of tree.

HOLLOWAY: Yes.

WINDERMERE: Famous in world.

HOLLOWAY: You are.

WINDERMERE: Doing God's will.

HOLLOWAY: Well...

WINDERMERE: Leader of nations.

HOLLOWAY: Listen, darling…?

WINDERMERE: Want to grind now?

HOLLOWAY: No.

WINDERMERE: (*Nodding.*) Must talk to people.

HOLLOWAY: Yes.

WINDERMERE: (*Laughing.*) Rather face enemy. Rather lead charge.

HOLLOWAY: I know but…

WINDERMERE: Sword flashing, guns blazing, darkies dropping…

HOLLOWAY: Listen…

WINDERMERE: Man of action.

HOLLOWAY: Yes.

WINDERMERE: Not words.

HOLLOWAY: Yes, but if you are to enter politics…

WINDERMERE: Others write words.

HOLLOWAY: Yes but…

WINDERMERE: Memorised speech.

HOLLOWAY: You said.

WINDERMERE: Took me all day.

HOLLOWAY: (*Quickly.*) You know, darling, that the executions take place in the…

WINDERMERE: Yes, the pants-pissing yellow bellies choke on their ropes!

HOLLOWAY: (*Removing second boot.*) Yes.

WINDERMERE: Throttled for faint-heartedness.

HOLLOWAY: The artist…

WINDERMERE: See him twist in rain. Eyes bulging, tongue bloated, lolling over chin.

HOLLOWAY: But I have managed to…

WINDERMERE: Heart not beating. Perhaps I paint him? (*A pause. He laughs.*) A joke!

HOLLOWAY: Yes.

WINDERMERE: Talent for watercolour.

HOLLOWAY: Yes.

WINDERMERE: When struggled through school!

HOLLOWAY: Yes.

WINDERMERE: Perhaps I paint him?! Paint him twist in rain!?

(*WINDERMERE's fit builds into absolute hysteria.*)

HOLLOWAY: I managed to persuade this man to work on our... (*the laughter continues.*) ...to work on our portrait... (*the laughter continues.*) He has begun the painting... (*the laughter continues.*) ...but the night after he'd begun... (*the laughter continues.*) ...they took him away... (*the laughter continues.*) He refused because of his policy never to... (*the laughter continues.*) ...but I offered to help him... (*the laughter continues.*) ...with medical care... He'd been badly beaten... (*the laughter continues.*) ...for his reluctance to... though, as you say, he would...in the event...have had to do very... (*the laughter continues.*) ...little of that... Are you listening? (*The laughter continues.*) I don't think you are listening. (*The laughter continues.*) And I was wondering...you could exert your...especially now... you might for me... (*the laughter continues.*) ...exert your influence...? There are union men, housebreakers... (*the laughter continues.*) ...there are others to bear the brunt of our rage. But this man...could be useful to you... (*the laughter continues.*) ...in all sorts of ways. He could commemorate your rise...to this position... The people need to celebrate. (*The laughter continues.*) He could be commissioned to erect...to erect a great monument of public celebration. They say he's a genius. Are you listening? (*The laughter continues.*) I don't think you are listening. (*Now on her knees and pulling off his blood-stained combat trousers, including his belt and holster.*) I was hoping...that we might be able to... Are you listening? (*The laughter continues.*) I don't think you are listening.

I find it so hard to...when you laugh like this... (*the laughter continues.*)...and you have been away...I found I could speak...I found my own words but now... (*the laughter continues.*) Are you listening? (*The laughter continues.*) I don't think you are listening.

(*At the end of his spasm, WINDERMERE now recovers and, semi-naked, stands. A silence.*)

WINDERMERE: Like jokes.

HOLLOWAY: I know you are fond of...

WINDERMERE: Make me laugh.

(*She goes to the bed and collects the suit. The screams are increasing.*)

Feel that? Ground vibrating. Bewildered herd.

HOLLOWAY: Yes.

WINDERMERE: It moos and it bellows.

HOLLOWAY: Here. (*She opens out his shirt for him.*)

WINDERMERE: Stamping its hooves. This freshly ironed?

HOLLOWAY: I managed to…

WINDERMERE: Nice feel of new cotton.

HOLLOWAY: Straight from your tailor.

WINDERMERE: Soft on my skin.

HOLLOWAY: It's the finest…

WINDERMERE: Softer than khaki. Itches and scratches.

HOLLOWAY: You are home now.

(*A silence as she dresses him.*)

WINDERMERE: So…how you been?

HOLLOWAY: I…

WINDERMERE: Kept yourself busy?

HOLLOWAY: I…

WINDERMERE: New projects and such?

HOLLOWAY: I…

WINDERMERE: Things for people?

HOLLOWAY: I…

WINDERMERE: Long, lonely days filled?

HOLLOWAY: I…

WINDERMERE: Wives of powerful. Time on their hands. Nothing to do.

HOLLOWAY: I…

WINDERMERE: (*Nodding.*) I understand.

HOLLOWAY: I…

WINDERMERE: Think we start family. Build nice new nation.

HOLLOWAY: I…

WINDERMERE: Lead by example. Fill up your days. Velvet black tie?

HOLLOWAY: (*Affixing tie.*) I…

WINDERMERE: (*Nodding.*) Mark of respect. Innocents slaughtered.

HOLLOWAY: I…

WINDERMERE: Now help me with lingo?

HOLLOWAY: Yes.

WINDERMERE: Mentioned before, did you? Drop parts of speech?

HOLLOWAY: May I speak then?

WINDERMERE: Problem with verbs, was it?

HOLLOWAY: I may speak then?

WINDERMERE: Definite…something?

HOLLOWAY: The definite article.

WINDERMERE: Yes.

HOLLOWAY: You drop it quite often.

WINDERMERE: I drop it quite often?

HOLLOWAY: But if you stick to what's written for you then…

WINDERMERE: (*Nodding.*) Stick to what's written.

HOLLOWAY: Here. (*She motions him to sit. He does so. She helps him into his socks. She speaks quickly.*) I have told you before, that when you deviate from the script and try to use your own words, you have a tendency firstly to drop both the definite and the indefinite articles and also, when utilising the verb, you generally omit both the personal pronoun and the auxiliary section. You leap straight to the participle. I don't know why this should be. Also your relative clauses…

(*He stands. She hands him his suit-trousers. He begins to dress into them.*)

…seem always to be whittled down to the bare bones of the phrase.

WINDERMERE: Whittled down…

HOLLOWAY: And your delivery is rather rapid.

WINDERMERE: Rapid.

HOLLOWAY: Try to breathe at each comma. Take your time.

WINDERMERE: Yes.

HOLLOWAY: And smile.

WINDERMERE: The smile, yes!

HOLLOWAY: Remember to smile.

WINDERMERE: (*Smile and pose.*) One may smile and smile and be a villain.

HOLLOWAY: Yes.

WINDERMERE: (*Different smile and pose.*) Smile and smile and be a villain.

HOLLOWAY: Yes.

WINDERMERE: (*Different smile and pose.*) Smile and smile and be a villain.

HOLLOWAY: Yes.

WINDERMERE: (*Different smile and pose.*) Smile and smile and be a villain.

HOLLOWAY: Good.

WINDERMERE: (*Different smile and pose.*) Smile and be a villain.

HOLLOWAY: And the look of concern…here… (*passing his shoes.*) is also essential.

WINDERMERE: (*Sitting and putting on shoes.*) The look of concern. (*Strikes pose.*)

HOLLOWAY: The expression of sympathy.

WINDERMERE: (*Striking pose.*) Yes.

HOLLOWAY: The tilt of the head, the compassion in your eyes…

WINDERMERE: Yes.

HOLLOWAY: …with perhaps your hands on your hips.

WINDERMERE: Yes.

HOLLOWAY: Informal, a friend.

WINDERMERE: Yes.

HOLLOWAY: Always full of thoughtfulness, always sympathetic.

WINDERMERE: Yes.

HOLLOWAY: Ready to listen.

WINDERMERE: Yes.

HOLLOWAY: The veneer of unthinking kindness.

WINDERMERE: Yes.

HOLLOWAY: You understand the pain of others.

WINDERMERE: I understand the pain. (*He stands.*)

HOLLOWAY: I have told you before… (*She holds open his jacket.*)…that humility is something which can always be simulated. (*She helps him into his jacket.*) Turn around.

(*He does so. She straightens the jacket.*)

One more thing…

WINDERMERE: Behind every great man…

HOLLOWAY: Your hair is all matted.

WINDERMERE: …there stands a great woman.

HOLLOWAY: Let me… (*She takes a brush and begins to brush his hair.*)

WINDERMERE: This, my friends, is only the beginning. We are a proud and victorious people.

HOLLOWAY: Hold still.

WINDERMERE: And I ask you all to join with me to build a new nation.

HOLLOWAY: There we are.

WINDERMERE: This, my friends, is only the beginning.

HOLLOWAY: You are ready.

WINDERMERE: This, my friends, is only the beginning.

HOLLOWAY: Now, take some deep breaths.

WINDERMERE: (*Doing so.*) Yes.

HOLLOWAY: (*Passing him a pair of very expensive and fashionable spectacles.*) And prepare to meet your people. (*He stands, now transformed into the respectable, civilised politician that he is. He walks forward, evidently anxious, but still grinning widely. A light change as he steps out onto a balcony. The cheers and screams increase immediately and he is momentarily blinded by the flashbulbs of a hundred cameras. Beaming enthusiastically, he raises his arms to calm the crowd. The noise abates slightly. The palms of his hands are covered in blood.*)

WINDERMERE: (*Heavily amplified, hands still raised.*) This, my friends, is only the beginning.

(*The noise of the crowd fades away.*)

(*Blackout on WINDERMERE as the lights change back to HOLLOWAY.*)

HOLLOWAY: I am the wife… the wife of the Governor. The Governor's wife. This is a role which, I have to confess, does have its appeal. I will now be able more easily to improve lives everywhere and to…yes, the wife of the Governor… it has a certain ring to it. A certain timbre. Which pleases me. (*She giggles.*) I feel strangely excited, I cannot deny it. Strangely empowered. I feel like a schoolgirl. The future is now one long, limitless possibility for me! With the people behind us... Ah, the wife of the Governor. The Governor's wife. 'Allow me to introduce the wife of the Governor'. It sounds...natural. 'And this beautiful lady here, as I'm sure you already know, is the Governor's wife.' (*She giggles.*) To think that I...me...? Who, while at school, was overlooked as head girl when it was commonly agreed that I was the obvious candidate. Content I had to be with school prefect and running the committees. Me...the Governor's wife?! They said I lacked the discipline and the imagination to go far in the world. They said that I was casual and lived too much for myself. That I was idle, directionless, aloof and egotistical. Well, look at her now! You timeservers, you line-towing lickspittles, you wretched, wretched middle classes...just look at this lazy, dull bitch-woman now! (*A pause.*)

Oh, how I long to be the centre of somebody's world!

(*Blackout on HOLLOWAY as the lights change back to WINDERMERE. He is still beaming, with the happy crowd cheering enthusiastically.*)

WINDERMERE: ...and so we have proved that we will not simply stand back and let terrorists everywhere brutalise the world! No, we will assume the moral high ground and endeavour to safeguard human rights all across the globe! And we will do this in the name of truth! And we will do this in the name of decency! And we will do this in the name of the humanist ideal and the civilised society!

(*Jubilation and cheering. Blackout on WINDERMERE as the lights change back to HOLLOWAY.*)

HOLLOWAY: (*Gathering up her husband's discarded clothes.*) Is it then the fate of the working woman to be endlessly staggering about like this, with armfuls of her husband's clothing? But the state allocates an army of servants to the Governor and his wife. 'The Governor's wife'. The phrase continues to charm. This irritating maidlessness of ours then will only be temporary. (*Looking at the gift.*) Oh, he is good to me. So…after I have offered my body to him, when I have been crushed under his naked weight and been pulped and pressed and savaged, his eyes always closed, a precise, measured violence, a hard, disciplined humping…that is the moment in which I shall claim my reward. I have the feeling that this will be something out of the ordinary. (*She circles the box.*) I cannot resist a peek. I am always unable to defer gratification. I suspect a nice little number in waxed cotton, perhaps in olive, with the daintiest of bows at the back? Or a sand-coloured suedette with a leopard fur lining? They do make such exquisite headgear, these peasants, putting smiles on the faces of ladies at races. No, I must wait. As is our custom. I must wait and suffer and then…my prize. Or perhaps he has gone for a small brim of distressed fur, charcoal or forest green, or a Panama with gerbera trim or what about something continental, out of buckskin? Oh, it is so awfully exciting. Perhaps something water-repellent with an adjustable drawstring tie, with a brim that can be formed to suit my mood, for the Governor's wife must wear a hat suitable for every possible occasion. Or perhaps for the summer a knotted rami straw in navy with a matching gingham trim, made from long strands of plaited straw, which those bitches in huts stitch so dextrously into a spiral? Why does the prospect of a hat make me chew the inner lining of my mouth in such a passion? I am intoxicated with curiosity. I swear I am salivating! I am Eve in the Garden of Eden and… No, it is a large brim velvet bonnet in lilac, garlanded in daisies and lilies of one hundred per cent silk, with a delicate netting, also in silk, hanging down over my face with its matchless bone structure and its… Or why not a traditional cloche in simulated moleskin or llama in a nice wine or a dusty rose? Or perhaps a fez-style in imitation hedgehog with a geometric heavy weave or floppy brim? Or an Angora with a self flower trim in plum, I think, or something in the 20s style in one hundred per cent velour, with a velvet band? Or, better still, a diamond-studded tiara, but nothing too showy, this will be subtle, nestling on my impeccably-combed hair, twinkling just slightly both with confidence and pride but not over-glamorous, I do not wish to rub their noses in their own disappointment...for it is I who am to be the Governor's wife. It is I! Yes, I!! And I lack the patience to wait for him! I must see what he has brought me even if I have to feign surprise afterwards. This is a temptation far too great to withstand!

(*She unties the bow on the box and then takes off the lid. As she does so, the sound of a woman's terrible grief hangs in the room.*)

Please...don't cry. Don't cry. Why are you crying? Please. I understand your sadness but really, there is a place for tears and that is in one's own room, firmly behind closed doors. Ah, why are you crying? These walls are so thin. The general public intrude upon my privacy with an infuriating regularity. But the Governor's residence has ample security and walls six feet thick, made of reinforced concrete, I am told, with cameras mounted on every wall, and men in peaked caps with dogs and sticks and... Oh really...that sobbing. Please. Do not destroy this for me. When I welcome a new hat into my collection, I like to savour the moment and look upon the item as one of my children.

(*The sobbing continues.*)

Oh, it is horrid. You will force me to use my ear-plugs if this continues... Why do you need to exhibit your pain like this? As I have said, there is a time and a place for such public circuses of emotion. But not here. And not today. Today your new Governor has returned from the wars and it is a public holiday, the schools and the offices are closed so please...stop this sobbing and put a smile on your face, you...

(*The sobbing continues.*)

Well, I shall ignore you. Yes. You will not unsettle me. I will not allow you to unsettle me. Now. I shall relish the feel of the tissue paper and…please go elsewhere with your tedious pain!…and then accept with gratitude this token of my husband's esteem.

(*She reaches inside and slowly removes a dark-skinned human head from the gift-box. She holds it up. The sobbing continues. Blackout on HOLLOWAY as the lights change back to WINDERMERE. The jubilant crowd are cheering and chiming in with continuing enthusiasm.*)

WINDERMERE: And I am the man who says to crime NO! Yes, I am the man who says…POVERTY, GO! Unemployment I'll keep to an absolute…LOW! Then I'll make our declining economy…GROW!

(*Blackout on WINDERMERE as the lights change back to HOLLOWAY. The sobbing continues as she examines the head.*)

HOLLOWAY: Though evidently lifeless, your eyes speak to me. They speak. Are you the cause of all this weeping, this wailing? This woman, is she your mother? Or perhaps your girl, your betrothed? Perhaps she was waiting for your return so that you might marry? In your close-knit little village with plenty of dancing and drinking the local schnapps and with no doubt eager cousins playing those dear three-stringed guitars? And smashing plates, throwing confetti? Outside the church? In the square? Yes, she was probably hankering to spawn a clutch of reeking, shrieking infants. How old are you? Eighteen? Twenty-two? And why this look of vague surprise? What did you see in your last moments that has made your eyebrows lift and lock like this?

(*The sobbing continues.*)

This woman, is she your mother? You people, really. You should think carefully before you try to take us on like this. You cause those that love you such…sorrow, such distress. But there is no anger about you. You do not look at me with hatred, do you? To think, a man like you in the master bedroom of the Governor and his wife! Looking upon all the taste and the culture you seek to destroy.

(*Guiding the head around.*) See, take a look around you. Do we not live beautifully? What do you think?

(*The sobbing continues.*)

Oh, this woman, this sobbing...hag! Please! You have made your point. Your agony has been recorded, now will you kindly...? You know...you have an extremely tempting mouth. I do of course make allowances for the congealed blood between your teeth and the light hint of blue in your lips, which are nonetheless quite full, cupid-bow lips, kissable really and...young. And your hair is soft, warm, though with just the slightest evidence of burning. It would be interesting to see you attached to the trunk and to the limbs. I have no idea of your height, or your build. Good-looking, I think, and I suspect your body was...taut. Wiry. A soldier's body. An infantryman. Lean through constant deprivation but well-muscled through gruelling physical exertion.

(*The sobbing continues.*)

Yes, yes...you again!? You object, do you, to me spending a little time with your son, with your...lad? The best thing for the bereaved is to suffer alone. Go home and lock yourself away. Work through your pain. But I cannot help you. I really cannot! But I do confess to being somewhat transfixed by your boy's gaze. It has a serenity about it, a calm I...I have never seen...no, I have never seen eyes quite as beautiful as this.

(*Blackout on HOLLOWAY as the lights change back to WINDERMERE. The crowd are still cheering and chiming in with enthusiasm.*)

WINDERMERE: I promise you all there'll be no new...

TAXATION!

I'll invest all your wealth in our...HEALTH, EDUCATION! I shall easily curb any rise in...INFLATION! So join with me now and let's...BUILD A NEW NATION!

(*Blackout on WINDERMERE as the lights change back to HOLLOWAY. She holds the head like a baby in her arms. The sobbing continues.*)

HOLLOWAY: Another thing which strikes me...my arms are aching a little, the unused muscles fizzing under the strain of it, but still...I am holding a man in my hands. And babies, how they repulse me! How I plaster on a smile whenever friends proffer their mewling, shitting slabs of meat at me. But you are vulnerable, yes? I go beyond the boundaries of nationhood and genetics and hold you to my breast with affection, do I not? And still you look up at me. With an expression of...what? You demand of me nothing. You are indifferent to me and you make no demands. And for that...I feel a terrible...a terrible love. No, that is ridiculous. But I hold you like this and you make my body warm. Like whiskey makes me warm. But I have not yet drunk today. Though later I shall.

WINDERMERE: (*Off.*) Fired up! Wired up! Need grind now!

HOLLOWAY: And now it is my turn to be mashed, to be invaded!

(*She replaces the head in the box and reties the bow.*)

WINDERMERE: (*Off.*) Have to stash my throbbing cock! Need to shoot bolt now!

HOLLOWAY: I am beginning to understand.

WINDERMERE: (*Entering.*) Need it in you now! Need you on it now!

HOLLOWAY: I...

WINDERMERE: (*Frantically undressing.*) Must insert it!

HOLLOWAY: I...

WINDERMERE: Big, hard, glistening prick!

HOLLOWAY: I...

WINDERMERE: Want to fuck now!

HOLLOWAY: I...

WINDERMERE: Want to right now!

HOLLOWAY: I...

WINDERMERE: Those fuckers, they love me!

HOLLOWAY: I...

WINDERMERE: They pant and they sigh...

HOLLOWAY: I...

WINDERMERE: ...as they eye up my packet!

HOLLOWAY: I...

WINDERMERE: Bitches in crowd!

HOLLOWAY: I...

WINDERMERE: All want me to fuck them!

HOLLOWAY: Yes, but...

WINDERMERE: I need to grind now!

(*Semi-naked, though still wearing his stylish spectacles, he holds her to him roughly. The sobbing.*)

HOLLOWAY: Listen!

WINDERMERE: Sweet hard body.

HOLLOWAY: Can you not hear it?

WINDERMERE: Taut, toned thighs.

HOLLOWAY: Please…

WINDERMERE: Bursting, bursting…

HOLLOWAY: Could we not…?

WINDERMERE: Spectacular arse.

HOLLOWAY: I beg you, darling…

WINDERMERE: Tight like a teenager's.

(*He pushes her onto the bed and pins her down.*)

WINDERMERE: Dreamed of this nightly.

HOLLOWAY: Yes.

WINDERMERE: Imagined intercourse.

HOLLOWAY: Please!

WINDERMERE: With you.

HOLLOWAY: Listen!

(*A silence. The sobbing peters out.*)

WINDERMERE: Some officers…strict secret this…some officers…away from bitches…turn arsefucker.

HOLLOWAY: You said.

(*He begins to fuck her.*)

HOLLOWAY: I have heard it posited…

(*WINDERMERE grunts.*)

That the act of love…

(*WINDERMERE grunts.*)

Is usually more rewarding…

(*WINDERMERE grunts.*)

Are you listening?

(*WINDERMERE grunts.*)

I don't think you are listening.

(*WINDERMERE grunts.*)

Yes, under these circumstances…

(*WINDERMERE grunts.*)

…it is generally accepted…

(*WINDERMERE grunts.*)
That when both parties…
(*WINDERMERE grunts.*)
When both parties are…
(*WINDERMERE grunts.*)
Darling?
(*WINDERMERE grunts.*)
When both parties are ready and receptive…
(*WINDERMERE grunts.*)
To the act…
(*WINDERMERE grunts.*)
…the act of love then…
(*WINDERMERE grunts.*)
Are you listening?
(*WINDERMERE grunts.*)
I don't think you are listening.
(*WINDERMERE grunts.*)
Then both participants are rewarded…
(*WINDERMERE grunts.*)
…with a more pleasurable experience.
(*WINDERMERE grunts.*)
Darling?
(*WINDERMERE grunts.*)
Whereas what we have here…
(*WINDERMERE grunts.*)
At this moment…
(*WINDERMERE grunts.*)
Is an assertion of will merely.
(*WINDERMERE grunts.*)
The strong over the weak merely.
(*WINDERMERE grunts.*)
Did you hear?
(*WINDERMERE grunts.*)
And you always close your eyes.
(*WINDERMERE grunts.*)
It would be nice if we…
(*WINDERMERE grunts.*)
Darling?

(*WINDERMERE grunts.*)
It might be nice if you looked at me.
(*WINDERMERE grunts.*)
Once in a while.
(*WINDERMERE grunts.*)
You seem in such pain.
(*WINDERMERE grunts.*)
But a loving regard might...
(*WINDERMERE grunts.*)
Might warm me to the deed.
(*WINDERMERE grunts.*)
But this I do not greatly enjoy.
(*WINDERMERE grunts.*)
I have to say.
(*WINDERMERE grunts.*)
It could even be...
(*WINDERMERE grunts.*)
...because you are so distant...
(*WINDERMERE grunts.*)
...that you are imagining that somebody else...
(*WINDERMERE grunts.*)
Somebody else...
(*WINDERMERE grunts.*)
...is being compressed beneath you.
(*WINDERMERE grunts.*)
And penetrated...
(*WINDERMERE grunts.*)
...in this most displeasing fashion.
(*He now bellows in relief. A long silence. He rises and walks from the bed.*)
WINDERMERE: (*Head down.*) Sorry.
HOLLOWAY: That's alright.
WINDERMERE: Want present now?
HOLLOWAY: Later.
WINDERMERE: Get carried away.
HOLLOWAY: I know.
WINDERMERE: Crowd pumped me up.
HOLLOWAY: Yes.

WINDERMERE: Feel ashamed.

HOLLOWAY: Don't worry.

WINDERMERE: Forgive?

HOLLOWAY: Forgive.

WINDERMERE: Still love me then?

HOLLOWAY: Of course.

WINDERMERE: Still best friend?

HOLLOWAY: (*She rises from the bed and walks to him. She has his revolver in one hand.*) But there is something that I have to tell you.

WINDERMERE: Feel ashamed.

HOLLOWAY: Something you must know.

WINDERMERE: Feel like beast.

HOLLOWAY: While you were away.

WINDERMERE: Feel like animal.

HOLLOWAY: While you were at the war.

WINDERMERE: Feel unclean.

HOLLOWAY: I made love to another.

(*A silence.*)

It was just once.

(*WINDERMERE is silent.*)

I can forgive you if you can forgive me.

(*WINDERMERE is silent.*)

It is always a risk the soldier takes. When he leaves his home for so long. Don't look so… Please, darling. Don't look so… I'm sorry. It was one night. I was lonely. But I still… We still… I still want to be your wife. The Governor's wife. You and I. We have the people on our side. We are young. We are beautiful. We are rich. We are popular.

(*WINDERMERE, like a child, begins to sob.*)

Please don't cry. Tears are always unnecessary. I have broken our trust and perhaps also your heart but the future is still bright. Come now. Let us look to the future. Forget all that's past. Here. Take my hand.

(*She holds out her hand towards WINDERMERE.*)

Let us forget everything.

(*WINDERMERE continues to sob silently, his head down.*)

Kiss me.

(*WINDERMERE continues to sob.*)

Kiss me. And look into my eyes.

(*He slowly turns his head towards her, in terrible pain.*)

Your face. The agony on your charming face. A kiss.

(*Close to him, she stares up at her husband. He tries to stifle his sobs.*)

Please…a kiss.

(*Choking back his tears, he brings his face towards hers. She raises the revolver behind their heads.*)

Look deep into my eyes, darling. Look deep into my soul.

(*They stare at each other.*)

Now…a kiss!

(*They kiss, slowly, gently, lovingly.*

The gun is fired.

Blackout.

The sound of waves crashing against a shore.)

Part III

The sound of the waves recedes slightly. The blinding light of an unnaturally hot summer's day. The verandah of a very desirable beach house. A table and several unopened crates and boxes, with folded deckchairs against the wall. The call of sea-birds, the chirrup of crickets. A ship horn sounds. GIESBACH, in the dirty clothing of the prisoner, steps out onto the verandah, looking around in amazement and bewilderment, shielding his eyes against the glare of the day. After a while, dressed smartly in shirt-sleeves, WINDERMERE enters in shades. He carries a briefcase.

WINDERMERE: (*Oozing decency, friendliness and excitement.*) There you are! I'm so glad they brought you here safely. What do you think? Lovely bit of beach, isn't it? (*Laughing.*) The sand looks almost real. Would you not say? And you are of course free to take a stroll down there at any time. Just inform the guards at the gate. (*Laughing.*) Though they don't of course recommend swimming.

GIESBACH: I...

WINDERMERE: So...how are you?

GIESBACH: I...

WINDERMERE: How are...things?

GIESBACH: I...

WINDERMERE: (*Opening briefcase.*) We're delighted, we have to say, that you've agreed to come here and take a look around. I expect it's a long time since you've actually seen the sea? (*Laughing.*) A good few years, is it not? And the sky? You approve, I can tell. It is such a lovely, deep blue today. Sea's a tad choppy, yes, but the sky...the sky is like a picture postcard. Tell me...have you ever lost anyone you truly love?

GIESBACH: I...

WINDERMERE: You approve of all this, do you?

GIESBACH: I...

WINDERMERE: We're so glad. Really. We are. (*Handing him a package.*) Here. We thought we ought to get you out

219

of those horrid clothes and find you something a little more casual. And we'll arrange an extensive new wardrobe for you just as soon as you say the word.

GIESBACH: I...

WINDERMERE: And have you looked inside the house yet? Rather opulent, no? Now, there are some of my colleagues who think we're going a little overboard here, that the money would be better spent on education or on housing, but since they tell me you are this country's last surviving dreamer, as it were, then we should...I am told that other governments treat their creative types like royalty...then we should show you, Mr G, a little...

GIESBACH: It is very grand.

WINDERMERE: (*Smiling.*) If you would kindly let me finish... (*Pause.*) Grand, you say?

GIESBACH: Inside.

WINDERMERE: You approve?

GIESBACH: I...

WINDERMERE: We're so glad. Really. We are.

GIESBACH: I'm not sure I...

WINDERMERE: We cannot have our geniuses languishing in our prisons, can we? You see, I can understand your reluctance to bear arms. (*Laughing.*) It takes all sorts to make a world. But now your country has called upon you in a different way. We want you to give your people a monument, a giant sculpture that will stand, hewn into the cliff-face for centuries to come or until the action of the ever-advancing waves has sent it crashing onto the beach below!

GIESBACH: A monument?

WINDERMERE: A great monument of public celebration!

GIESBACH: I...

WINDERMERE: And we have a chauffeur, (*laughs*) who is I'm afraid a light-fingered Scouser unfortunately, but he will pick you up from here each morning and drive you back from the site at night, (*laughs*) cracking jokes all the way quite possibly, we have a cook and a rather firm-buttocked young maid, and all are fully-briefed and ready to start work for you on Monday morning.

GIESBACH: I...

WINDERMERE: You see up there? The cliffs up there? Where those cranes are, and the JCBs? That is where the site is even now being prepared. It will be the largest construction this land has ever known. And the big cliff there? In the centre? That is what, we hope, you are to transform into a five hundred-foot-high statue of immense beauty, which will welcome visitors to this land, striking an open-armed and friendly pose, and will serve as a symbol of all that is good, all that is true, and all that is... You stand, Mr G, wide-eyed and awestruck before all this natural splendour which will, should you agree to this scheme, be your very own back garden!

GIESBACH: I...

WINDERMERE: Now... I expect you have one or two questions that you'd like answered?

GIESBACH: I...

WINDERMERE: You know I lost my wife some time ago, Mr G?

GIESBACH: Yes.

WINDERMERE: You heard?

GIESBACH: It was a national...

WINDERMERE: It was a tragedy with which I am still coming to terms.

GIESBACH: Of course.

WINDERMERE: It shattered me.

GIESBACH: Yes.

WINDERMERE: Completely.

GIESBACH: Yes.

WINDERMERE: I have to say. (*Pause.*) You approve of all this then?

GIESBACH: I...

WINDERMERE: We're so glad. Really. We are.
(*WINDERMERE beams at GIESBACH for a time. GIESBACH is on edge.*)

GIESBACH: Would it be possible to...?

WINDERMERE: I imagine that the country has changed... (*laughing*) for the better naturally...in the years you have spent incarcerated?

GIESBACH: I understood I was to be...

WINDERMERE: I don't know how closely the criminal follows the national news, Mr G, but things have not been at all easy for me. Which is rather grating as I have bent over backwards to appeal to as many people as is humanly possible.

GIESBACH: I...

WINDERMERE: As you may recall...leadership was rather thrust upon me and, though I am told my bereavement at that time won me the sympathy of the elderly and the middle-aged, the unfortunate death of my wife at the outset of my term of office... (*He breaks off.*)

GIESBACH: Sir?

WINDERMERE: It's quite alright.

GIESBACH: You evidently loved...

WINDERMERE: Tell me...do you like the way I talk?

GIESBACH: I...

WINDERMERE: The way I articulate?

GIESBACH: I...

WINDERMERE: Communicate?

GIESBACH: I...

WINDERMERE: Enunciate?

GIESBACH: I...

WINDERMERE: I have a handle on the language, no?

GIESBACH: You...

WINDERMERE: It is something I have learned over the period of my stint as Governor. I receive expert tuition. A little each day. It was my late wife who began the process for me. My humanising, as it were. My wife, she...

GIESBACH: She...?

WINDERMERE: When I was a soldier, a mere fighting man, I confess I was something of a lout. I was certainly no grammarian. (*Laughing.*) Not by a long chalk, I can assure you.

GIESBACH: I...

WINDERMERE: But now I so relish the sensation of the words as they are composed in my mouth, the resonances of the syllables, the permutations of the adjectives, nouns, verbs and adverbs, the amassing and refining of the vocabulary, that I find it rather difficult to pause. Do you love language, Mr G?

GIESBACH: I...

WINDERMERE: (*Producing wallet.*) I have in my possession one or two photographs but unfortunately she looks rather too solemn in them, always this unremitting sadness behind the eyes. I fear she rather enjoyed simulating melancholy whenever a camera was pointed in her direction. What we need however for this statue, Mr G, is something a little more accessible, a little more congenial. This country is open for business, as it were. Are you good at smiles?

GIESBACH: I'm still not...

WINDERMERE: I have always firmly believed that the function of your sort is to offer the people hope. We all know, and I of course know more than most, that life is arduous, that it is a journey of hardship, anguish and despair but we want this monument to be life-affirming, to be a beacon in the darkness of people's squalid little lives. I feel I can be candid with you, Mr G. You think you might lend your sculpture a positive aspect?

GIESBACH: I...

WINDERMERE: We're so glad. Really. We are.

GIESBACH: I...

WINDERMERE: This whole project will be, as I say, a celebration. There will be a full-scale mediaeval castle up there, intrepidly peering out over the sea, the size of a small town, Mr G. It will be a living community. There will be a funfair, a circus and a business park to demonstrate firstly our pride in ourselves and then to the rest of the world it will show that...

GIESBACH: It is...

WINDERMERE: If you would kindly let me finish? (*Pause.*) You will agree that we cannot be faulted for a lack of ambition?

GIESBACH: I...

WINDERMERE: Do you play golf at all?

GIESBACH: I...

WINDERMERE: We are trying to lure the dollar and the yen by building numerous courses down there. Across the bay, see? There is one already operational...

GIESBACH: I have never...

WINDERMERE: If you would just let me finish my sentence? Thank you. (*Pause.*) Between thee and me, Mr G, we are beginning to detect a little public discontent and I do not seem... For some reason I am not so loved as once I was. And so we want to give to the electorate, admittedly through their own taxes, a wonderful gift, a gift that will put the smiles back on their faces, give their grandchildren something to look back on and say 'our grandparents gave us this, left this piece of history for us!' (*Pause.*) You say you can do happy, Mr G?

GIESBACH: I...

WINDERMERE: We're so glad. Really. We are.

GIESBACH: I wonder, Captain Windermere, if I might...

WINDERMERE: Tell me...do you have anybody you would actually call a close friend?

GIESBACH: I...

WINDERMERE: Anyone whose death or disappearance would cause you distress?

GIESBACH: I...

WINDERMERE: I imagine not. Prison life is a struggle not only to embrace the solace of solitude but also to escape the agony of loneliness?

GIESBACH: I...

WINDERMERE: Government is a tremendous responsibility.

GIESBACH: Yes?

WINDERMERE: The adulation of others so quickly turns to suspicion.

GIESBACH: Yes.

WINDERMERE: But I really do feel we should all be speaking in one voice. I think I am a good man.

GIESBACH: I...

WINDERMERE: Would you not say?

GIESBACH: I...

WINDERMERE: I should like to be well thought of.

GIESBACH: You...

WINDERMERE: You suppose I am well thought of?

GIESBACH: I...

WINDERMERE: My colleagues are happy that we use my late wife as a model for your sculpture. As a mark of respect both to my grief and to her memory. Did you ever see my wife in the flesh?

GIESBACH: I...

WINDERMERE: She was a remarkably beautiful woman.

GIESBACH: I...

WINDERMERE: And I loved her very much.

GIESBACH: Yes...

WINDERMERE: You saw her, did you? Perhaps on our wedding day? Just before the foreign war? Or perhaps at one of her charitable functions?

GIESBACH: I...

WINDERMERE: More likely you saw her on television? But that never did her justice. Oh, how it flattens and squashes. In reality she emanated elegance, grace and tradition. You think you will be able to undertake the commission?

GIESBACH: I...

WINDERMERE: We imagine you will need several years to complete it and we have a hundred-odd chisellers and scaffolders and other tattooed types already hired. They will all be directly under your command. You are excited about the challenge, I can tell?

GIESBACH: I...

WINDERMERE: We're so glad. Really. We are.
   (*WINDERMERE beams at GIESBACH for a time. GIESBACH is on edge.*)
   Please. Try on your clothes.

GIESBACH: Then...am I free?

WINDERMERE: Sorry?

GIESBACH: Am I...free?

WINDERMERE: Free?

GIESBACH: Yes.

WINDERMERE: Are you free?

GIESBACH: Yes.

WINDERMERE: You are asking me?

GIESBACH: Yes.

WINDERMERE: If you are free?

GIESBACH: Yes.

WINDERMERE: We are all free, Mr G.

GIESBACH: Yes.

WINDERMERE: Your freedom is what we are striving
    night and day to preserve.

GIESBACH: Yes.

WINDERMERE: Please. Your clothes.

GIESBACH: Yes.

(*A bewildered GIESBACH begins to remove his prison*
uniform.)

WINDERMERE: (*Inhaling deeply.*) Ah, the smell of the salt.
    The salt from the sea. Do you like seagulls at all?

GIESBACH: I…

WINDERMERE: Here they are the size of Labradors.
    There are moves afoot, however, to have them culled.

GIESBACH: I…

WINDERMERE: They tend to bomb their thick white
    excrement into people's gardens.

GIESBACH: Birds are, I suppose…

WINDERMERE: That's it. Remove those rank and filthy
    garments. Personally, I like to change my clothes at least
    five times a day.

GIESBACH: Yes.

WINDERMERE: My late wife once managed eleven
    separate changes.

GIESBACH: I…

WINDERMERE: (*Laughing.*) What do you think of that,
    Mr G?

GIESBACH: Well, I…

WINDERMERE: And they tell me you are something of a
    socialist?

GIESBACH: I…

WINDERMERE: Is that true?

GIESBACH: I…

WINDERMERE: (*Laughing.*) One wonders where all your 'comrades' are now!

GIESBACH: I...

WINDERMERE: (*Laughing.*) In their furry beaver hats!

GIESBACH: I...

WINDERMERE: (*Laughing.*) And with their breath stale with cheap vodka and the stench of those filterless cigarettes!

GIESBACH: I...

WINDERMERE: How peculiar, Mr G!

GIESBACH: I...

WINDERMERE: You think then that your countrymen should not eat?

GIESBACH: I...

WINDERMERE: Is that it?

GIESBACH: I...

WINDERMERE: Or that the industrious should not be rewarded?

GIESBACH: I...

WINDERMERE: The entrepreneurial?

GIESBACH: I...

WINDERMERE: Is that it, Mr G?

GIESBACH: I...

WINDERMERE: Most peculiar!

GIESBACH: I...am...not...sure...I...

(*WINDERMERE looks at GIESBACH, now in colourful and undignified beachwear.*)

WINDERMERE: (*Laughing.*) That suits you rather well, Mr G!

GIESBACH: I...

WINDERMERE: Such wonderful, lively colours, no?

GIESBACH: I...

WINDERMERE: (*Laughing.*) Don't forget the sandals there!

GIESBACH: (*Stepping into them.*) No.

WINDERMERE: That's good!

GIESBACH: I...

WINDERMERE: So...welcome to your new home!

GIESBACH: I...

WINDERMERE: Your new life! We're so glad. Really. We are.

(*WINDERMERE beams at GIESBACH for a time. GIESBACH is on edge.*)

Here. (*He opens a deckchair.*) Take a seat.

GIESBACH: I...

WINDERMERE: Please. Be my guest.

GIESBACH: Well...

WINDERMERE: We want you to think of yourself as on a permanent holiday.

GIESBACH: I... (*He cautiously sits in the deckchair.*)

WINDERMERE: The picture is complete.

GIESBACH: Yes.

WINDERMERE: How does that feel?

GIESBACH: I...

WINDERMERE: Do we not respect you?

GIESBACH: I...

WINDERMERE: Revere you?

GIESBACH: I...

WINDERMERE: All this belongs to you!

GIESBACH: It's very...

WINDERMERE: Here. (*He passes GIESBACH a photograph.*) Do you think you could work from that?

GIESBACH: Well...

WINDERMERE: You can capture her beauty?

GIESBACH: I...

WINDERMERE: What do you think of her?

GIESBACH: She is...

WINDERMERE: What do you think of her face, her bone structure?

GIESBACH: It is... good.

WINDERMERE: Good?

GIESBACH: Yes. She...

WINDERMERE: And her hair?

GIESBACH: It is...

WINDERMERE: She holds herself attractively, does she not?

GIESBACH: The photograph is...

WINDERMERE: Is what, Mr G? Is what?

GIESBACH: She is rather obscured.

WINDERMERE: Obscured?

GIESBACH: By a man.

WINDERMERE: Is she?

GIESBACH: By a man in uniform whom I take to be...

WINDERMERE: You think she is obscured?

GIESBACH: Whom I take to be you, sir.

WINDERMERE: Yes, but what do you think of her?

GIESBACH: She is, as you say...

WINDERMERE: You see what I mean about the mournfulness?

GIESBACH: Yes.

WINDERMERE: A constant snarl on the lips.

GIESBACH: Yes.

WINDERMERE: She had, at great expense I should add, a syringeful of poison injected into her forehead to remove that frown.

GIESBACH: Ah.

WINDERMERE: You think you could translate that image into the cliff?

GIESBACH: I have never...

WINDERMERE: Three dimensions?

GIESBACH: Never worked with chalk before.

WINDERMERE: And five hundred foot high?

GIESBACH: The calcium carbonate is...

WINDERMERE: With a warming smile?

GIESBACH: And the rock is...is very soft and is prone... prone, as you say, to rather rapid...erosion.

WINDERMERE: You need something else?

GIESBACH: It is, as I...understand it, composed chiefly of minute fragments...fragments of fossil shells and... organic remains...and so...

WINDERMERE: I expected as much.

GIESBACH: ...and so therefore the action of the chisel...

WINDERMERE: (*Moving towards the large crate centre-stage.*) Please. Over here.

GIESBACH: It crumbles easily and...

WINDERMERE: If you would?

GIESBACH: (*Rising.*) Yes.

WINDERMERE: I do not wish you to breathe a word of this.

GIESBACH: I...

WINDERMERE: To anyone.

GIESBACH: I...

WINDERMERE: Is that understood?

GIESBACH: I...

WINDERMERE: It is part of our agreement.

GIESBACH: I...

WINDERMERE: Now then. (*He opens the hinged top of the crate. He moves away.*) Take a look.

(*GIESBACH approaches the crate and peers in. There is a long silence. His expression slowly changes as he takes in what he sees.*)

I want you to replicate everything. In perfect proportion. The contours, the curves, the way the flesh sits on the bone, the smoothness of the skin, the high and delicate cheeks. It must be in perfect proportion. Yes? I want it exact in every detail. You have a responsibility to tell the truth. That is right, is it not? I want this woman remembered! Remembered until the end of time. Are you married?

GIESBACH: I...

WINDERMERE: But you had a girlfriend, did you?

GIESBACH: I...

WINDERMERE: She desert you when you were banged up?

GIESBACH: I...

WINDERMERE: (*Laughing.*) You don't look like an arsefucker!

GIESBACH: I...

WINDERMERE: Because let me tell you, Giesbach, let me tell you something...there is nothing more tragic in the life of a man than when he loses the woman in his life and only then...only when she is dead and gone...only then does it dawn upon him how much he was loved and how much, Giesbach, how much he himself loved. This is a fate I would not wish on anyone. Let me tell you that. I shall let you have that for nothing.

(*A silence as GIESBACH stares into the crate and WINDERMERE stares out to sea.*)

I have achieved much in my life. And I am, I know, still relatively young. And why is that, I ask myself? It is because I work hard and I am fair and I know how to play by the rules. I may not be an academic, Giesbach, I may not be some firebrand intellectual but I know what's right and I know how to go about getting what I want. Is that a crime? You think that is a crime? And I love my country. I love its traditions, its people. I love its countryside. Its trees, its fields, its beaches. I love what my ancestors achieved. I love their self-belief, their sense of duty and they were civilised. Civilised, Giesbach. You know what that means? You know how to paint that? How to sculpt that? You can do responsibility, can you? You can do honour? Justice? Your art has a conscience, does it? That is me in that crate, Giesbach. That is me. Packed in the ice there. My life. My heart. That is my pain. Can you do pain?

GIESBACH: I can do pain.

WINDERMERE: Yes?

GIESBACH: Yes.

WINDERMERE: I will leave her with you for a night. You will absorb her. The fact of her. Make any drawings you need to make. Memorise her face. Examine her body.

GIESBACH: Her body.

WINDERMERE: But do not touch.

GIESBACH: Her face is…

WINDERMERE: I will not have her touched.

GIESBACH: The lips.

WINDERMERE: She belongs to me.

GIESBACH: Her mouth.

WINDERMERE: Yes?

GIESBACH: With her eyes closed.

WINDERMERE: You will not lay a finger on her.

GIESBACH: As if frozen in a kiss.

WINDERMERE: You understand?

GIESBACH: She…

WINDERMERE: But I do insist on the smile.

GIESBACH: Would that not be to create a fiction?

WINDERMERE: We must always tell the truth.

GIESBACH: But it seems she rarely smiled?

WINDERMERE: This is for public consumption.

GIESBACH: Yes.

WINDERMERE: And immortality.

GIESBACH: Yes.

WINDERMERE: And so...happiness and hope, if you please.

GIESBACH: Yes.

WINDERMERE: You approve of the plan?

GIESBACH: Yes.

WINDERMERE: We're so glad. Really. We are.

GIESBACH: She is...

WINDERMERE: (*Closing the crate.*) Let her rest for now.

GIESBACH: Yes.

WINDERMERE: In her icy bed.

GIESBACH: Yes.

WINDERMERE: (*Laughing.*) I am becoming something of a poet, Mr G!

GIESBACH: Ah?

WINDERMERE: Oh, yes. I have taken to reading poetry, novels.

GIESBACH: Yes.

WINDERMERE: Do you like poetry at all?

GIESBACH: I...

WINDERMERE: It makes me think it is possible to achieve anything. In this life.

GIESBACH: Yes.

WINDERMERE: Providing one has the application.

GIESBACH: Yes.

WINDERMERE: And the discipline.

GIESBACH: And I am to live here?

WINDERMERE: Tell me, Giesbach... since you are evidently one of those who condemn action of any sort... answer me this: You are walking down a busy high street, soon you come across a man beating a woman violently, savagely. What do you do? Do you act? Or do nothing?

GIESBACH: You...

WINDERMERE: You act of course!

GIESBACH: You do...

WINDERMERE: You act.

GIESBACH: ...no harm.

WINDERMERE: Between thee and me, Mr G, I have seen footage. Of the foreign war. (*Laughing.*) What we did was to kill the man. And then the woman. And all the bystanders. And the families of the bystanders. And we destroyed all the houses. All the shops. The bridges.

GIESBACH: I...

WINDERMERE: (*Leading him away, with his arm over his shoulder, removing his shades.*) But that is between thee and me, Mr G. I feel I can talk candidly? I feel I can confide in you?

GIESBACH: I...

WINDERMERE: I may be a chieftain but I do have a conscience!

(*A woman laughs, surreal, distorted.*)

You follow?

(*The woman laughs. WINDERMERE grows increasingly unsettled as his grip on reality gradually slips.*)

Not true: we sleep like babies. At night.

(*The woman laughs.*)

But inertia, Giesbach, it destroys credibility.

(*The woman laughs.*)

In eyes of world.

(*The woman laughs.*)

If we vacillate.

(*The woman laughs.*)

Have to have run-ins.

(*The woman laughs.*)

And vital to triumph.

(*The woman laughs.*)

You follow?

(*The woman laughs.*)

To flex muscles.

(*The woman laughs.*)

When wretches defy us.

(*The woman laughs.*)

Refuse to conform.

(*The woman laughs.*)

Scream for autonomy.
(*The woman laughs.*)
Virus of independence.
(*The woman laughs.*)
From our kind control.
(*The woman laughs.*)
Gives others ideas.
(*The woman laughs.*)
Also strategic.
(*The woman laughs.*)
Need base for our people.
(*The woman laughs.*)
Keep watch over workers.
(*The woman laughs.*)
Boost defence spending.
(*The woman laughs.*)
Military systems.
(*The woman laughs.*)
Aerospace buoyant.
(*The woman laughs.*)
Avionics equipment.
(*The woman laughs.*)
Rebuild what we flatten.
(*The woman laughs.*)
Big reconstruction.
(*The woman laughs.*)
Nice bit of money.
(*The woman laughs.*)
So shareholders happy.
(*The woman laughs.*)
We are enlightened.
(*The woman laughs.*)
Their new government thinks so.
(*The woman laughs.*)
Opened their markets.
(*The woman laughs.*)
We peddle our software.
(*The woman laughs.*)
Our trainers, our burgers.

(*The woman laughs.*)

And lovely, cheap labour!

(*The laughter ceases.*)

You find me amusing?

GIESBACH: I...

WINDERMERE: Think me a comic?

GIESBACH: No, I...

(*They stare at each other. A silence.*
A fist knocks on wood twice.
WINDERMERE, in his declining mental state, looks to
GIESBACH in alarm.)

WINDERMERE: I think we are friends now?

GIESBACH: Yes.

(*A fist knocks on wood twice.*)

WINDERMERE: You and I, friends?

GIESBACH: Yes.

(*A fist knocks on wood twice.*)

WINDERMERE: Need someone to trust.

GIESBACH: Yes.

(*A fist knocks on wood twice.*)

WINDERMERE: Because I want to do good.

GIESBACH: Yes.

(*A fist knocks on wood twice.*)

WINDERMERE: Us all to be happy.

GIESBACH: Yes.

(*A fist knocks on wood twice.*)

WINDERMERE: New order in world.

(*A fist knocks on wood twice.*)

Love one another.

(*A fist knocks on wood twice.*)

Stay with me?

GIESBACH: Yes.

WINDERMERE: Stay with me?

GIESBACH: Yes.

(*Behind them, the top of the crate is slowly opened.*)

WINDERMERE: Stay with me?

GIESBACH: Yes.

WINDERMERE: Build nice new nation?

GIESBACH: Yes.

(*HOLLOWAY, in a blood-spattered nightdress and with a large bullet-hole in her temple, stands up in the crate. She is sporting an expensive-looking hat.*)

WINDERMERE: Stay with me now.

GIESBACH: I...

WINDERMERE: Get these attacks.

GIESBACH: I...

WINDERMERE: Need you to stay.

GIESBACH: I will...stay.

(*HOLLOWAY now begins to laugh. She laughs like a schoolgirl and approaches WINDERMERE. She closes in on him and adopts the same position with him as when we last saw her, in the kiss. She laughs hysterically.*)

WINDERMERE: (*Very quickly as if to repel the vision, the mantra echoes around.*)

And I am the man who says to crime...no!

Yes, I am the man who says poverty...go!

Unemployment I'll keep to an absolute low!

Then I'll make our declining economy grow!

I promise you all there'll be no new taxation!

I'll invest all your wealth in our health, education!

I shall easily curb any rise in inflation!

So join with me now and let's build a new nation!

(*HOLLOWAY, still laughing, disappears from view.*
In a state of mental collapse, WINDERMERE again looks at GIESBACH, who looks back at him, uncomprehending.
A long silence. The waves crash against the shore.)

GIESBACH: Sir?

WINDERMERE: (*Recovering slightly.*) Come now, Mr G. Let us look to the future. Forget all that's past.

(*They stand, staring out front.*)

Here. Take my hand.

(*WINDERMERE holds out his hand towards GIESBACH.*)

Let us forget everything.

(*They do not move for a time and continue to stare out front. Slowly and uncertainly, GIESBACH raises his hand. He extends it towards WINDERMERE. As their hands reach towards each other, the lights fade to blackout.*
Birdsong.)

THE BIGGLESWADES

Characters

BRIAN BIGGLESWADE
an office worker

THE WIFE
a housekeeper

THE FRIEND
a widower

The Biggleswades was first produced at The White Bear Theatre, London on 6 November 2001. The full cast details were unavailable at the time of going to press.

Morning

A living-room which is entirely grey in colour. The only colourful area is a large map of the world which hangs from the back wall. A grandfather clock ticks throughout the play (at increasing speed throughout) and stands towards the rear. At the moment it is eight o'clock. Ranged along the back wall are seven large piles of newspapers, all of equal height. Bookshelves. There is a window in the left wall out of which BRIAN, who is any age over fifty, occasionally fires his shotgun. The wall is also covered in chalk marks, as in a prison. There is a large chest of drawers upstage left. Cut into the back wall map is a small hatch through which THE WIFE, who is also any age over fifty, occasionally produces food. There is a door, that has a bolt, upstage right. BRIAN's large armchair is situated centre-stage, in front of the clock. There are also various housekeeping items visible: ironing board, vacuum cleaner, washing line, clothes basket etc. Also some shelving. THE WIFE is a ceaseless worker and irons, puts clothes away, dusts, cooks etc. throughout the play. She spends a good deal of time in the kitchen and so speaks these lines through the hatch. As the play begins, BRIAN is taking aim out of the window. Eventually he fires twice. He looks through the binoculars, that always hang around his neck, to see if he has had any success. It becomes apparent he has not. He aims again and fires two more shots. Again no luck. He shakes his head, leans the gun against the wall and ambles back to his chair. He removes the morning paper and then sits. As he opens the paper, a small brown package falls to the floor. This event is enough to make man and wife regard each other anxiously. She stops ironing. He bends down and starts to open it. He wears grey nightgown, pyjamas, slippers and nightcap, THE WIFE plain grey clothes.

THE WIFE: Anything interesting, Brian?

BRIAN: I beg your pardon?

THE WIFE: Is that a letter from the outside world?

BRIAN: Of sorts, yes. It is my passport.

THE WIFE: At long last.

BRIAN: Despite the vagaries of our increasingly unreliable postal service, it has arrived. And I have to say that I am very pleased about that.

THE WIFE: Are you? (*She resumes the ironing.*)

BRIAN: Yes. I am very pleased indeed. (*A pause.*) Contented.

THE WIFE: As long as you are contented then so am I.

BRIAN: It enables a man to travel.

THE WIFE: Nearly done now.

BRIAN: To travel from country to country. And, if he deems it necessary, from continent to continent.

THE WIFE: Throughout the known world.

BRIAN: (*Rising and approaching back wall.*) There are numerous continents to be found upon the face of this earth.

THE WIFE: (*To herself.*) I admire a man that travels.

BRIAN: (*Pointing.*) Firstly there is, of course, India: a large and developing continent and one through which I intend to roam. In the fullness of time.

THE WIFE: Try as I might this crease will not be defeated.

BRIAN: (*Pointing.*) Secondly there is a far away continent known by the name of Australia...or the Sunny Antipodes. This is a happy, smiling continent in the shape of an island where the inhabitants bounce about on their heads like kangaroos.

THE WIFE: And you would like to go there?

BRIAN: Again...in the fullness of time. (*A pause.*) There are, in addition, two half-continents: Higher and Lower America. I'm sure I have already told you that most of the decisions affecting our everyday lives are made in Higher America.

THE WIFE: Not Lower America?

BRIAN: Certainly not. In Lower America people eat drugs and sit around in puddles staring at their hands.

THE WIFE: Poor things.

BRIAN: They are not fit to make decisions which affect themselves let alone their more illustrious, neighbouring continents.

THE WIFE: Two half-continents?

BRIAN: And, as you probably know, two halves must surely make a whole.

THE WIFE: They surely must.

BRIAN: (*Pointing.*) And then there is Africa. Like India, this is a developing continent (some would say more so) but it is also very hot. Its inhabitants, more importantly, have a slack economy and indulge in tribal warfare.

THE WIFE: Must be hard.

BRIAN: It will be noted that the babies unfortunate enough to be born under an African sun will die of thirst, malnutrition or a basic lack of facilities. This is a shame because Africa is a continent which looks aesthetically pleasing in the summer twilight.

THE WIFE: That's the best I can do.

BRIAN: Then comes the European continent. A vast, sprawling continent made up of many different nation states, which occasionally involve themselves in massacres and border skirmishes.

THE WIFE: (*Staring at map.*) I like all the different colours.

BRIAN: And then, finally, we have our own continent. An independent and fearless continent, it stands alone… a pillar of sanity in a hopelessly illogical world. Some say that our nation has become a spineless whore, brainlessly intoxicated by the dark-suited murderers who run Higher America. A fawning lapdog, which…

THE WIFE: I expect you are looking forward to using…?

BRIAN: If you would just allow me to finish my sentence! (*A pause.*) This accusation is of course both adolescent and over-simplistic.

THE WIFE: (*After a wait.*) I see.

BRIAN: (*Returning to seat and opening passport.*) The inscription reads: Her Britannic Majesty's Secretary of State requests and requires…excellent phrasing…in the Name of Her Majesty…let them argue with that if they dare…all those to whom it may concern to allow the bearer…in this case my good self, Brian Biggleswade… to pass freely without let or hindrance and to afford the bearer such assistance and protection as may be deemed necessary.

(*A long silence.*)

THE WIFE: And when will you be using your new passport?

BRIAN: In the fullness of time, my dear. In the fullness of time.

(*A long silence.*)

THE WIFE: And is there anything interesting in the paper?

BRIAN: (*Behind paper.*) Only the news.

THE WIFE: Only the news.

BRIAN: (*Smiling.*) And what is the *news* vis-a-vis Brian Biggleswade's morning repast?

THE WIFE: Your breakfast this morning will consist of the following: two hens' eggs, scrambled with milk, mixed herbs and butter served over two slices of lightly-toasted wholemeal bread.

BRIAN: Plenty of salt and pepper if you please.

THE WIFE: If that is what you require.

BRIAN: It is what I require. (*A pause.*) It would make me contented.

THE WIFE: As long as you're contented then so am I.

BRIAN: And I'd also like a cup of tea.

THE WIFE: If that is what you require.

BRIAN: I do. I require it.

THE WIFE: Then it shall be done.

BRIAN: Then I shall be contented.

THE WIFE: Then so shall I.

BRIAN: (*Reading.*) Assassinations in Somalia, massacres in Marrakesh, carnage in the Cameroon, purging in Petrovka, slaughter in San...Jose...de...Beun...avista...

THE WIFE: (*Shaking her head.*) I don't know.

BRIAN: And butchery in Baghdad.

THE WIFE: Why don't they do something?

BRIAN: These Muslims represent an enormous danger to world unity. Whilst we strive for peace and stability, they seem hellbent on destroying civilised values everywhere.

THE WIFE: Civilised values are a very good thing.

BRIAN: And, closer to home, our national news today...we have...homicide in Holbeach, fratricide at Felixstowe...

THE WIFE: I used to love the Big Dipper at Felixstowe.

BRIAN: ...matricide in Market Deeping, parricide in Peterborough...

THE WIFE: These goings-on are all quite local, aren't they?

BRIAN: ...and uxoricide in Uttoxeter.

THE WIFE: What's that?

BRIAN: It's when a man takes it upon himself to murder his wife.

THE WIFE: But why should he want to do that?

BRIAN: And, finally, there was a spate of suicides in Spalding and the usual flurry of infanticide in Leighton Buzzard.

THE WIFE: I blame the parents.

BRIAN: But, it seems, nothing untoward in Biggleswade.

THE WIFE: There is never anything untoward in Biggleswade.

BRIAN: In the fullness of time there may well be.

(*A long silence as THE WIFE irons and BRIAN turns pages.*)

THE WIFE: (*Nervously.*) I assume then that today is not going to be the day?

BRIAN: (*Rising and clearing his throat, he walks to the window.*) As the dawn broke through into my bedroom and the gentle sunbeams stroked me awake with their comforting fingers, I did ponder upon it. For a few moments I did feel a strange stirring, a disconcerting sensation in my blood, a ripple of excitement crackling through the calcium of my bones and I thought that this day might, perhaps, be the one.

THE WIFE: (*Excitedly.*) Really?!

BRIAN: However, since it has progressed, this particular day does not, much to my chagrin, seem to have the makings of that all-important existence-altering day for which I have been so patiently waiting. Yet I do feel it will be quite soon.

THE WIFE: Do you?

BRIAN: The day approaches. It is in the air.

THE WIFE: It has been a long time now. That you have been waiting.

BRIAN: It has been a moderate stint.

THE WIFE: Since the days when you walked naked under the sun, you have been biding your time.

BRIAN: And that most patiently.

THE WIFE: And I have stood by your side, through thick and thin, have I not? (*No answer.*) Day by day I have loved and cherished you during the long, lonely hours of your attendance?

BRIAN: You have been a loyal companion.

THE WIFE: You are confident the event is imminent?

BRIAN: Why all these questions? What on earth is becoming of you? You are asking far too many questions and challenging the existing order. That is not what I require. Not what I require at all!

THE WIFE: I'm sorry.

BRIAN: And so you will be silent and leave me to my thoughts?

THE WIFE: I will be silent.

BRIAN: Then I shall be contented.

THE WIFE: Then so shall I.

(*She has now just about finished preparing her husband's grey suit and he continues to flip disinterestedly through the paper. She motions to him that his clothes are ready and he rises, placing the paper neatly on one of the piles. The dressing ritual begins. This sequence should be akin to a knight being clad in his armour by a squire. It is very intricate and, obviously, much-practiced. He stands in the centre of the room and she helps him off with his gown; he then raises his arms and she pulls his pyjama top off and a string vest is revealed. He raises one foot and then the other and his slippers are removed followed by his pyjama bottoms. A pair of baggy grey Y-fronts are revealed. He raises one arm to receive some spray and then the other. She helps him on with his shirt, trousers, tie, jacket, socks and shoes. The following dialogue covers the action.*)

BRIAN: I think I forgot to tell you but I received a letter from the Mablethorpes last week.

THE WIFE: The Mablethorpes?!

BRIAN: Indeed.

THE WIFE: We have not heard from the Mablethorpes for a very long time.

BRIAN: Apart from the odd Yuletide communication it has been nearly two thousand days.

THE WIFE: Extraordinary.

BRIAN: He wanted to know whether or not we intended holidaying with them this summer.

THE WIFE: And do we?

BRIAN: He suggests Horncastle or Woodhall Spa whereas I would prefer a resort like Newport Pagnall, Hitchin...

THE WIFE: Hemel Hempstead?

BRIAN: We holidayed in Hemel Hempstead last year.

THE WIFE: Did we?

BRIAN: We stayed in that hotel just off the A41.

THE WIFE: So we did. By that canal.

BRIAN: The Grand Union Canal.

THE WIFE: I saw a great-crested grebe.

BRIAN: We visited Bovingdon Aerodrome.

THE WIFE: We saw some planes taking off.

BRIAN: We saw many planes landing.

THE WIFE: Landing, of course.

BRIAN: We wandered through the cemetery at Potten End and picnicked on the east bank of the river Gade as it meandered through Little Gaddesden.

THE WIFE: There was a wedding there.

BRIAN: A late fourteenth-century church.

THE WIFE: A beautiful young girl.

BRIAN: They were repairing the steeple.

THE WIFE: The bridegroom had a crew-cut. Tattoos.

BRIAN: A storm had blown off many of the slates.

THE WIFE: But the face of an angel.

BRIAN: I remember thinking they were lead slates but I wasn't entirely sure.

THE WIFE: They were smiling.

BRIAN: The scaffolding looked very precarious to me.

THE WIFE: Holding hands.

BRIAN: I spoke to the man. He wasn't used to repairing storm damage as he was a shuttering carpenter by trade.

THE WIFE: The sun was shining.

BRIAN: His brother had been a ceramic tiler.

THE WIFE: She was so beautiful.

BRIAN: But he'd been electrocuted fixing somebody's television aerial. In the rain. (*A pause.*) He had a squint. (*A pause.*)

THE WIFE: So...will we be holidaying with the Mablethorpes?

BRIAN: I prefer to holiday alone.

(*She has now nearly finished dressing her husband and is helping him on with his jacket. After a while:*)

THE WIFE: (*Nervously.*) I too received something this morning.

BRIAN: You did?

THE WIFE: Just a paragraph on a piece of red card.

BRIAN: (*Concerned.*) From whom?

THE WIFE: It was sent anonymously.

BRIAN: What did it say?

THE WIFE: (*Flatly whilst brushing down his suit.*) Oh the comfort, the inexpressible comfort of feeling safe with a person, having neither to way thoughts nor measure words, but to pour them all out, just as it is, chaff and grain together, knowing that a faithful friend will take and sift them, keeping what is worth keeping and then, with the breath of kindness, blowing the rest away. (*A pause.*)

BRIAN: I do. I prefer to holiday alone.

THE WIFE: (*As to a child.*) You are all ready now.

BRIAN: Here. (*Gives her nut.*) Now...make haste.
(*She rushes off and takes a large book and a pencil from the bookshelf. She gets ready for the dictation whilst BRIAN walks with self-importance around the room. A businessman to his secretary.*)

THE WIFE: Dream six thousand, six hundred and thirty-four. I'm ready for you.

BRIAN: (*Clearing throat.*) Last night's dream was truly auspicious. It was in the days when I walked naked under the sun, during the days of the Friend, during the days of the mountains and the lakes and the grass... (*A silence as his dream comes back to him.*) There is a large wooden table, laid out for a small banquet or festivity of sorts. A brass band is playing old favourites. There is much jollification and tomfoolery afoot and a host of partially-clad temptresses are dancing on the tables, moving their young and thin and long and supple and tanned limbs, their flat-like-marble stomachs in time to the music. Whilst their cherry-red lips are pouting at the revellers, their luscious tongues intermittently darting out of their mouths and delicately stroking the top of their teeth.

Their hips sway, their hands caress the area between their legs, moving up to the soft brown breasts, slightly covered by the long tresses of dark, creamy chestnut hair. (*He breaks off, panting slightly.*) The Friend was with me. Attired as garishly as ever. These were the days of the singing and the dancing, these were the pre-wife days when the countdown had not yet begun, these were the days...(*He breaks off.*) What was that?

THE WIFE: (*Writing.*) The...countdown...had...not...yet... begun.

BRIAN: I distinctly heard a sound.

THE WIFE: A sound?

BRIAN: Faint yet audible.

THE WIFE: I heard nothing.

BRIAN: (*Walks to the window, uses binoculars.*) This is irregular. This is highly irregular. It was a sound of despair.

THE WIFE: Can you see anything untoward?

BRIAN: I can see shapes moving in the distance. By the graveyard. Dark shapes moving about at the periphery of my vision.

THE WIFE: Could they not be just the shadows cast down from the trees?

BRIAN: We are not alone.

THE WIFE: Will you be forced to use the gun?

BRIAN: In the fullness of time.

THE WIFE: In the fullness of time.

(*She replaces the book and then dismantles the ironing board before exiting to the kitchen. BRIAN still keeps watch.*)

BRIAN: A pitiful sound. A pitiful sound of despair.

THE WIFE: (*Opening hatch.*) Pitiful. (*Closes hatch.*)

BRIAN: (*Still keeping watch.*) You do know, don't you?

THE WIFE: (*Opening hatch.*) I beg your pardon?

BRIAN: You do know...that...I love you. Don't you?

THE WIFE: Yes. (*Closes hatch.*)

BRIAN: I just thought you should know.

THE WIFE: (*Opening hatch.*) Thank you.

BRIAN: I am moderately unnerved by that sound of despair. I am moderately unnerved.

THE WIFE: Your breakfast meal will, I expect, calm your moderately unnerved disposition. (*Closes hatch.*)

BRIAN: I will not be requiring my breakfast meal this morning.

THE WIFE: (*Opening hatch, shocked.*) You will not!?

BRIAN: Instead I shall go and investigate the disturbance over by the trees at the periphery of my vision.

THE WIFE: But the eggs have already been cracked!

BRIAN: There is no time to lose.

(*He picks up his case and sports bag and makes for the door with purposeful stride. He notices his shoes and stops in his tracks.*)

Come here, please!

(*She closes the hatch and then enters through the door.*)

THE WIFE: Yes?

BRIAN: Kneel at my feet.

THE WIFE: (*Doing so.*) Yes.

BRIAN: And what do you see?

THE WIFE: Your feet.

BRIAN: Encasing my feet are…?

THE WIFE: Your shoes.

BRIAN: My unpolished shoes, to be more precise.

THE WIFE: Yes.

BRIAN: My unpolished shoes. Do you understand?

THE WIFE: Yes.

BRIAN: It seems you are becoming old. Old and forgetful.

THE WIFE: I'm sorry.

BRIAN: And… (*snaps fingers.*) quickly!

(*She rises and rushes out, quickly returning with polish and cloth which she frantically applies to her husband's shoes.*)

I will devise grave punishments for thee. In the fullness of time.

THE WIFE: Yes.

BRIAN: Make haste! Make haste!

THE WIFE: Yes.

BRIAN: There is no time to lose.

(*Blackout. The clock ticks in the darkness.*)

Evening

THE WIFE alone. She stands in the centre of the room, applying red lipstick inexpertly to her lips and pouting unseductively. The clock shows five to six. After a while BRIAN enters wearing grey sports gear. Her surprise at his entrance causes her to make a mess of her embellishments. She quickly returns to her present task: dusting the large, coloured map of the world. BRIAN puts down his case and bags and chalks off the wall.

THE WIFE: You are a good while early.

BRIAN: I beg your pardon?

THE WIFE: It has not yet struck six.

BRIAN: I stopped off at the Fortification Store. It is absolutely essential...(*Cocks an ear and listens with concentration. He picks up his gun and walks to the window. He scours the landscape. Eventually he aims and then fires twice. Looks again. Shakes his head.*)

THE WIFE: Did you miss again?

BRIAN: At least it frightens them off. If only temporarily.

THE WIFE: How was your day?

BRIAN: (*Waking to the bag.*) I have here some necessities. (*Producing items.*) Some wood...some nails...a hammer... a roll of barbed wire. And for you...

THE WIFE: Hens' eggs. Thank you. (*Takes them and exits to the kitchen. Off.*) And how many times did you lollop around the red, shale racetrack tonight?

BRIAN: I beg your pardon?

THE WIFE: You lolloped around the red, shale racetrack how many times?

BRIAN: In the area of twelve.

THE WIFE: And did you enjoy yourself?

BRIAN: I tired after the eighth lap.

THE WIFE: Shame.

BRIAN: Many others, it has to be said, tired a lot sooner.

THE WIFE: And how would you like your eggs this evening?

BRIAN: (*To himself.*) I intend to construct a fence, a large perimeter fence, over by the trees, the trees at the periphery of my vision. In the hopes that a repeat of this morning's disturbing occurrence will not be...repeated. (*He kneels and examines his purchases.*) This will probably not suffice.

THE WIFE: Have you no preference?

BRIAN: Griddled.

THE WIFE: Griddled eggs?

BRIAN: With a touch of basil.

THE WIFE: Rosemary, surely.

BRIAN: With basil! With basil!

THE WIFE: If that is what you require.

BRIAN: That is what I require.

THE WIFE: Then that is what I shall do.

BRIAN: Then I shall be contented.

THE WIFE: Then so shall I.

(*BRIAN raises his arms and awaits his wife's assistance.*)
(*Rushing in.*) Forgive me.
(*She peels off his sweaty shirt and applies talcum powder to his chest and under his arms. She kneels to remove shorts, shoes and socks. Clothes go in the basket. She helps him dress into grey gown and pyjamas. The following covers the change.*)

BRIAN: Due to the fact that my passport has arrived I have been planning my Great Adventure.

THE WIFE: Oh yes?

BRIAN: (*Rapidly.*) My outward journey will be to walk down the B1040 towards Sutton, past the golf course and then up towards Gamlingay. I shall be breakfasting in the village of Waresley before proceeding via Great Gransden and Little Gransden down the B1046 to Longstow. I shall then be inspecting the traffic on the A14 as it roars northward towards Godmanchester and due south towards Royston. Then I shall be visiting either Wimpole Hall or the windmill at Caxton. That, of course, depends on weather conditions. Whatever the outcome, I shall venture in a northeasterly direction onward through Kingston, Toft and Barton (where I will take refreshments.) before I join the M11 at junction 12 by the village of Comberton. I shall inspect the traffic here, junction 12 providing an excellent vantage point,

before I cross over and march into Cambridge. I shall
fish in the River Cam for tench and trout and, naturally
enough, I will visit the aerodrome situated a stone's
throw from Cherry Hinton.

(*A pause.*)

THE WIFE: And will you swim in the oceans under
tropical skies?

BRIAN: Possibly.

THE WIFE: And will you dine with princes and princesses
in palaces of vast majesty whose towers reach to the
stars?

BRIAN: I would certainly imagine so.

THE WIFE: And make love to dusky maidens in the
untouched sand, as the invigorating surf caresses your
passionate, naked bodies?

BRIAN: All in the fullness of time. (*A pause.*) When the day
makes itself apparent.

THE WIFE: And that day is just around the corner?

BRIAN: It is definitely in the air.

(*A silence.*)

Can I help you at all?

THE WIFE: I'm waiting for my reward.

BRIAN: There will be no nut on this occasion.

THE WIFE: No nut!?

BRIAN: Now…you continue with your duties whilst I
wonder aimlessly about the room.

(*She clears up and then takes basket away and goes through
to the kitchen. He wonders about, picks up objects, studies
map, looks for dust on shelves, stares out of window, polishes
gun. He then returns, picks up his DIY equipment and makes
for the door. He soon realises he is not suitably dressed.*)

BRIAN: What function are you fulfilling at present?

THE WIFE: (*Opening hatch.*) I am preparing, for your
contentment, griddled eggs with a touch of basil.

BRIAN: It appears that a minor oversight has arisen.

THE WIFE: Really?

BRIAN: You think I am suitably attired for outdoor
carpentry?

THE WIFE: Are you not?

BRIAN: You have been reckless in your work.

THE WIFE: Must the fence go up tonight?

(*A pause.*)

BRIAN: You obviously do not appreciate the danger we are presently facing. We are not alone. We must be protected.

THE WIFE: I shall change you immediately.

BRIAN: Then I shall be contented.

THE WIFE: Then so shall I.

(*She enters with jeans, sweater, duffel coat etc. He raises arms and another precision dressing routine ensues. The following covers this action.*)

BRIAN: My homeward journey takes me through uncharted territory: westward out of Cambridge, through the villages of Coton and Hardwick and Caldecote Highfield by the A45 as the traffic thunders its barbarous way towards St Neots. If I did not inspect the windmill at Caxton on the outward leg, I shall pay it a visit at this juncture. Otherwise I shall hike intrepidly onward to Papworth Everard where I plan to rest for the night. At sunrise I will be found worshipping in the tiny church of Papworth St Agnes (the end of my pilgrimage, so to speak), before rejoining the B1040 back through Eltisely, Waresley and Gamlingay and eventually reaching home on the seventh or eighth day.

THE WIFE: Don't forget your compass.

BRIAN: The true explorer is guided by the stars, the great guiding stars of the twinkling firmament.

THE WIFE: Like Marco Polo.

BRIAN: Christopher Columbus.

THE WIFE: Captain Scott.

BRIAN: Marco Polo, Captain Scott…

THE WIFE: And Christopher Columbus.

BRIAN: It was the spirit of adventure that forged our worthy empire. It was the spirit of adventure which first inspired our brave and honourable sailors to put out to sea, circumnavigating the globe all those centuries ago. It was the spirit of adventure…

(*Screams of despair. Distant. They stop. A silence.*)

There. Again. That sound. At the periphery of my hearing.

THE WIFE: I heard nothing. (*She has now finished dressing him.*) I await my reward. (*No reward.*) Am I to have no nut again?

BRIAN: Silence! Silence as I strain my ears! (*He does so.*)

THE WIFE: There is a slight tear in the instep of your left boot.

BRIAN: (*Walking to window, binoculars poised.*) This is highly irregular.

THE WIFE: Can you see anything untoward?

BRIAN: Shapes. By the graveyard. Moving in the distance. Dark shapes moving about at the periphery of my vision.

THE WIFE: Could they not be the shadows cast down from the trees?

BRIAN: Highly irregular.

THE WIFE: Will you be forced to fire your gun wildly into the darkness?

BRIAN: In the fullness of time. (*A pause.*) It was a scream of despair. Distant but clear.

THE WIFE: (*Exiting.*) I shall return to the hens' eggs.

BRIAN: And you must wipe these dust-encrusted lenses!

THE WIFE: (*Off.*) I shall give them a wipe.

BRIAN: You do know, don't you?

THE WIFE: (*Opening hatch.*) I beg your pardon?

BRIAN: You do know...that I love you.

THE WIFE: Yes. (*Closing hatch.*)

BRIAN: I just thought you should know.

THE WIFE: (*Opening hatch.*) Thank you. (*Closing hatch.*)

BRIAN: For I am fractionally intimidated by that sound of despair.

THE WIFE: (*Off.*) Your evening refection will, I hope, soothe your fractionally-intimidated temperament.

BRIAN: Griddled eggs! With a touch of basil!

THE WIFE: (*Off.*) A good brace of hens' eggs!

BRIAN: And when I inspected this morning's disturbance, over by the trees at the periphery of my vision, I found only...trees.

THE WIFE: (*Opening hatch.*) I beg your pardon?

BRIAN: I found only the trees and the graves and the grass, in need of a trim, and the hedgerows lined up like soldiers, lined up as far as the eye can see, way over the meadow, the hedgerows, like soldiers in a line, in the gentle breeze and the summer sun, about to do battle, about to wage war…

THE WIFE: I'm sure it's just the shadows cast down from the trees.

BRIAN: Like the little tin soldiers I had as a boy. (*A pause.*) But now the night is upon us.

THE WIFE: You think it is safe to venture out tonight?

BRIAN: The barricade must be constructed. We must not delay. (*Notices boots.*) Come here!

THE WIFE: (*Closes hatch and enters.*) Yes.

BRIAN: Kneel at my feet!

THE WIFE: (*Doing so.*) Yes.

BRIAN: What do you see?

THE WIFE: Your boots.

BRIAN: Note the tear.

THE WIFE: It is noted.

BRIAN: (*As to a child.*) You have noted it, have you?

THE WIFE: I have.

BRIAN: (*Snapping fingers.*) Exchange and repair!

(*She pulls at the damaged right boot and eventually removes it. She then rushes into the kitchen and returns with another boot, which is in fact a left boot, and helps her husband on with it.*)

BRIAN: Make haste! Make haste! There is no time to lose.

(*Blackout. The clock ticks ever faster in the darkness.*)

Morning

THE WIFE alone. Grey clothes are pegged onto the washing line which now spans the stage. She has laid a small camping table with crockery and cutlery. She wears far too much red lipstick, rouge and also a red scarf. It is eight o'clock. As ever, the morning paper lies on the central chair. She sits by the table repairing the boot. Soon BRIAN enters wearing his pyjamas, gown etc. THE WIFE is slightly less animated.

THE WIFE: Good morning. (*No answer.*) Did you sleep well?

BRIAN: I did not.

THE WIFE: No?

BRIAN: I could not rid myself of a specific thought. One single thought had me tossing and turning the whole night through.

THE WIFE: And what was that?

BRIAN: Simply this: there are many people upon this earth whom I will never meet. Not in my entire life will I meet them.

THE WIFE: I would have thought that was a good thing.

BRIAN: And there are many women I will never hold in my arms.

(*A pause.*)

THE WIFE: Your breakfast is bubbling away on the rusty stove.

BRIAN: These are sobering thoughts to carry with one for a whole day.

THE WIFE: Hens' eggs. Two of them. Poached.

BRIAN: I must inspect the newly-erected perimeter fencing at the periphery of my vision. (*He does so.*) Served over lightly toasted wholemeal bread?

(*A pause.*)

THE WIFE: No.

BRIAN: No?

THE WIFE: They are to be served over lightly-toasted crumpets this morning. (*A pause.*) Would that make you contented?

(*A pause.*)

BRIAN: (*Seriously, thoughtfully.*) Crumpets? Crumpets? (*A long pause.*) Yes. Yes it would.

THE WIFE: As long as you are contented, Brian, then so am I.

BRIAN: (*To himself.*) Crum-pets. Crum-pets.

THE WIFE: And your boot is almost repaired.

BRIAN: Last night you sent me out into the night with two left boots on my feet. And not, as is customary, one left boot and one right boot.

THE WIFE: Did I?

BRIAN: You are becoming old. Old and forgetful.

THE WIFE: Yes.

BRIAN: And not a little incompetent.

THE WIFE: Yes.

BRIAN: And sloppy.

THE WIFE: Yes.

BRIAN: And forgetful.

THE WIFE: Yes.

BRIAN: And old.

THE WIFE: Yes.

BRIAN: And fat.

THE WIFE: Yes.

BRIAN: And forgetful.

THE WIFE: Yes.

(*A pause.*)

BRIAN: And...fat.

THE WIFE: (*Upset.*) Yes.

BRIAN: (*Binoculars aimed out of window.*) There are shapes. Dark shapes. By the graves. There seem to be tracks. Yes. Footprints...or pawprints. Just inside the barbed wire fence. Alarming. (*No response.*) I said that it is alarming. And, over to the right, over by the weeping willow and the loganberry bushes, I can see treadmarks. They look like treadmarks. (*No response.*) Am I alone? Am I all alone? (*No response.*) Answer me!!! Am I alone?

THE WIFE: (*Exiting.*) No.

BRIAN: And beyond the loganberry bushes, over the rolling green meadow, past the cornfield and the lake where the kingfisher lives, I can see smoke billowing out of the chimney of the neighbour's house. They are possibly burning coal. I would have thought that this morning's temperature is hardly low enough to justify the burning of coal. (*No response.*) I said it is scarcely justifiable. (*No response.*) Am I alone? (*No response.*) Am I all alone!?

(*He sees he is alone and, as is customary, he begins to panic.*) You have left me! You have left me alone! You have abandoned me!

THE WIFE: (*Rushing in.*) What is it?

BRIAN: (*Sitting, upset.*) You left me! You left me!

THE WIFE: (*Holding him.*) It's alright. I'm here now.

BRIAN: Hold me tightly!

THE WIFE: It's all going to be alright. Nothing to worry about. There. Come on now. Put your gun down.

BRIAN: Am I all alone then? Am I all alone?

THE WIFE: You are not alone. I am with you.

BRIAN: You are here, aren't you? You are here with me?

THE WIFE: (*Rocking him.*) I am here.

BRIAN: (*Recovering slightly.*) You do know, don't you?

THE WIFE: I know that you love me.

BRIAN: You know that I love you?

THE WIFE: I know.

BRIAN: I just thought you should know.

THE WIFE: Would you like me to read to you?

BRIAN: Yes. Whilst I am feeding.

THE WIFE: Would you like me to read you a dream?

BRIAN: Yes. A dream from the past might soothe my nerves.

THE WIFE: Let go then. And I shall fetch your breakfast.

BRIAN: (*Releasing grasp.*) It may remind me of my direction. Illuminate the path which I must tread.

(*THE WIFE is on the point of exiting.*)

Here!

THE WIFE: (*Turning.*) Yes?

BRIAN: (*Holding out a nut.*) I have something for you.

THE WIFE: (*Taking the nut erotically in her mouth.*) A delicious nut!

BRIAN: (*Appalled.*) What *do* you think you are doing?

THE WIFE: I am accepting my reward.

BRIAN: I will devise grave punishments for thee.

THE WIFE: (*Exiting.*) I will return to my duties.

BRIAN: Whilst I pace nervously around the table. (*He does so.*)

THE WIFE: (*Off.*) Be seated. The poached hens' eggs are ready.

(*He sits and takes napkin from the table and tucks it into his pyjama top. He rubs his hands in expectation. She enters and places plate in front of him along with a mug which says 'Brian' on it. She then fetches the large book.*)

BRIAN: (*Nervously.*) Where are you going?

THE WIFE: To fetch the Dream Log.

BRIAN: Hurry. (*He begins to eat noisily, cutting his food into insanely small pieces.*)

BRIAN: The dream. (*Snaps fingers.*) Proceed.

THE WIFE: (*Flicking through.*) Dream...one thousand nine hundred and sixty-eight?

BRIAN: Sufficient. A calming dream, that one. (*Snaps fingers.*) Proceed.

THE WIFE: (*Flatly.*) It is an early evening in summer and there has been a heavy fall of rain, causing a sweet-smelling mist to shroud the landscape with a dense white cloak. The damp clings to my face, flecking my skin with wet...

BRIAN: (*Mouth full.*) No...no...no! I need more inflection. I need more feeling. You read it as if it meant nothing to you. There is so much colour in the language, so much depth and tone. I want to hear the beauty of the words. I want to hear the music. But you, you are so flat. There is no joy, no rhythm. No passion, woman. I want passion. I want you to sing the words to me. It is a celebration! Let me hear you sing! Sing! Sing! Sing! Do you understand? (*No response.*) Do you?

THE WIFE: Yes.

BRIAN: Then...(*Snaps fingers.*) Proceed.

THE WIFE: ...flecking my skin with a wet...

BRIAN: And, incidentally, these eggs are inadequate.

THE WIFE: They are?

BRIAN: The whites are unpoached and the yolks are tasteless.

THE WIFE: I'm sorry.

BRIAN: They taste as if you laid them yourself.

THE WIFE: They are hens' eggs.

BRIAN: *Are* you a barnyard hen?

THE WIFE: I'm not.

BRIAN: Let me hear you cluck if you are.

THE WIFE: I'm not a hen.

BRIAN: Come on. Cluck! Cluck!

THE WIFE: I am too tired.

BRIAN: Let me hear you cluck like a hen!

THE WIFE: I cannot cluck.

BRIAN: And these crumpets are burnt.

THE WIFE: Lightly-toasted.

BRIAN: There is ample salt yet not enough pepper.

THE WIFE: The pepper mill...

BRIAN: The tea is cold.

THE WIFE: It cannot be cold.

BRIAN: (*Pushing plate away.*) There is not sufficient seasoning.

THE WIFE: A little tarragon...

BRIAN: Fat and forgetful. Fat and forgetful. This is yet another example...

(*Screams of despair. Closer. They stop. A silence. BRIAN stands and cocks an ear. He is rattled.*)

Ssssh!

(*A long, tense silence.*)

Did you hear that?

THE WIFE: (*Tearful.*) I heard nothing.

BRIAN: You are telling untruths! That sound. Closer. Louder. That sound. It was a sound of despair. Highly irregular. (*Peeps nervously out of window.*) Why won't they leave me in peace?

THE WIFE: Will you be forced to use your gun again?

BRIAN: That sound of despair has left me...

THE WIFE: If you finished your breakfast...

BRIAN: Do not interrupt!

(*A silence. She takes plates into kitchen.*)

I must set traps. Yes, I will forgo your unpalatable hens' eggs and use the allotted time to inspect yet again the trees at the periphery of my vision. (*Notices her absence.*) Hello! Hello! Hello! (*No answer.*) Hello! Hello!

THE WIFE: (*Opening hatch.*) Yes?

BRIAN: Come here! (*A pause.*) Please. (*A pause.*) Please come here.

THE WIFE: (*Closing hatch then entering.*) What is it?

BRIAN: You do know, don't you? That I love you. (*No answer.*) I just thought you should know.

THE WIFE: (*Tired.*) Yes. Thank you.

BRIAN: (*Holding out nut.*) Here.

THE WIFE: (*Not moving.*) I am sated with nuts.

BRIAN: Take the nut.

THE WIFE: I don't want the nut.

BRIAN: Take the nut.

THE WIFE: I don't want the nut.

BRIAN: Take the nut!

THE WIFE: I don't want the nut.

BRIAN: Take it!!

(*A pause.*)

THE WIFE: (*Nervously.*) No.

BRIAN: Then I shall eat it myself.

(*He eats the nut and returns to his scrutiny of the outside world.*)

THE WIFE: I am going to continue with my duties whilst you stare out of the window at the distant shapes.

(*She resumes her cleaning.*)

BRIAN: I must set traps. (*A pause.*) There. I see you.

(*He takes aim and fires twice.*)

THE WIFE: What is it?

BRIAN: I saw a figure. In the distance.

THE WIFE: I'm sure it is only the shadows cast down from the trees.

BRIAN: There will be no surrender.

THE WIFE: Are you ready?

BRIAN: I am.

(*He raises his arms in the centre of the stage and the same dressing sequence as before takes place. She is noticeably less proficient.*)

THE WIFE: (*Nervously.*) I received a letter this morning.

BRIAN: You did?

THE WIFE: Just a paragraph on a piece of red card.

BRIAN: (*Concerned.*) From whom?

THE WIFE: It was sent anonymously.

BRIAN: What did it say?

THE WIFE: (*Flatly.*) Oh the comfort, the inexpressible comfort of feeling safe with a person, having neither to weigh thoughts nor measure words…

(*Blackout. The clock ticks ever faster in the darkness.*)

Evening

THE WIFE alone. She is taking off the grey apron and replacing it with a red one. The clock shows five to six. She sees a newspaper on the chair and cautiously goes to pick it up. She flicks through it. Its contents repulse her. Each turn of the page provokes a larger reaction. By the end she is almost retching. She then places the paper on one of the piles. BRIAN enters, wearing grey sports clothes and carrying his bag and case. He chalks up the wall. His agitation has increased and he immediately scours the landscape with his binoculars.

THE WIFE: You are early.

BRIAN: It is not just me. Fear has spread.

THE WIFE: Like a virus.

BRIAN: I have been buying more fortifications. There was a long queue. I overheard conversations. Somebody else had seen a movement by the graveyard.

THE WIFE: And how many circuits of the…?

BRIAN: There was also an earthquake.

THE WIFE: An earthquake?

BRIAN: Fallen masonry litters the pavements and the zebra crossing will need a touch of paint.

THE WIFE: I did feel a tremor.

BRIAN: The epicentre was just outside Downham Market.

THE WIFE: And what have you brought home to me tonight?

BRIAN: What do you think you're doing?

THE WIFE: (*Producing box of eggs.*) Hens' eggs!!

BRIAN: Do not tamper with my acquisitions. Leave well alone, woman. Leave well alone.

THE WIFE: I apologise.

BRIAN: Return those hens' eggs to me!

THE WIFE: (*Doing so.*) And what is that menacing contraption there?

BRIAN: (*Producing a man-trap.*) This is a device which will, I am told, prove a further deterrent to the trespassers.

THE WIFE: I wonder, Brian, if…

BRIAN: Unfortunately it is dysfunctional.

THE WIFE: It seems to me that...

BRIAN: I have scattered a dozen of them throughout the garden, inside the barbed wire perimeter fencing which surrounds the house, just by the trees, the trees at the periphery of my vision.

THE WIFE: It seems to me that...

BRIAN: Normally when one opens the trap like so (*opens it*) these teeth are set by this catch here. And there it lies, by the fishpond, by the large terracotta urn, by the stepping-stone pathway, wherever one chooses, it awaits its prey.

THE WIFE: Just like a tawny owl or a small tabby cat stalking a mouse.

(*A pause.*)

BRIAN: (*Annoyed.*) But, should the foot of some unsuspecting terrorist happen to depress this plate here. Like this...

(*The trap shuts fast. A long silence.*)

THE WIFE: It doesn't appear to be dysfunctional at all.

BRIAN: I was told this one had a faulty mechanism.
    I bought it for half the standard price.

THE WIFE: Then it seems you have a bargain.

BRIAN: (*A slight smile.*) A bargain? Yes, it does, doesn't it?
    (*A pause.*) Now...you may proceed with your duties whilst I scrutinise today's paper. (*A pause.*) Can I help you?

THE WIFE: I am waiting for you to raise your arms.

BRIAN: There is no need to change me yet.

THE WIFE: No?

BRIAN: I intend to sit, festering in my own sweat for a while.

THE WIFE: Then I shall cook your evening meal.

BRIAN: Where is my paper?

THE WIFE: The paper?

BRIAN: Today's paper, yes. I am totally ignorant of yesterday's events. I can't possibly tackle my supper in such a state. (*No answer.*) I am waiting.

THE WIFE: I must have moved it.

BRIAN: You moved it?

THE WIFE: And placed it on the pile.

BRIAN: You placed it on the pile?

THE WIFE: I am sorry.

BRIAN: In the fullness of time I will devise grave punishments for thee.

(*A silence.*)

THE WIFE: I assume there will be no nut for me on this occasion?

BRIAN: Your assumption is well-founded.

THE WIFE: Well-founded.

BRIAN: Upon which of these piles did you place the paper?

THE WIFE: I cannot remember.

BRIAN: You cannot remember?

THE WIFE: I cannot.

BRIAN: (*Selects paper and reads headline.*) Was it upon this pile? 'Chatteris Traffic Warden Dismissed'?

THE WIFE: I do not know.

BRIAN: Or this one: 'Smokers Ejected From Melton Mowbray Patisserie'?

THE WIFE: I don't know.

BRIAN: Or this one: 'Dinner Lady Sparks Canteen Riot'?

THE WIFE: I cannot remember.

BRIAN: (*Throwing papers in the air.*) Or this one? Or this one? Or this one? Or this?

(*Screams of despair. Closer. They stop. A silence.*)

Now that. That you must have heard.

THE WIFE: I heard nothing.

BRIAN: What do you mean, you heard nothing? What do you mean? It was as clear as crystal. Vivid. There were screams. There were pitiful screams. You cannot be deaf to those screams. You cannot, you must not, be deaf to those screams. (*Looks out of window.*) Screams. I cannot see... Nothing untoward. Smoke. Graves. Dark. So dark. There is rain.

(*THE WIFE has left the room.*)

I must check the traps...I must... There are shapes...I can make out...There is wind and rain...We are not alone... We must be protected. (*Aims gun blindly.*) There will be a high price to pay for this. (*Shoots twice.*) Why can you not leave me in peace!? Why must you be out of your houses at this time!? (*Turns.*) Am I all alone? (*No *answer.*) Hello! Hello! Am I alone then? Am I all alone? (*No answer. He is almost weeping.*) Hello! Hello! Where are you? Why have you abandoned me like this? Where are you? Where are you?

THE WIFE: (*Opening hatch.*) I am here.

(*A pause.*)

BRIAN: You…you do know, don't you?…That I love you. (*No answer.*) Because I do. I love you very much. (*No answer, smiling nervously.*) That sound…those screams… they have unnerved me rather. (*No answer.*) I think you'd better undress me now. Little one. (*Raises his arms.*) I think so. (*She does not move.*) Did you hear what I said? (*No answer.*) I said I think you'd better undress me. (*No answer.*) I thought you should know. That I love you. Very much. (*She closes hatch.*) And I have decided…one night of being oblivious to the goings-on of the outside world will not harm. (*She enters at doorway.*) Ah…you have some red lipstick on. It is most…becoming. (*He raises arms again.*) I am ready for you. (*She does not move.*) I'll start. Here. (*He pulls his jacket over his head and there it rests.*) I am in difficulty. (*He struggles pathetically.*)

THE WIFE: I am feverish.

BRIAN: (*Muffled.*) Help me.

THE WIFE: I am sick at heart.

(*Blackout. The clock ticks ever faster in the darkness.*)

Morning

THE WIFE alone. Some time has elapsed. The room is far messier, denoting the woman's declining state of health. There are clothes and newspapers everywhere. She sits alone and stares impassively ahead. Her lipstick has faded and she seems paler. BRIAN enters, even more disturbed than before, wearing his night attire. The clock shows eight o'clock.

BRIAN: My passport is missing a number of its pages. There were a good twenty on its arrival and now I can count only five. My horizons are being limited. What

have you done with them? (*No answer.*) This restricts my
movements. You are deliberately imprisoning me,
woman. Your cloying femininity is a weapon with which
you suffocate me. You dampen my adventurous spirit.
I am wise to your deviousness. You are scared of being
on your own. But I want the missing pages returned by
this evening. Do you hear? (*No answer.*) All my life I
have been waiting for the knock of opportunity. For the
time to be right. I have been looking to the future with
expectation. Waiting my turn. My silent patience would
be a lesson to the saints. And now...now that the time is
at hand...you, with your underhandedness, are hellbent
on preventing my hour of glory.

THE WIFE: (*Weary.*) Oh.

BRIAN: Time is passing. We may only get the one chance.
I need you to ready yourself.

THE WIFE: (*Who has not been listening.*) To have seen the
face of a child, my own child, to have seen the bright,
clear eyes, the delicate hair and the smile. The beaming
smile on the face of a child.

BRIAN: You are barren.

THE WIFE: To have felt the skin, the soft skin and feel the
stare from her glowing eyes and to have held her with
love, unspoilt, to have cradled her tiny head in my arms,
with all the love inside me. All the love in the world. For
the child.

BRIAN: Your sterility is a blessing from the gods.

THE WIFE: I would have loved her so. I would have loved
her so much that...

(*BRIAN checks his watch, his favourite toy, and makes a note.*)

BRIAN: Day ten thousand. These are milestones, woman.
Points of hope.

THE WIFE: I would have sung to her.

BRIAN: How we have progressed over these thousands of
days.

THE WIFE: Lullabies.

BRIAN: (*Scrutinising watch.*) I see the seconds go ticking by.

THE WIFE: I would sing her to sleep.

BRIAN: Tick Tick Tick.

THE WIFE: Every night.

BRIAN: Tick Tick Tick.

THE WIFE: And forever.

(*BRIAN notices the mess and begins to rummage about. He looks at dates and tries to rearrange papers onto correct piles.*)

BRIAN: This is a disgrace.

THE WIFE: Rockaby baby on the tree top,
When the wind blows the cradle will rock,
When the wind blows the cradle will fall...

BRIAN: So many Thursdays. So many Mondays.

THE WIFE: And down will come baby and cradle and all...

BRIAN: You must keep things in order. Without discipline then chaos ensues. And when chaos ensues anarchy reigns. And when... Just look at this crockery. It is a disgrace. And what about my clothing? What about my breakfast? (*No answer.*) I am becoming tired of your games now. One must have the maturity to know when one has taken a joke too far.

(*He notices that his work clothes are lying in a heap on the floor.*)

This is an outrage! A total outrage! Look at this! My shirt! My jacket! My trousers! You are slovenly! Yes. You. You are lazy. Yes. You are ugly, you are. And fat! Stupid! Fat! Slovenly! Slut! (*She does not react.*) Confess! Confess! (*No answer.*) You cannot spend the rest of your days staring into space. There is work to be done. We all have our contributions to make. You must fulfil your half of the marriage-bargain just as I fulfil mine. I have erected the fence, set the traps, dug the moat and am even now discussing plans for the drawbridge. This is time-consuming work, woman. And time is precious. Yes, it is a gift from the gods. And I give up my time to earn the bread. I give up my time to plant the booby-traps and position the tripwires. You are not aware of the gravity of the situation. We are on the brink of all-out war.

THE WIFE: We are on the brink.

BRIAN: And at times like this, a man and his wife must pull together. We must shoulder the burden together.

This is no time to shirk one's responsibilities. It is time to roll up one's sleeves and to muck in with the rest of the community.

THE WIFE: We are on the brink. It is time to muck in.

BRIAN: And for the work to come I must remain fit and healthy. So the doctor telling me that I have lost too much weight, my blood pressure is up and my complexion is suffering is no great cause for comfort. I am not, apparently, receiving the correct vitamins and am in danger of overdosing on albumen. I am becoming diabetic, anaemic, leukaemic, rheumatic, paralytic, syphilitic, bronchitic, allergic, asthmatic, pyretic, dysenteric and bilious. Think carefully. If I were to develop pneumonia, diptheria, septicaemia, dyspepsia… if I were to become mortally deficient in some way and find my soul carried off into the great void beyond… where on earth would that leave you?…Hmm? Have you thought about that?… Where would that leave you? (*No answer.*) You must think. (*No answer.*) Now…onto matters more everyday… I trust you have a second suit for me to wear to work? (*No answer.*) I cannot wear these articles quite obviously. I could not appear at my place of work looking like something the cat has been dragging through the hedgerow. So… (*He raises his arms.*) I am waiting.

THE WIFE: I am tired.

BRIAN: *You* are tired!? *You* are tired?!?

THE WIFE: I am too tired to dress you this morning.

BRIAN: *You* are tired!? *You* are tired!?

THE WIFE: There is no second set of clothes and I have not started your breakfast.

(*Silence.*)

BRIAN: You have not?

THE WIFE: No.

BRIAN: That is unacceptable. (*Almost tearful.*) I do not understand. I want my hens' eggs. I need my hens' eggs. It was to be hens' eggs boiled in water. With soldiers. With little eggy soldiers.

THE WIFE: I am so tired.

BRIAN: *You* are tired!? What about me? Have you any idea…

THE WIFE: You will have to try…

BRIAN: Do not interrupt!

THE WIFE: You will have…

BRIAN: Do not interrupt me!!! (*A pause.*) Help…me.
(*She does not move.*)
I will have to face the humiliation of working in soiled garments today. On this occasion I will forgive you.
(*She does not move.*)
Move!!
(*She slowly rises and approaches him. He dumps his clothes into her arms.*)
And…(*Snaps fingers.*) proceed.
(*The usual sequence takes place though now she is not so polished. She stumbles occasionally and her work is sluggish. Mistakes are made which BRIAN suffers with all the self-control at his disposal. The following covers the change.*)

BRIAN: The day draws closer with every breath. And last night's dream was a sign. The Friend appeared again, with tears in his green eyes. There were tears. (*A pause.*) There was also a girl, incidentally. A young girl. In the dream. She was young and she was exceptionally beautiful. Smooth skin, do you hear? Long, long legs. Her belly was flat, flat like the surface of a lake on a windless afternoon. She came to me, do you hear? Do you hear?

THE WIFE: I hear.

BRIAN: She came to me. Her eyes burned into mine, her cherry-red lips curled into a licentious smile and I knew. I knew that she wanted me. Her hair was chestnut brown. Oh yes. It cascaded down onto her slim shoulders and she moved closer to me, do you hear? She moved so close to me, I could taste her honeyed breath in my nostrils. Oh yes. Let me assure you she was panting with expectation. Hmm? Do you know what that's like? Hmm? Her hands encircled my waist, do you hear? Her young, fine hands. Yes? Delicate fingers, do you hear?

She stroked my back, she stroked the back of my thighs, unbuckling my belt, murmuring words of desire, gently nibbling at my ear. And then I unbuttoned her snowy-white shirt, revealing her soft, brown breasts, I pulled it off her and she smiled. She smiled at me knowingly, pouting she was. Do you hear? Pouting. And her slim brown body was brushing against my chest, woman. Do you hear?

(*Silence as BRIAN loses himself in memory.*)

And there we were, oh yes, both as naked as the day we were born. I holding her quivering young body in my arms...she moaning in a frenzy of lust. And then...do you know what she did? Do you? Do you know what she did then? She slid her angelic face down my body and she took my organ in her mouth.

(*THE WIFE should be kneeling to fix trousers at this point.*)

Did you hear what she did? She took my organ in her mouth! Can you imagine that, woman? And then...then I laid her down in the grass, a baking hot afternoon, naked under the sun, and I copulated with this girl, this young slim and beautiful girl, for what seemed like an eternity.

(*BRIAN's chest is heaving with the pleasure of his dream. His eyes closed.*)

THE WIFE: And then you woke up, Brian?

BRIAN: (*Sad.*) Then I woke up.

THE WIFE: To find me.

BRIAN: I found you.

(*Furious that his wife should shatter his illusions, he looks for an outlet for his rage.*)

And, incidentally, your appearance is becoming a cause for concern. A woman should take pride in the way she presents herself to the wider world. Your face is lurid, your eyes are bloodshot and your skin is drawn so tightly over your skull that you resemble a Gorgon.

(*A pause.*) I *was* intending to take you out tonight...

THE WIFE: You were?

BRIAN: We were to sit at a table by the window, in silence, staring at our drinks the whole night through.

THE WIFE: And now...?

BRIAN: As your standards are so evidently slipping...

THE WIFE: I would dearly love a visit to the...

BRIAN: It is too late.

THE WIFE: My heart is so heavy.

BRIAN: Instead I shall keep watch tonight.

THE WIFE: I crave so much the sound of a human crowd.

BRIAN: It is in the air.

THE WIFE: I would love to walk through the town.

BRIAN: My patience is finally to be rewarded.

THE WIFE: We could sit in the square and watch life
flowing past us. And perhaps we could...

BRIAN: Am I ready now?

THE WIFE: ...drink a little.

BRIAN: I said...

THE WIFE: You are ready.

BRIAN: A wholly incompetent performance.

THE WIFE: Drink a little...

BRIAN: I stumbled on at least four occasions. The first...
(*Screams of despair. Closer. They stop. A silence. After a while,
BRIAN slowly walks to the window. Again he surveys the
landscape with his binoculars and grips his gun. He is more
upset than before.*)
This time, then! This time! You cannot say you were deaf
to those screams. (*No answer.*) Pitiful! They were pitiful.
Tell me you heard them! (*No answer.*) Unacceptable! I am
far from being contented. Yet I cannot see anything but
the dark shapes moving about at the periphery of my
vision...

THE WIFE: (*Tired.*) They are most likely...

BRIAN: Do not! Do not say they are just the shadows cast
down from the trees! Don't you dare say that! You can
say anything but that! How can they be shadows? How
can they be? Idiot! Hmm? You are an ugly fat idiot, are
you not? You must not say that! You cannot say that!
(*A pause.*) I must now fire shots blindly into the
wilderness. (*He does so. Then a long silence.*) I love you so
much. You know? You are my world. My life. (*No answer.*)
I thought you might like to know. (*No answer.*) Hmm?

You understand? (*No answer.*) Answer me when I'm
talking to you!!! (*Silence.*) You know, don't you?

THE WIFE: Yes.

BRIAN: That I love you?

THE WIFE: Yes.

BRIAN: You know it?

THE WIFE: Yes.

BRIAN: You are aware?

THE WIFE: Yes.

  (*Silence.*)

BRIAN: And...?! And...?! And....?!

THE WIFE: (*Quiet, head down.*) I love you too.

(*Blackout. The clock ticks ever faster in the darkness.*)

Evening

*THE WIFE alone, seated. She is now totally exhausted. Her breathing
is heavy and she can hardly keep her eyes open. All her movements
are vague, heavy and painful. She stares forward and her head
occasionally falls onto her chest. A bottle of spirits stands on the table
and she pours herself a glass. She is already quite drunk. The clock
shows midnight.*

THE WIFE: The whole of Biggleswade is gripped by fear.
From Biggleswade to...Basingstoke and from
Basingstoke to...Bridlington and from Briddlington back
to Biggleswade again, we are barricaded...behind...bars.
Well, I'm not frightened. That's all I can say on the
matter. I'm not as frightened as everybody else. (*A pause.*)
Well, dear...to your eyes! (*Drinks.*) 'And, incidentally,
these eggs are inadequate.' (*Laughs.*) 'The whites are
unpoached and the yolks are tasteless.' (*Pours.*) The yolks
are tasteless! The yolks are tasteless! He should have
such tasteless yolks. Well...to your eyes, my friend.
To your bloodshot eyes! (*Toasts herself.*)
(*BRIAN, in night-attire and gripping his gun tightly, enters
and stares in horror at what he sees. He is pointing the gun
at his wife.*)

BRIAN: What are you doing? At this hour? This is totally unacceptable. Did you hear? (*No answer.*) You left me alone in that bed. This is totally unacceptable. Confess! Confess! (*No answer.*) You are drinking! You are drinking! (*No answer.*) You are…

THE WIFE: (*Without turning.*) Do you remember the days when we first met? Do you? Can you cast your mind back to those halcyon days, those carefree days when our futures stretched out before us like a clear blue river on a lovely summer's day? (*No answer.*) Because I can. I was just thinking of them. Those days. And you…I can see you now. Your face, your little child-like face with all its pretty innocence. Little hopeful beady eyes. Sweet little giggle. You had such a glow about you. A little golden glow, grinning with health and happiness. And it was then, when we sat down after a dance…we danced a lot in those days, Brian…it was then that you told me of the event that was to befall you, the overwhelming revelation that was to alter your life forever. Something momentous, something fantastic. It was going to light up your days and tie up all the loose ends. Wasn't it, Brian? Hmm? (*A pause.*) And you took me into your confidence. You said you needed a friend, a loyal friend to accompany you, to hold your hand through the endless hours of your search. (*A pause.*) And all those days. All those long, long days. Day after day after day after day. Each one running into the next. All those days. Those days, those days and still they pass. In a constant stream. A constant stream of day changing into night, of night changing into day, of day into night, of night into day, of day into night, of night into day, of day….

BRIAN: Enough!!!

(*There is a short silence.*)

(*Quieter.*) That is enough.

(*He wades through all the mess and comes closer to his wife. He lifts up the bottle and smells it. It does not agree with him. He puts it down and screws on the lid.*)

BRIAN: I want this place in order.

THE WIFE: (*Holding up pages.*) And you tore out those pages yourself. I found them in your box under the bed. (*A silence.*)

BRIAN: (*Pacing.*) I will devise grave punishments… We danced a lot in those days, you say? (*A pause.*) On your feet!! (*She does not move.*) Move!!! (*She slowly rises, hardly able to stand.*) You remember when we used to dance, do you?

THE WIFE: I do.

BRIAN: The time is etched on your memory?

THE WIFE: I am so tired.

BRIAN: You are tired?

THE WIFE: So very tired.

BRIAN: You are drunk.

THE WIFE: No.

BRIAN: You are drunk.

THE WIFE: No.

BRIAN: Drunk like a slut.

THE WIFE: Brian…

BRIAN: Like a drunken slut.

THE WIFE: Please.

BRIAN: It is the middle of the night.

THE WIFE: I had one drink.

BRIAN: One drink!? Where is the rest of the liquid then? I'll tell you. It has been drained away by a drunken slut. And how many times have you been slithering like a serpent from the safety of our conjugal bed and then swilling like a pig from the bottle? (*No answer.*) Answer!! Answer!! Confess!! Confess!!

THE WIFE: I need…

BRIAN: (*Snapping fingers.*) I'd like a waltz.

THE WIFE: A waltz?

BRIAN: Dance me a waltz.

THE WIFE: I am tired.

BRIAN: You are not tired. You are drunk.

THE WIFE: I am worn out.

BRIAN: And… (*Snaps fingers.*) Dance!!

(*She does not move so he snaps fingers again.*)
Dance!!
(*She slowly moves to centre of room.*)
Clear a space. For the dancing.
(*She slowly picks up clothes and puts them on the table.*)
Now…(*Snaps fingers.*) Dance!!
(*She slowly waltzes around the room. It is a lethargic performance. Soon she stumbles and crashes painfully to the floor.*)
You have stumbled.

THE WIFE: Yes.

BRIAN: You are graceless and ungainly.

THE WIFE: Yes.

BRIAN: Watch. It's step-together-together. Do you understand? Step-together-together. Are you ready?

THE WIFE: I can't.

BRIAN: And…(*Snaps fingers.*) Dance!! (*She slowly dances.*) Faster!! (*He starts to clap.*) Faster! Faster!
(*She dances faster.*)
Step-together-together!! Move, slut! Move! Step-together-together! Faster!
(*She dances faster.*)
And feel the dance! Feel the dance! Yes. The dance of life. Put your soul into it! Can you feel it? The dance, yes. Enjoy the dance! Move to the rhythm! The rhythm of the dance! The rhythm of life! It is a celebration, woman! A celebration of life! Can you feel the energy? A midnight dance. And step-together-together! Yes, step-together-together! Yes! Yes! Yes! Feel the rhythm of the waltz pumping through your arteries. That's it! Yes. And dance like a nigger, woman!! Dance like a nigger!!
(*She now collapses to the floor again, knocking over the table, chairs and crockery in the process. There is a silence.*)
It is quite the right place, don't you think, for a drunk? The floor. (*No answer.*) And… (*Snaps fingers.*) Rise!!
(*She does not move.*)
Rise!!!

THE WIFE: I cannot.

BRIAN: You cannot?

THE WIFE: I cannot.

BRIAN: You cannot?

THE WIFE: No.

BRIAN: Rise!!!

THE WIFE: Help.

BRIAN: Rise!!!

THE WIFE: Help.

BRIAN: On your feet!!

THE WIFE: Please, Brian...Help me.

BRIAN: You must learn to help yourself, woman. It is life's greatest lesson.

THE WIFE: I feel so weak. I am sick.

BRIAN: Weak?! You are weak-willed. Sick?! You are sick in the head.

THE WIFE: I am aware of my heart beating. I am aware of the sound of my heart beating.
(*Screams of despair. Closer. They stop. A silence.*)

BRIAN: That you heard! That you most definitely heard!

THE WIFE: My heart.

BRIAN: (*Searching mess for binoculars.*) Where are my binoculars? Where have you hidden them? What have you done with them? It is so dark outside. Why is it so dark? I must fire blindly into the night. (*Fires but no shots are heard.*) What has happened to my gun?

THE WIFE: Help.

BRIAN: It appears to be dysfunctional.

THE WIFE: (*Weakly.*) If you love me, Brian...if you have ever loved me, then please help me!

BRIAN: (*Exiting.*) There are some spare cartridges in my box under the bed.
(*Silence.*)

THE WIFE: Have a little...mercy. Have a little...Have a little...mercy. Have a little...Have a little...mercy. Have a little...

(*Blackout. The clock ticks ever faster in the darkness.*)

Morning

THE WIFE alone, slumped over the table. After a while BRIAN enters in night attire, nervously holding his gun.

BRIAN: I have been keeping watch. From the bedroom. There is definitely something untoward, something untoward stirring at the periphery of my vision. Did you hear? (*No answer.*) And, as I kept watch…I have to confess that I came to some conclusions. (*No answer.*) But first I had better be dressed. I do not want to be in a hurry this morning. (*Consults watch and clock.*) Perfect synchronisation. Day ten thousand and one. Yes. A new beginning. So…(*He waits but she does not move.*) And I have a hunger. I have not eaten, it seems for a whole day. So a good brace of hens' eggs…prepared anyway you like…(*No answer.*) I would be grateful for a little assistance. (*She does not move.*) You are tired, aren't you? I understand. I will attempt to dress myself this morning. (*He wonders how to begin.*) I take the gown off like so…? (*He struggles free from gown with some difficulty.*) And do I step out of the slippers? (*He slowly does so.*) And the cap is a straightforward procedure, is it not? (*Removes it.*) And I unbutton this? (*His pyjamas pose a further conundrum.*) Now…should I work from the bottom upwards or the top downwards? (*No answer.*) I am in difficulty. I have to confess.

(*He continues to undress himself with the dexterity of an infant and then frantically tries to find his suit from the chaos on the floor. He puts on his trousers back to front, his jacket inside out, wrong shoe on wrong foot, failure to affix tie. The following covers the change:*)

And whilst I scoured the landscape in the early hours and surveyed the stillness of the night air, my mind began to reflect upon certain issues we raised last night during our little discussion. And, as the sun came up and the dawn chorus began and I picked off the sparrows and the pigeons as they lined up on the wire, bursting their pissy little heads apart with the accuracy of my shooting, it came to me that I might have been a little severe in my chastisement of you last night. (*A pause.*) I apologise.

(*No answer.*) Did you hear? I apologise. (*No answer.*)
Because I do love you. Dear. Very much. And I know
that I tell you on a frequent basis but I wish you to know
that I mean it. I mean it from the bottom of my heart.
This jacket is filthy!! You must clean it!! You must!! You
must!! (*A pause.*) And so I would be grateful if you would
accept my offer of apology so that I can go about my
business with a clear conscience. You know how much I
have had on my mind of late. I am in a quandary with
these trousers. Yes, what with the Fortification Project
and all the hours ticking by and the impending arrival of
The Great Day, I may have neglected some of my duties
as a husband. And for that, too, I ask forgiveness.
(*Two knocks on the door. A silence.*)
(*Petrified.*) There were two knocks upon the door!!!
(*Two more knocks. A silence.*)
There were a further two knocks upon the door!!!
(*A silence.*)
You heard the knocks, woman?
(*Two more knocks.*)
Somebody is knocking upon the door. We must wait for
it to cease.
(*Two more knocks.*)
I cannot answer these knocks!! I am as yet not suitably
dressed for the answering of knocks. Who can it be?!
Nobody has come knocking on our door for some
considerable time.
(*Two more knocks.*)
(*BRIAN holds gun tightly and goes to rouse THE WIFE.*)
Tell them to leave us!! Tell them to leave us in peace!!
THE FRIEND: (*Off.*) Is anybody at home? (*No answer.*)
I am unarmed and would like to talk to you.
BRIAN: (*Weakly.*) Who's there?
THE FRIEND: (*Off.*) A friend. An old friend. Is that you,
Brian? (*No answer.*) Hello.
BRIAN: You know my...name?
THE FRIEND: (*Off.*) Of course.
BRIAN: Who are you? What do you want? I have received
my passport. Thank you. It was a little late and my wife
tears out the pages but...

THE FRIEND: (*Off.*) I am not from the Passport Office.

BRIAN: You are delivering hens' eggs?

THE FRIEND: (*Off.*) Neither am I from the Farm.

BRIAN: Then you are the Journey Planner?

THE FRIEND: (*Off.*) I am none of these things. I am just a friend.

BRIAN: A friend?

THE FRIEND: (*Off.*) Yes. (*A pause.*) May I come in?

(*After a while BRIAN slowly moves to the door, holding gun. He unbolts the door.*)

BRIAN: I must be at work shortly.

THE FRIEND: (*Off.*) Then I will be brief.

(*The door is opened and BRIAN raises his gun. THE FRIEND stands in the doorway. He is a colourfully-dressed man, stepping into this monochrome world. There is a long silence.*)

Hello, Brian.

BRIAN: Is it you?

THE FRIEND: Who else could it be?

BRIAN: You are exactly as I dream of you.

THE FRIEND: Won't you put your gun down?

BRIAN: I beg your pardon?

THE FRIEND: Your gun. I have come to ask you to lay down your arms.

BRIAN: Enter.

(*THE FRIEND wades into the room.*)

THE FRIEND: What has happened here?

BRIAN: My wife has been a little tired and consequently her work has been suffering.

THE FRIEND: She is asleep?

BRIAN: Yes. We danced at midnight…

THE FRIEND: You danced?

BRIAN: (*Proudly.*) We danced a waltz.

THE FRIEND: (*Approaching her.*) It must be a very deep sleep. Hello there! Are you alright? Can you hear me?

BRIAN: You can wake up now. We have a visitor.

THE FRIEND: (*Gently shaking her.*) She is not responding. Have you called her a doctor?

BRIAN: (*Trying not to laugh.*) She is not a doctor. Why would I want to call her one?

THE FRIEND: You must call a doctor.

BRIAN: But I am the one in need of medical assistance.

THE FRIEND: (*Feeling her pulse.*) Mrs Biggleswade? I can feel nothing. She is quite cold. (*Opens her eye.*) You must call a doctor. There is no time to lose.

BRIAN: From where could I call a doctor even if we had one?

(*A silence.*)

THE FRIEND: I think that perhaps it's not necessary.

BRIAN: I have always felt that the telephone is an expensive extravagance.

THE FRIEND: Your wife is dead.

(*A silence.*)

BRIAN: Dead?

THE FRIEND: I am so very sorry.

BRIAN: (*Laughing.*) How can she be dead, you fool? She was alive last night!! (*A pause.*) Dead!? The very idea. (*Goes to THE WIFE.*) Come on now. It is time to stop all this. Wakey-wakey!! Rise and shine!! Always playing these silly little games with me. (*Holds up her head.*) We have a visitor!! Don't be so rude now!! (*Slaps her face.*) We have a visitor!! We need the room tidied and the tea brewed!!

THE FRIEND: Brian!

BRIAN: (*Pulling her off chair, like a rag-doll in his arms.*) This is ridiculous. Come on!! Come on!! You are making a fool of yourself in front of our guest. Pull yourself together!! Rise and shine!! Rise and shine!! (*Starts to drag her round the room.*) Shall we dance then!? Shall we dance!? Come on! (*Spins her round in circles.*)

> I could have danced all night,
> I could have danced all night,
> And still have danced some more,
> I could have spread my wings,
> And done a thousand things,
> That I've never done before.

That's it. Whirl like a dervish!! Whirl like a dervish!! But you have no grace. No style. You have two left feet this morning. Is it because we have an audience?

THE FRIEND: I beg you!!

BRIAN: And step-together-together and step-together-together!! Feel the dance, remember! The spirit of life!! We must celebrate! Celebrate! And step-together-together!! You remember! And step-together…
(*Screams of despair. Closer. They stop. A silence.*)
Did you hear that?

THE FRIEND: Lay your wife's body down.

BRIAN: It was a sound of despair!! It was a sound of despair!!

THE FRIEND: I heard nothing. Now, please. Put your wife down.

BRIAN: She will not dance with me!!

THE FRIEND: No. She will not.

BRIAN: But I want her to dance with me. I just want her to dance with me. Why won't you dance with me? Woman!! Did you hear? I only wanted us to dance together. Naked under the sun. Naked like the day we were born. Just you and I. And now you will not dance!!

THE FRIEND: Let me. (*Takes the corpse.*)

BRIAN: She cannot dance, can she?

THE FRIEND: She will not dance again.

BRIAN: This is unacceptable.

THE FRIEND: I think she has been dead for some time.

BRIAN: But she was alive last night!!

THE FRIEND: I'm sorry.

BRIAN: Highly irregular. I have not yet had my hens' eggs.

THE FRIEND: Why don't you sit down?

BRIAN: And I am not suitably attired for work. I cannot go like this.

THE FRIEND: Please.

BRIAN: I shan't be able to affix my tie single-handedly.

THE FRIEND: Perhaps you should not go to work this morning.

BRIAN: I am shaking, look.

THE FRIEND: I think you should sit down.
(*BRIAN sits.*)
Now…how can I let your work know you won't be coming in today?

(A long silence in which BRIAN stares at THE FRIEND in amazement.)

BRIAN: Are you quite mad?

THE FRIEND: You have experienced a great shock.

BRIAN: People depend on me there. I carry a lot of responsibility.

THE FRIEND: Your wife has died. You are in no fit state.

BRIAN: I have my responsibilities.

THE FRIEND: Can I get you something to drink?

BRIAN: I have a sense of duty.

THE FRIEND: Is your kitchen through here?

BRIAN: I will not shirk.

THE FRIEND: Would you like a cup of tea?

BRIAN: You will have to ask her how it's done.

THE FRIEND: I can manage.

BRIAN: You'll need to heat the water. Heat the...the cup.

(THE FRIEND exits.)

(A silence. The clock is ticking at speed.)

We have a visitor. An old friend. He looks older but otherwise he is exactly the same person as before. He is making us all a nice cup of tea. *(No answer.)* Don't worry. No need to worry. You stay there and rest. He says he knows how to make the tea. He is a clever man. Don't you think? *(No answer.)* Do you think he's a clever man? Hmm? *(No answer.)* What do you think? *(No answer)* Am I all alone then? Am I all alone? *(No answer.)* You are funny. I admit you have been amusing but it's time to put an end to all this. Do you understand? You gain nothing from ostracising me like this. What can you possibly gain from it? We must pull together at times like these. And you have made your point. Do you understand me? You have proved your point. *(No answer.)* And he won't make the tea like you do. You make such...such nice tea. *(No answer.)* I have always enjoyed the tea you have brewed. *(No answer)* Am I all alone then?! Am I all alone? *(No answer so he draws close to her and screams in her ear, shaking her.)* Hello!! Hello!! Hello!! Rise and shine!! Rise and shine!! Am I all alone then!? Am I all alone?!

(*THE FRIEND opens the hatch.*)

THE FRIEND: What is it?

BRIAN: (*A wronged child to his mother.*) She is ignoring me. She is refusing to speak.

THE FRIEND: Yes.

BRIAN: She is treating me with cruelty. With absolute cruelty and I will not put up with it.

THE FRIEND: I don't think you understand...

BRIAN: It is heartless. That is all. We danced. She danced a waltz and I clapped out the rhythm with my hands. That is all. And now this. This conspiracy of silence. It is an outrage, that's what it is. An absolute outrage. An absolute disgrace.

(*A silence. Then quietly, broken:*)

> We could have danced all night,
> We could have danced all night,
> And still have danced some more,
> We could have spread our wings,
> And done a thousand things,
> That we've never done before...

(*Blackout. The clock ticks ever faster in the darkness.*)

Evening

BRIAN alone, eating a boiled egg.

BRIAN: (*Mouth full.*) I am so hungry.

THE FRIEND: (*Entering.*) How is the egg?

BRIAN: It is the yolk. It is bland.

THE FRIEND: Bland?

BRIAN: Yes. Tasteless. Insipid in the extreme.

THE FRIEND: I'm sorry.

BRIAN: It is not of the correct...consistency.

THE FRIEND: I see.

BRIAN: She always makes them just as I like them. Not too hard and not too soft. These yolks are like raw sprouts.

THE FRIEND: They are too hard?

BRIAN: And the toast is all bendy. Look. See how it bends. It is not adequately crisp.

THE FRIEND: Perhaps I…

BRIAN: And I am used to having soldier slithers with my hens' eggs.

THE FRIEND: Soldiers?

BRIAN: She cuts the toast into strips and I dip these strips into the egg. One at a time.

THE FRIEND: Could you not cut the toast you already have into strips?

BRIAN: What, this bendy toast? Are you a fool? It is dripping in margarine. If I tried to dip a soldier cut from this toast it would fold up like a piece of string in the egg.

THE FRIEND: Should I make you some more toast?

BRIAN: If I had to wait for that long, the eggs would be stone cold as well as rock hard.

THE FRIEND: I see.

BRIAN: Equally, there is no little mound of sea salt.

THE FRIEND: Sea salt?

BRIAN: I like a little mound of sea salt by the egg cup. Just there, look.

THE FRIEND: I could get you some.

BRIAN: Too little too late, fool. Too little too late.

THE FRIEND: Listen, Brian…

BRIAN: I think I will have that mound of sea salt after all.

THE FRIEND: You will?

BRIAN: On second thoughts, no. (*He eats noisily.*)

THE FRIEND: Would you like me to tidy up for you now?

BRIAN: In the fullness of time, dear.

THE FRIEND: And you are quite sure you…?

BRIAN: This is how I sometimes amuse her in the mornings. I take an empty egg shell and invert it like so when she is either unaware or out of the room, and see… You'll notice it resembles a fresh, uncracked egg. Can you see? And so…when she enters the room, I say 'Look, look, I am about to start eating the egg, I am about to start eating the egg'!! And then, when she is watching me, I stab the spoon right through the shell like so, like this, smash, smash, smash, causing her to start with alarm. (*A silence.*) The other day she made me griddled eggs. With a touch of basil.

THE FRIEND: My wife was a wonderful...

BRIAN: And, at Eastertide, I draw an amusing face on the shell. With a crayon.

THE FRIEND: She too is dead. She died recently. So if you need...

BRIAN: It was a red crayon.

THE FRIEND: I understand how you...

BRIAN: Yes, dear.

THE FRIEND: I too have known pain. I too...

BRIAN: I draw one of those faces. You know, that if you have the egg one way up, it is a happy, smiling face and then if you turn it on its head, the face looks at you filled with sadness. (*A pause.*) And now they have taken to advertising cheap-rate morning calls on the egg shells. It is, however, wasted on me. (*Laughing.*) I cannot deny that I am a consumer of eggs but, not having a telephone, I am not really a consumer of cheap-rate morning calls.

THE FRIEND: No.

BRIAN: Or any calls for that matter. (*A pause.*) Not a bad bit of albumen, that.

(*A silence.*)

THE FRIEND: Brian...I must leave you shortly.

BRIAN: You must leave me?

THE FRIEND: I'm afraid I must.

BRIAN: You must not.

THE FRIEND: I must.

BRIAN: I can't have that.

THE FRIEND: I play in a band. The trombone. We must practice.

BRIAN: You are not to leave.

THE FRIEND: We are playing tonight. Why not...?

BRIAN: You are not to leave.

THE FRIEND: It might do you good.

BRIAN: You are to stay.

THE FRIEND: It's a friendly atmosphere.

BRIAN: You are to stay.

THE FRIEND: We play music and the audience...

BRIAN: You can play your music here. You can practice here.

THE FRIEND: I must go.

BRIAN: You must not.

THE FRIEND: I must.

BRIAN: You are to stay.

THE FRIEND: I cannot.

BRIAN: You are wrong.

THE FRIEND: I'll say goodbye…

BRIAN: (*Frantic.*) You play the trumpet, you say?

THE FRIEND: The trombone.

BRIAN: Fascinating.

THE FRIEND: I am so sorry…

BRIAN: You play music?

THE FRIEND: Yes.

BRIAN: You play music?

THE FRIEND: Yes.

BRIAN: You play…music?

THE FRIEND: Yes.

BRIAN: Fascinating.

THE FRIEND: So…

BRIAN: Absolutely fascinating. Not the trumpet then?

THE FRIEND: No.

BRIAN: Nor the tuba?

THE FRIEND: No.

BRIAN: Nor the trombone?

THE FRIEND: I play the trombone.

BRIAN: Fascinating.

   (*In the distance, the opening strains of 'The Star-Spangled Banner' can now be heard.*)

THE FRIEND: I must go…

BRIAN: But why do you? Why do you? Why? Why? Why?

THE FRIEND: I…

BRIAN: Why do you waste your time on such trivialities?

THE FRIEND: I'm not sure it's…

BRIAN: The tuba, the trombone, the trumpet…

THE FRIEND: Yes.

BRIAN: And you play old favourites?

THE FRIEND: I must go.

BRIAN: Requests?

THE FRIEND: Yes.

BRIAN: Fascinating.

THE FRIEND: Goodbye.

BRIAN: Absolutely fascinating.

THE FRIEND: If you need…

BRIAN: You play the trombone, you say? The trumpet?!

THE FRIEND: Please…

BRIAN: (*Blocking doorway.*) Trum-pet. Trum-pet.

THE FRIEND: (*At door.*) Excuse me.

BRIAN: The yolk was too hard!!

THE FRIEND: I'm sorry.

BRIAN: There were no soldiers!!

THE FRIEND: I'm sorry.

BRIAN: We danced a waltz!!

THE FRIEND: You said.

BRIAN: I clapped out the rhythm!!

THE FRIEND: I know.

BRIAN: You play the trumpet, you say? The trombone, you say?

THE FRIEND: I must pass.

BRIAN: Fascinating.

THE FRIEND: Excuse me.

BRIAN: Trum-pet!! Trum-pet!!

THE FRIEND: Excuse me.

BRIAN: Trum-pet!! Trum-pet!!

THE FRIEND: Please.

BRIAN: Don't touch me!! Don't touch me!! You fool!! You fool!! You fool!!

(*BRIAN pushes THE FRIEND over violently and he is sent sprawling onto his back. BRIAN, still screaming, sits on the man's chest and begins to strangle him in his now overflowing rage. 'The Star-Spangled Banner' is now much clearer and closer.*)

Fool!! Fool!! Fool!! I've seen you!! I've seen you!! Don't think I haven't seen you!! You fool!! Over by the graves!! The graves at the periphery of my vision!! Don't think I haven't seen you!! I have!! I know, you fool!! I know!! You and your flowers on the graves, you and your flowers. Wiping the tears away as you kneel. I've seen you talking, fool! I've seen you talking to the grave!! Weeping like a child!! You're a grown man, you fool!! I've seen you!! I've seen it all!! Flowers, tears, talking!! I've been watching you. And now!! You invade us here!! Me and my wife!! You've taken her from me!! Yours is dead and now you want to steal mine away!! You're a fool then! A fool! You can't take mine!! You can give her back!! I'm close to the Day now. I'm close to the Great Day and you cannot steal what belongs to me. Fool!! I'm too smart for you!! You can make the tea alright but you're not as smart as you think!! Fool!! Fool!! Fool!!

(*BRIAN looks round the room at the chaos of his life, at the heap of newspapers, clothes and crockery. The clock is ticking at great speed at this point. He looks at the dead man beneath him. Then, something registers in his eyes. The Day has finally dawned. He is horror-struck. The 'Star-Spangled Banner' builds to a deafening crescendo, while the scream of his soul likewise builds to its hideous climax.*)

(*Blackout.*)

THE LAST DAYS OF DESIRE

a comedy

Characters

FROST
Forties/fifties, a civil servant (m)

ANDERSON
Fifties/sixties, an entrepreneur (m)

McCALL
Forties, an adulteress (f)

STENNING
Twenties, an unappreciated genius (m)

LAW
Forties, a highly-cultured critic (f)

To be delivered with relentless energy

The Last Days of Desire was commissioned by the BBC in July 2000 and was recorded on 5-6 June 2001 for broadcast on 18 July 2001 as an afternoon play on Radio 4. The cast was as follows:

FROST, Ian Lindsay

ANDERSON, Bill Stewart

McCALL, Carolyn Backhouse

STENNING, Ian Pepperell

LAW, Jennie Stoller

Producer, Karen Rose

Studio Manager (grams and spot), Keith Graham

Studio Manager (on panel), Anne Bunting

Broadcast Assistant, Vivien Rosenthal

Scene One

A city street. The noise is deafening: a cacophony of helicopters, angry traffic and indecipherable public address announcements. Voices have to scream to be heard above the pandemonium. We hear the sound of a man running.

FROST: Excuse me! Are you…are you the fat man?!

ANDERSON: What does it look like!?

FROST: Well, yes. I suppose you do stand out a little.

ANDERSON: (*Moving.*) Follow!!

FROST: (*Moving.*) As it were.

ANDERSON: Mind your back!!

(*They do not speak as sirens begin to scream.*)

FROST: Haven't been in this neck of the woods since I…

ANDERSON: (*Wheezing.*) Sorry?!

FROST: Nothing.

TANNOY: (*American.*) *Customer information: would any witnesses to this recent outrage please contact Miller & Reynolds Law Enforcement Associates as soon as possible on two seven zero three five four five three seven. A one hundred thousand dollar reward is being offered for any information leading to the liquidation of the guilty. This sum is due to the generosity of Tennessee Trading Partners (for Cheap and Friendly Financial Planning). Thank you for your time.*

ANDERSON: Stock Exchange!!

FROST: Anyone killed?!

ANDERSON: And Jimmy Reynolds is a bloody amateur!!

FROST: Sorry?

ANDERSON: That contract won no doubt through sheer arse-licking!

(*A helicopter flies overhead.*)

FROST: I'm reminded why I rarely venture out of doors these days!

ANDERSON: You what!?

FROST: I said…

ANDERSON: (*Wheezing.*) This way!

COMPUTER: (*Italian.*) *Welcome to Crossing 41A, sponsored by Toscadelli Ice Creams, The Genuine Italian Article. Please insert your card now.*

(*A card is swiped.*)

ANDERSON: Watch you don't catch anyone's eyes!!

COMPUTER: *Thank you. When you hear the music, please cross the road. We realise you can choose where you cross the road so grazie and a big ciao for now!*

ANDERSON: Keep your head down!

FROST: Whatever you say!

(*The computer emanates opera, the singer sings only the word 'Toscadelli'. They cross the road. Nobody speaks for a time.*)

I say!! Don't you ever get apprehensive...living in this part of...

ANDERSON: Take more than a couple of bombs to intimidate someone like me!!

FROST: Yes!! Good!!

(*A helicopter flies overhead. They run off.*)

(*Credits.*)

Scene Two

ANDERSON's office. A little later. A door closes. The sound of footsteps. We can still hear the odd, muffled helicopter and siren outside the window.

FROST: You're right...it is a quite amazing view. (*Weak laugh.*) I only earn enough to live on the twenty-fifth myself. Business is evidently booming for you?

ANDERSON: (*Out of breath.*) Alcohol?

FROST: Not for me.

(*Drink is poured.*)

So...that's the famous park then?

ANDERSON: All that remains of what used to be known as Kent. The Garden of England apparently.

FROST: I could stare out of this window all night. We are so high up. The lights are quite...

ANDERSON: Perhaps I should point out that I do charge by the minute and...

FROST: Of course.

ANDERSON: ...and I'm not especially cheap, I know.

FROST: No.

THE LAST DAYS OF DESIRE

ANDERSON: But if you'd rather we admire the twinkling metropolis for…

FROST: You're quite right.

ANDERSON: So…your spouse…?

FROST: Oh God.

ANDERSON: I need an image. I need to know her routines.

FROST: Here. Taken last year.

ANDERSON: Very nice. She has what I like to call…poise.

FROST: She does, yes.

ANDERSON: I think that, due to your respectable rank within the Civil Service and, how shall I phrase it?…the rather pleasing appearance of your good lady wife, I think that this is a case which I will undertake personally. At no extra charge.

FROST: You will?

ANDERSON: So tell me…when did you first suspect her of being untrue? Of her being, as it were, penetrated by another man.

FROST: Oh God…

ANDERSON: And do you have any idea of her lover's name?

FROST: Listen…

ANDERSON: You suspect a much younger man?

FROST: Maybe she…maybe I have this all wrong. I could be wrong?

ANDERSON: One finds that this is usually the case. (*Pause.*) My function is to put your mind at ease. The trenches of anxiety scored along your forehead lack…dignity.

FROST: And I adore my wife, I…

ANDERSON: You are aware that if I do discover she is a whore then it is the standard practice to incarcerate her?

FROST: Yes, I am aware.

ANDERSON: And then, should the admittedly prohibitive bail conditions not be met, to exterminate her?

FROST: (*After a pause.*) Yes.

ANDERSON: For thirty years Anderson Private Penitentiaries Ltd has prided itself on helping to safeguard the sanctity of matrimony and preserve the integrity of the marriage vow. We are the undisputed market leaders in the Government's crusade to eliminate the abomination of adultery and to reinstate traditional family values. We believe…

FROST: You can spare me the sales pitch, Mr Anderson. You come highly recommended and your reputation speaks for itself.

ANDERSON: What I mean is…once you start the ball rolling I am honour-bound to see the case through to its bitter conclusion…

FROST: I understand.

ANDERSON: You are at liberty to walk away right now. You will lose only your deposit which, I am sure you'll agree, is a mere token. (*No answer.*) I am appallingly brutal, Mr Frost, but I do work only with the facts. You seem unsure?

FROST: I wish…to proceed.

ANDERSON: Then expand.

FROST: Well, where can I start? She is beautiful. She is kind. Intelligent. A wonderful mother to our daughters. She is gentle, she is witty, she is selfless…she…

Scene Three

STENNING's bedroom. Dogs barking somewhere off. Shouts of violence intrude throughout.

McCALL: We can't do this again.

STENNING: Of course we can.

McCALL: It's destroying me!

STENNING: Relax.

McCALL: Don't tell me to relax. I'm riddled with guilt, my heart feels heavy… I keep…even while we're…when we're…

STENNING: (*Laughing.*) You can say it.

McCALL: …I see his face, I see the faces of my daughters and….we simply have to end this….this treachery.

STENNING: (*Laughing.*) Treachery!

McCALL: And kindly stop laughing!

STENNING: Come here...

McCALL: And I am old enough to be your...

STENNING: (*Laughing.*) Spare me!

McCALL: And you simply must stop all this killing!

STENNING: (*Laughing.*) When my writing is recognised, only then will I lay down my sword.

McCALL: And you earn nothing from any of it!

STENNING: Tragedy is what changes society. When my work starts making its point I...

McCALL: You are irresponsible, you are lecherous and impoverished. You are arrogant and self-centred and idle. (*A window is smashed somewhere off.*)
What is more, you laugh far too much. It is dangerous. I have seen people...

STENNING: (*Laughing.*) I write tragedies, I blow up capitalists. The laugh does not frighten me!

McCALL: And you are faithless. Quite faithless.
(*A kiss.*)
No, I'm sorry...but this has got to finish.

STENNING: (*Laughing.*) You always have to talk.

McCALL: Talk?

STENNING: Let us just kiss and then...

McCALL: Of course I must talk! What else can I do? I have to broadcast my private anxieties. You are silent because you don't care. When I eventually leave this freezing, stinking bedroom of yours...

STENNING: (*Laughing.*) Stop talking.

McCALL: ...you'll no doubt find some quivering virgin somewhere who is desperate to...

STENNING: You ache for me.

McCALL: I can't keep pace with your...appetites.

STENNING: (*Laughing.*) It is I who generally struggles to keep pace with yours.

McCALL: And will you stop this...laughing!?

STENNING: (*Laughing.*) I can't! You're so...comical.

McCALL: And the laugh is so unappealing, so resonant with misanthropy. It rarely masks the misery of the man who emits it.

STENNING: (*Suddenly serious.*) You alliterate well. Let me make a note.

McCALL: And yet I...I rarely laugh...and there never was such a miserable woman as...

STENNING: We have a perfect arrangement, do we not? You love your husband (or rather...his soul-sapping circularities have corrupted you for so long you now believe he is somehow a part of your personality) but of course you no longer find him desirable. You find me on the other hand...what did you say?...self-centred, was it?...and irresponsible...

McCALL: That's not all that you are!

STENNING: (*Laughing.*) And yet you and I together...What we enact here in this bed, it cannot be denied...

McCALL: It is lies, it is falsehood, it is...

STENNING: ...is nothing less than the truth. You may be married, you may have two musically-gifted daughters, you may be older than my mother...

McCALL: What?

STENNING: ...but this lovemaking of ours blasts all that into insignificance.

McCALL: How much older am I?

STENNING: Your body looks superb in this light.

McCALL: Don't touch...

STENNING: Do you always have to pretend like this? That your hunger is somehow less than mine?

McCALL: I am older than his mother. Older than his poor, dear mother.

STENNING: (*Laughing.*) I love the way you refer to me in the third person.

McCALL: Do I?

STENNING: As if we had an audience.

McCALL: Oh God...

STENNING: (*Suddenly, excited.*) Look at the time!

McCALL: It's time I should go.

STENNING: No. Wait.

(*A silence.*)

You see? Your body distracts me from my work.

McCALL: I don't want to know.

STENNING: What I do turns you on.

McCALL: No!

STENNING: That I have blood on my hands, it sends your pulse racing, the lust churning through your arteries, your bowels…

McCALL: Just kiss me!

STENNING: Wait!

(*A silence.*)

A few more seconds…

McCALL: I do not wish to know.

STENNING: …and a hundred more sneering bankers will go to their graves.

McCALL: I wish to remain completely in the dark.

STENNING: Their foetid flesh blending with the whitewashed office walls. Plasterboard and muscle. Blood and brick.

McCALL: Oh, your purple prose!

STENNING: The sweet agony of disintegration.

(*A silence. Then a distant explosion.*)

McCALL: Just once more. And then I go.

STENNING: Of course.

McCALL: My daughters will soon be home from music practice.

STENNING: Lucky girls to have a mother like you.

McCALL: I am evil, I am depraved, I am…

STENNING: Beautiful.

McCALL: …and totally without… Ah, your lips. I…suck your youth from them, they…revitalise me. Yes, I could sink into these lips, this mouth. I could sink into your soul and lose myself forever.

(*They kiss.*)

Scene Four

The family dining room. A clock ticks.

FROST: I think, my daughters, that we may soon be forced to start eating without her. (*A silence.*) I appreciate the fact that you have both taken time away from your

Rachmaninov to step in for your mother on this occasion. (*A silence.*) It seems that you, Louisa, have prepared the meat, whilst Emily here has taken care of the vegetables. (*A silence.*) Yes. I am grateful. (*A silence.*) Try not to look so worried, Emily. I am sure she will have a perfectly legitimate explanation for this. (*A silence.*) As for myself, I had a good day. Nothing unusual to report. Ah, Louisa, I seem to be short of a knife. If you would be so kind…

(*A chair scrapes.*)

Thank you. (*A pause.*) You dress well, Emily. You look just like your mother did when we… (*He stifles an emotion as cutlery is placed on a table.*) Ah, the knife! Many thanks. (*A silence.*) I trust that, while we wait, neither of you will mind if I take a look at the evening paper? (*A weak laugh.*) It's so hard these days to find the time to catch up on events in the wider sphere.

(*A newspaper rattles.*)

(*A key in the door.*)

Ah, she is home.

McCALL: Forgive me, forgive me. I beg you to forgive!

FROST: You were held up?

McCALL: I was.

FROST: A stroll in the park?

McCALL: A stroll in the park, yes!

FROST: Your daughters are hungry.

McCALL: Yes.

FROST: Your husband is hungry.

McCALL: Forgive!

FROST: I feel…tense.

McCALL: Your face *is* rather red.

FROST: I am attempting to control the rage, the frustration I am feeling.

McCALL: Well, this all looks lovely.

(*A chair scrapes.*)

How are you, my darlings?

FROST: I think on reflection it would be wiser for them to leave the dining area. Allow their parents to resolve this situation in private.

STENNING: You don't need to check up on me. I'm
  meeting her now. The civil servant's wife. I'm…

LAW: And this hideous council flat. (*Pause.*) Then I shall
  come with you.

  (*A distant, violent shout.*)

STENNING: (*On the move.*) God, how I hate!

LAW: (*Following.*) We must talk about your next assignment!

STENNING: I hate…with a passion.

LAW: The free-marketeers are running scared, Mr Stenning.

STENNING: A passion that is unsurpassed…

LAW: And we are the ones who are making them run!

STENNING: …in this hideous land.

  (*A can is kicked down the corridor. Shouts.*)

LAW: And so for the sake of the revolution I am destined to
  spend my valuable time with a mere boy like you…

STENNING: For I am the only one who understands…

LAW: In an environment of such squalor, such degradation!

STENNING: Yes, my hatred is what I need!

LAW: I don't think I can hear this again. Your hate speech.
  Really. I can't.

STENNING: It sharpens my pen!

LAW: Look at me. I am forty-three years of age! And a
  highly-respected critic of literature!

STENNING: And distils the outpourings of the intellect…

LAW: And this place. The graffiti, the pools of vomit. Ach,
  these syringes, Mr Stenning!

STENNING: …so that what is left on the page…

LAW: I should stick to writing reviews. I should never have
  got involved in trying to bring down the Government.

STENNING: …is sheer quality.

  (*A window is smashed. A child starts to wail.*)

LAW: Oh, how you spit out your words, Mr Stenning!

STENNING: I'm an angry young man.

LAW: Yes, but your anger clouds your…

STENNING: Don't say it!

LAW: …your respect for form.

STENNING: Not listening!

LAW: For structure!

  (*They start walking down some stairs.*)

Yes, your latest novel was...how can I put this kindly?
...rather epic.

STENNING: No!

LAW: And your short stories are like novels!

STENNING: Never, never!

LAW: Ignoring as you do the adjective inherent...

STENNING: I'm deaf to your...

LAW: ...in the very description of the medium. Look, slow
down! These shoes are Italian and terribly expensive.
These heels are simply not designed for...

STENNING: I'm late and this woman lives by the clock!

LAW: We've things to discuss!

STENNING: And what do *you* know anyway? You who
command killing from behind a desk!

LAW: I could help you!

STENNING: And yet *you* lecture *me*! *You* seek to advise *me*
...it is utterly laughable...in the ways of the pen!

LAW: You must package your anger in...

STENNING: (*Scornfully.*) '...innocuous wrappings.'
(*Another window is smashed. Screams. Shouts. Sirens.*)

LAW: (*Having to shout.*) Oh, so I repeat myself then?!

STENNING: (*Likewise.*) Often!!

LAW: Then it is a crime we are both guilty of since you
have after all only ever written the one novel!

STENNING: Who asked you anyway?!

LAW: ...only ever written the one play!!

STENNING: I have written over twenty!!

LAW: The difference being the title only!!

STENNING: I have covered every aspect of human
experience!!

LAW: Same characters, same plot!!

STENNING: There is never a plot!! I do not restrict myself
to mere narrative!!

LAW: Then this horrendous plotlessness is the same in each
case!!

STENNING: Ah, what do you know, you...philistine
butcher, you...!!

LAW: You must hide your anger and your desire for chaos
within a framework of...!!

STENNING: I'm not listening!!

LAW: ...a framework of order!!

STENNING: That reeks of...!!

LAW: It is *not* compromise!!

STENNING: The true artist has no respect for the whining (yet at the same time curiously indifferent) demands of his public!!

LAW: Then the pages of your novels will remain unthumbed, the painfully-crafted syllables of your poetry will never fall upon a single ear and your plays will either collect dust on the shelves of the Institutions or, at the very most, be acted out by amateurs on tiny stages before an audience of beer-stained wooden benches! People are staring at me!!

STENNING: (*Screaming.*) Let them stare!! We are beautiful!!

Scene Seven

Back in the bar. The tape clicks on.

ANDERSON: (*Into tape.*) One twenty-three. She is now smoking a cigarette. Offered to her by some chortling student. She does not inhale. Smokes like a princess. Smokes like a queen. (*A loud series of whoops, laughter and cheers.*) And, what is more appealing, she remains quite unmoved by all these unsubtle invitations to cackle. Just sits there, as if in terrible pain, drawing gazes from the youthful, dimpled wretches. As they gurgle and backslap in their intoxication. They are terrified of her. And so am I. She shifts in her seat, her delicate rump caressing the creaking leather of the bar-stool. She is waiting for someone. So much is clear. What manner of man gains access to such treasures? And why am I condemned always to watch from afar? The eternal spectator! (*He slams his fist on the bar.*) Another, if you please! Ah, spare me the look of concern. I'm an adult. I do not need protecting!

(*A drink is poured. The laughter.*)

Scene Eight

FROST's office. He is tapping on his keyboard.

FROST: Not long to lunch now. Five minutes and thirty-six
seconds. Not long to go.
(*He makes a call.*)
Any messages? Are you quite sure? Right. Thank you.
(*End of call.*) Jesus Christ!
(*He knocks a glass off his desk. It shatters. A silence.*)
Oh God. Blood. I cannot stand the sight of… Oh, there
is blood all over my keyboard, all over my screen and…
Oh God…

Scene Nine

Back in the bar. Laughter all around.

ANDERSON: This laughter, this laughter! It gives me a
stitch. Ah, so she has waited long enough! The eyes and
the gawping gobs follow her out. She will now pound the
streets, her snout in the gutter, her eyes to the drains,
when she could be at home bathing in scented oils or
sleeping in crisp, cool linen. I sound like I'm in love. I
am too old for this. Too old and too fat. But now, in this
city, where it is impossible to find even a half-decent
whore, I… (*Up and on the move, wheezing.*) And so I too
must follow. I think I could follow this woman to the
ends of the earth.

LAW: (*As they enter the bar.*) Do you mind?!

STENNING: Oh, how I detest the obese!

LAW: He nearly knocked me off my feet!

STENNING: She's not here!

LAW: I'm sure I know this man.
(*A photograph is taken.*)

STENNING: She is punctual. She is patient. Whereas I…
What are you doing?

LAW: A precautionary measure.

STENNING: Why do you need a picture of him?!

LAW: Go to the hotel then! Round the corner. I still have thirty minutes!

STENNING: I am not a gigolo!

LAW: (*Back into the noisy street.*) I'll be there shortly. I need to check something out!

STENNING: No. I...am a talented artist.

LAW: Yes, but you are so...

STENNING: Killing capitalists is merely a sideline.

LAW: ...thin.

STENNING: The written word is my true passion.

LAW: Your hips jut out rather, they threaten to slice open your trousers...

STENNING: I just need to be given a chance!

LAW: ...which incidentally could do with pressing. Excuse me, lady!

STENNING: And I will never demean my work by following rules!

LAW: You are wasting away. Now, will you please...

STENNING: Rules are for the rabble.

LAW: Rather like your talent.

(*A helicopter flies overhead.*)

Oh, I see I have offended you. I apologise.

STENNING: I am not offended.

LAW: It is odd that one so skilled in the ways of savagery should be so terribly...thin-skinned.

STENNING: I am a subtle blend of fury and sensitivity. Which is, I am told, a combination very attractive to women.

LAW: A young man like you should play to his strengths. And I suspect your particular strengths lie in the brutalities of murder rather than in the finer points of literature. Now, will you go to the hotel?!

STENNING: You say that but one day and soon I will burst... (*He moves away.*)

(*A computer is tapped. Numbers are dialled.*)

LAW: (*Into phone.*) I want an ID on this man. I'm sending the image now. Report back to me immediately. We may need him followed.

Scene Ten

ANDERSON is on the move. We hear his wheezing. FROST is on the other end of his phone.

FROST: Yes, but what is she doing?

ANDERSON: (*Wheezing.*) Walking. Listen, Mr Frost…

FROST: Where is she going?

ANDERSON: I don't know.

FROST: You don't know!?

ANDERSON: (*Patiently.*) And this is the reason I am following her.

FROST: Well, is she alone?

ANDERSON: Yes.

FROST: Thank God.

ANDERSON: Mr Frost, you will have to stop calling me like this. I'm finding it difficult to…

FROST: So what is she wearing?

ANDERSON: Well…

FROST: Does she look good to you? Has she made an effort or…

ANDERSON: She looks…

FROST: How does she look, for God's sake!?

ANDERSON: She looks…good.

FROST: What?

ANDERSON: Attractive.

FROST: God!

ANDERSON: Very…attractive.

FROST: Alright, alright! I get the point!

(The phone call is suddenly over. ANDERSON lets out a sardonic laugh and continues walking and wheezing.)

Scene Eleven

The hotel bedroom. A door closes.

STENNING: Where have you been?

LAW: The fat man. In that bar. If you see him again I want you to tell me.

STENNING: Fat men don't frighten me.

LAW: His name is Anderson. He runs a Penitentiary.

STENNING: Listen…

LAW: He is also a pornographer.

STENNING: Will you just listen for a minute?! (*An expectant silence.*) I have finished my latest play. Almost.

LAW: You write them as fast as I can read them.

STENNING: It will be my finest work to date.

LAW: As usual you are struggling with your ending?

STENNING: I have to get it just right. You will have it by early next week.

LAW: And I see you've gone for the master bedroom again?

STENNING: I craved a little luxury.

LAW: You are proving to be an expensive hobby, Mr Stenning.

(*A keyboard is tapped.*)

Now…business before pleasure. Yes, another commendable success yesterday afternoon. You have created one more mob of widows, whose oh so touching grief will no doubt be slightly assuaged by the health of their husbands' bank accounts. Good. Now, tell me… how are things progressing with this Mr Frost, this Government pen-pusher, this pot-bellied paper-shuffler?

STENNING: (*Laughing.*) Well, I enjoy violating his wife.

LAW: Try not to enjoy her too much as we need him dispatched rather promptly. There are other more significant people we need you to turn your attention to.

STENNING: I shall begin the surveillance proper tomorrow.

LAW: Good. You may now remove your clothing. I shall prepare myself in the en suite bathroom. (*She moves off. A pause.*) Come along. I have to be back at the office within a matter of minutes. I must write a review on yet another novel, in diary format naturally, about an ageing woman who drinks too much, eats too much and is unable to find herself a boyfriend.

(*A door is opened and then closed.*)

Scene Twelve

A park. A fusion of birdsong and human voices. The odd helicopter/
siren overhead.

McCALL: Yes, Mr Stenning, but you didn't show up. You
    left me in that hideous bar. You know I cannot stand
    comedy of any sort!

STENNING: I must have just missed you. I'm sorry.

McCALL: Too much laughter is dangerous! I've told you!
    I've seen people…

STENNING: I'm sorry. I was…waylayed.

McCALL: And a man has been following me.

STENNING: Men are always following you.

McCALL: A drunken, bloated, wheezing buffoon, he
    staggers from lamppost to lamppost. He thinks I do not
    see him. Yesterday all day. Then in the bar he…

STENNING: Why do we have to come here?

McCALL: I need the green.

STENNING: It's always so full.

TANNOY: (*American.*) *Would any customers wishing to sit*
    under the shade of the tree this lunchtime please form an
    orderly queue at the sign. Friday rates apply. Thank you.

McCALL: This way.

STENNING: Where are we going?

McCALL: Through here.

STENNING: I rage against these crowds.

McCALL: They have the same right to be here as…

STENNING: They are Establishment lickspittles and
    deserve to die!

McCALL: Sssh!

STENNING: The haircuts the same, the suits all the
    same…

McCALL: Here! Now, sit.

STENNING: Your nails are puncturing my skin.
    (*A silence.*)

McCALL: I…I am in love with you.

STENNING: And…?

McCALL: And I want you. In my life. I want you.

(*He laughs.*)

Why are you laughing?

(*He continues.*)

I expose my soul and all you do is laugh!

STENNING: Return to your timeserver.

McCALL: Please…

STENNING: (*Laughing still.*) You have already chosen your life whereas I…

McCALL: I choose you!

STENNING: …I am still young and I intend to choose…

McCALL: (*Suddenly scared.*) It's him!

STENNING: Who?

McCALL: The fat drunk! There by the…Listen!

(*A distant wheezing can be heard.*)

STENNING: (*Laughing.*) This man is so fat!

McCALL: I told you 'bloated'! I said 'bloated'!

STENNING: (*Laughing.*) He actually waddles!

McCALL: Let's go back to your room.

STENNING: My palms are bleeding. You are clawing me!

McCALL: This way!

STENNING: This is the same man who… Ow!

(*They move off quickly. Boots over gravel.*)

I fear that our little passion may soon…

McCALL: Soon what? You *must* learn to finish your sentences!

STENNING: …may soon have to come to an end.

McCALL: Please…be quick!

Scene Thirteen

FROST's office.

FROST: Take a seat.

ANDERSON: (*Wheezing.*) I prefer to stand.

FROST: As you wish.

ANDERSON: As sometimes when I sit I am unable to stand up again.

(*A silence.*)

FROST: My secretary will bring you coffee if you…?

ANDERSON: Alcohol? (*Unscrews.*)

FROST: I don't.

(*ANDERSON laughs.*)

I amuse you?

(*ANDERSON swigs.*)

Listen, I've been thinking...perhaps we...

ANDERSON: (*Matter of fact.*) He is very young. Twenties. Good-looking...if a little emaciated. I cannot at this stage prove that she has shared his bed but it seems...feasible. He has, it would appear, literary ambitions...though he is unlikely to make any mark since his particular enthusiasms are not the kind which sit easily with the spirit of the times.

FROST: I see.

ANDERSON: If it is any consolation...your wife is not his only diversion since I have now noticed one other... I believe she reads his scripts for him.

FROST: I need to see it. Their lust, their... I need to observe.

ANDERSON: Then there would of course be no way back. For thirty years Anderson Private Penitentiaries Ltd has prided itself...

FROST: I want the image of it. I want to feel...

ANDERSON: The pain?

FROST: Yes. (*A pause.*) Yes.

ANDERSON: And afterwards...the lover?

FROST: Well, what is normal? In these circumstances?

ANDERSON: I could have him stabbed outside a bar.

FROST: I see.

ANDERSON: Or I could burn him in his bed.

FROST: Well...yes.

ANDERSON: Make his skin peel and bubble.

FROST: Well, whatever. You must do whatever you think is appropriate.

ANDERSON: Your card will be debited exactly one month after the event. Thirty thousand dollars. This way our customers feel a little more detached from the murder. (*Pause.*) She's an attractive woman, your wife.

FROST: Yes.

ANDERSON: I look forward to witnessing her…undoing.

FROST: This is all so…

ANDERSON: It's something I am very much looking forward to.

Scene Fourteen

LAW's place of work. Footsteps down busy corridors. They are on the move.

STENNING: (*Urgently.*) To say that he is a man of routine would be to understate the case. He is a slave to it. Are you listening, Law?

LAW: Go on.

STENNING: The treadmill is his mistress. His working week follows the same pattern almost to the second and I have no reason to believe that it has changed at all in the twenty-one years he has been working there. Why are we walking so rapidly?

LAW: We need to talk.

(*An elevator door opens with a sound. It closes with a sound.*)

ELEVATOR: (*American.*) *Thanks for choosing SwiftLift. Please insert your card now. Standard rates apply.*

(*A card is swiped. The elevator moves at great speed.*)

STENNING: (*Quieter.*) He rises at six thirty-five, breakfasts alone while his wife and daughters sleep and then he surveys the news briefly.

(*The door opens with a sound.*)

ELEVATOR: *It was a pleasure to lift you. SwiftLift bids you a fond farewell. We realise you had a choice…*

(*The door closes with a sound.*)

STENNING: (*On the move.*) He's in his vehicle at seven and then makes the hour-long journey, following the same route each time, to his place of work.

LAW: (*To someone passing.*) Yes, Bishop, you can leave your review in my tray, thank you!!

STENNING: He is behind his desk and shuffling papers by eight.

LAW: Nice boy is Bishop. Likes his musicals.

STENNING: He never leaves the building for lunch and prefers to eat the delicacies on offer from the company vending machine. I intend to use him as a character in a play.

(*A door closes and they are in LAW's office. A pause.*)

It will be a tragedy.

LAW: Sit down.

STENNING: I will end his life on Friday evening. The car-park will be full of his colleagues at that time. Fleeing back to the sanctuary of family life. As soon as he touches the vehicle door, however, both he and they will rest safely in the arms of oblivion. What's wrong? You look...severe.

LAW: (*Severely.*) This script. This last script.

STENNING: Yes?

LAW: It is a work of...if one can safely use the word nowadays...genius.

STENNING: (*Humbled.*) Thank you.

LAW: You have a talent for comedy which is wonderful.

I was in an agony of laughter from beginning to end.

STENNING: Comedy?

LAW: The jokes are clever and unpredictable.

STENNING: The jokes?

LAW: The characters are strong and clearly recognisable.

STENNING: You are wrong! It is a serious attempt...

LAW: In this scene, for example...

(*A page turns.*)

...where the housewife offers herself to the hero, the clown character, in the park. It is so... (*She laughs.*)

STENNING: He is no clown!

LAW: ...so funny.

STENNING: It is a tragedy, I tell you!

LAW: And the way the clown is being trailed by the...

STENNING: Listen...

LAW: Leave it to me. You should feel very proud of yourself. The money this kind of thing commands...

STENNING: I no longer need your money.

LAW: (*Trying to stop the laugh.*) Oh, this is killing me!
Killing me!

STENNING: Since I have sold my soul to the fat man.
(*The laughter suddenly stops. A pause.*)

LAW: The fat man?

STENNING: Anderson. I am now a man of means.

LAW: (*To herself.*) Oh no.

STENNING: I have been forced to betray a passion but…

LAW: This man is dangerous.

STENNING: He is too fat to be dangerous.

LAW: The fatter they are, the thinner their hearts.

STENNING: His offer was generous.

LAW: Your naivety…

STENNING: Here is his cheque.

LAW: You call *that* 'generous'!!

STENNING: It's ten times what you pay me for a single
homicide.

LAW: Compared to what they'll pay you for your writing…

STENNING: You don't understand!

LAW: This man will murder you!

STENNING: (*Laughing.*) Such melodrama!

LAW: You are now too precious a talent to be exposed to
such people! This is the man who has grown fat on the
immense profits that his private penitentiary…

STENNING: And we all know that these days melodrama
has no place in the repertoire.
(*He laughs on.*)

LAW: (*Seriously.*) Did no-one ever tell you that a woman
loathes being laughed at?
(*The laugh peters out.*)
For I can assure you that she does not like it at all.

Scene Fifteen

A busy restaurant.

FROST: (*To a waiter.*) And I'll have the turbot. Thank you.

McCALL: Oh, darling. Why don't you have something else
for a change?

FROST: I am very particular to the turbot they serve here.

McCALL: I know you are.

FROST: It has a distinctive flavour.

McCALL: I know but the menu is extensive and yet you...

FROST: I am content with my selection.

McCALL: I know but...

FROST: I am a man who knows what he likes.

McCALL: We have been coming here every week for eighteen years.

FROST: Yes?

McCALL: And yet you always choose the turbot.

FROST: (*To waiter.*) And the usual Chardonnay, please. Thank you.

McCALL: Why not try the glazed oysters with Champagne and Sevruga caviare?

FROST: Because I enjoy the turbot.

McCALL: Or the salad of seared Devon scallops with spiced leaves?

FROST: I am happy with my turbot.

McCALL: (*More annoyed.*) Or the feuillete of quails eggs with the mushroom mousseline and the asparagus tips?

FROST: I'll stay with the turbot.

McCALL: (*More annoyed.*) Or the grilled Scottish lobster?

FROST: The turbot if you please...

McCALL: (*More annoyed.*) Or perhaps the sea bass with braised fennel?

FROST: I want to eat the turbot!!!

(*A pause.*)

You have made me lose my temper.

McCALL: I apologise.

FROST: People are now staring.

(*Pause.*)

(*To waiter, quietly.*) The turbot. Thank you.

(*A laugh somewhere off.*)

McCALL: What's wrong?

FROST: (*Alarmed.*) That ghoulish boy! At the table by the plant. Don't look round!

McCALL: What is it?

FROST: Writing in a notebook. Shaking his head, giggling like a schoolboy. He's been watching us.

McCALL: Where?

FROST: Don't! I'm sure I know this man.

McCALL: Who is…?

(*A pause.*)

FROST: You know him?

McCALL: (*After a pause.*) No.

FROST: But you have turned quite pale.

McCALL: It's nothing.

(*The laugh again.*)

FROST: He is laughing at us.

McCALL: I'm sure that's not the case.

FROST: Don't look round again!

McCALL: Darling, really…

FROST: We will have to move tables.

McCALL: But this is the table we always…

FROST: I cannot enjoy my turbot if I know someone is watching us.

McCALL: You are being paranoid.

FROST: You don't know what it's like. At work. Every day. Every moment of every day…someone is watching me. From round a corner, from behind a computer screen. Waiting for me to fail. With an eye on my position. Those above me constantly judging, silently judging me. Those below, anxious that I make some error which will…

McCALL: You have been telling me this same thing every day for twenty…

FROST: And now you…you resent the fact that I…that I…

McCALL: Darling, you have the turbot. It's fine. I just thought you might like to…

FROST: I feel tense.

McCALL: Yes.

FROST: Perhaps we should go?

McCALL: If that's what you…

(*The laugh again.*)

FROST: I will not have some emaciated loser, whose mode of dress I would have supposed inappropriate to this

319

particular establishment, I will not have him… He is
writing again! What is he writing?
(*Chairs scrape.*)

McCALL: (*To waiter.*) Excuse me! We are leaving. Could we
cancel our order?

FROST: (*To waiter.*) And that shabby lout…by the plant. He
should not have been granted entry here! I will speak to
the manager tomorrow!

McCALL: This way. Give me your hand.

FROST: (*Upset.*) In eighteen years…in eighteen years. I
have never…we have never…left this place without
dining. Never…we have never…

McCALL: (*Gently.*) Come on…

FROST: Never…never…I have never…

Scene Sixteen

*STENNING's bedroom. The barking dogs, the crying babies, the
shouts and screams. ANDERSON is setting up his equipment.*

ANDERSON: And this one goes up here.

STENNING: But these cameras are so small!

ANDERSON: Technology will reduce the size of
everything.

STENNING: And this one is no bigger than a fly.

ANDERSON: Now, I think we will need to move the bed.

STENNING: Won't that arouse her suspicions?

ANDERSON: Why should it?

STENNING: Well…

ANDERSON: We just need to angle it slightly so that we
have as clear a view of your…ardour as possible.

STENNING: Well if you lift that side then I…

ANDERSON: I'm afraid my back is out.

STENNING: Is it?

ANDERSON: Doctor's orders are that I refrain from…

STENNING: I see.

ANDERSON: It is due, you understand, to my colossal
weight.

STENNING: Then I must...

(*STENNING exerts himself and moves the bed.*)

ANDERSON: A little more to the left, I think.

STENNING: There?

ANDERSON: Just let me have a quick look...

(*He taps on his keyboard.*)

Camera one placed on the headboard, camera two concealed in the light shade, while camera three...

(*He taps on his keyboard.*)

...affords a splendid view from behind the mirror.

STENNING: Do you not feel that all this is rather excessive?

ANDERSON: One must always give the paying customer value for money.

STENNING: We will be so exposed.

ANDERSON: I am assuming of course that you do not generally perform beneath the sheets?

STENNING: Well...in winter we...

ANDERSON: And I wonder also if it would be at all possible to give the place a quick clean?

STENNING: Why?

ANDERSON: Well...just to give the spectacle a touch more dignity, a little polish.

STENNING: I suppose so.

ANDERSON: I have to say, Mr Stenning, you are most obliging.

STENNING: What can I say? Your offer was...

ANDERSON: Do you not know who I am?

STENNING: I have been advised...

ANDERSON: And you are fully aware of the reason for this operation?

STENNING: Of course.

ANDERSON: Tell me...your lover, your soon-to-be betrayed lover...she is a very...nice woman. I have... formed something of an attachment to her. Emotionally, you understand?

STENNING: You have?

ANDERSON: But you...you are young whereas I am old, you have a certain skeletal charm whereas I am weighed

down by all this flesh, accrued over the years by my
ghastly self-indulgence, and you have an enviable
success with women whereas I…

STENNING: You are reduced to…?

ANDERSON: Images. Yes.

STENNING: (*Laughing.*) You could try losing some weight?

ANDERSON: It is not that. I am stout, of course, but it is
not this unsightly bulk of mine which repels them.

STENNING: No?

ANDERSON: It is because I lack…conversation.

STENNING: You do?

ANDERSON: And also when I drink, which is relentlessly,
I become… If you could just pass me the screwdriver…

STENNING: Here.

ANDERSON: Thank you …maudlin.

STENNING: Ah.

ANDERSON: Yes, I have spent a lifetime in this profession
and I have done uncommonly well but I cannot help
sometimes feeling a certain…regret. Destroying lives
like this is not without its drawbacks.

STENNING: I know.

ANDERSON: And you…I have been watching you. You
have been trailing the husband.

STENNING: (*After a pause.*) No.

ANDERSON: Yesterday evening you even followed them to
their favourite eating place.

STENNING: Well…

ANDERSON: Forcing them to leave before they had
enjoyed even a single sip of wine.

STENNING: Look, I am writing a tragedy and for that it is
necessary to…

ANDERSON: The man works tirelessly for the good of his
country. Surely he should be allowed to…

STENNING: For someone who lacks conversation you
rarely seem at a loss for something to say.

ANDERSON: Words, as they…

STENNING: Are we not done yet?

ANDERSON: And I feed this wire through here and
now…invisible. See?

STENNING: You are very clever.

ANDERSON: I know.

STENNING: Now, may we…

ANDERSON: You press this here, under the bed like so, and the cameras will then be noiselessly activated. She will anyway be so immersed in her desire that the rest of the world will for her be quite…annihilated.

STENNING: Good.

ANDERSON: I wish you joy of her.

STENNING: Thank you.

ANDERSON: And I do ask you to remember one thing.

STENNING: What's that?

ANDERSON: This is likely to be her last adventure. In this life. Her final fling.

STENNING: I understand.

ANDERSON: So…be a gentleman.

STENNING: Of course.

ANDERSON: Be a gentleman. That is all I will say.

(*A door closes.*)

Scene Seventeen

FROST's front room. The sounds of a dining table being cleared away. The clock ticks.

McCALL: (*Slightly off.*) You are becoming something of an expert in the kitchen, Louisa. That was a delicious meal. (*Calling.*) And if you make sure you leave the silver to one side, Emily, as it needs to be polished. Thank you.

FROST: It is ready.

McCALL: Leave that till later, darling. Your father wants us all to watch a film together. It will be just like the old days. If you could just pass that…thank you. Why the long face, darling? Is it a sad film we'll be watching?

FROST: It is a tragedy.

McCALL: Good. How I hate to be entertained. How they presume, these people.

FROST: It is the tale of a woman…

McCALL: They presume that their infantile observations will somehow lighten our darkness.

FROST: ...who valued love more than life.

McCALL: Nearly done now. If you would go and join your father by the screen.

(*Footsteps.*)

I assume it is suitable viewing for...?

FROST: It is.

McCALL: But your expression, darling... Have you been crying?

FROST: Not at all.

McCALL: You look as if...

FROST: Please. Let us just watch the film.

McCALL: As you wish.

FROST: If you would turn off the lights. We will need the dark for this.

(*A light is switched. Footsteps.*)

McCALL: Now...you have our full and undivided attention.

FROST: You are all sitting comfortably?

McCALL: (*Cheerfully.*) We are.

FROST: Then I shall begin.

(*The TV kicks into life. We hear the tinny, recorded voices of STENNING and McCALL.*)

McCALL: Darling...why have you stopped?

STENNING: I can't do this...

McCALL: Don't stop. I beg you...don't stop.

STENNING: I...

McCALL: What...are you crying?

STENNING: No.

McCALL: I have never seen you cry before.

STENNING: Please...

McCALL: You are breaking my heart.

STENNING: You have to go.

McCALL: Never!

STENNING: This cannot...I have done something that...

McCALL: Stop talking. Just kiss me!!

STENNING: Please...

McCALL: Just kiss me, just kiss me, just kiss me...

McCALL: Go to your room, girls!

FROST: They must stay where they are.

McCALL: Go to your room! Now!

(*Footsteps. A door opens and then is closed.*)

FROST: Would you not like to see how it turns out?

McCALL: Why...why do you seek to humiliate me in front of my children?

(*The TV is turned off. We hear the Rachmaninov from another room.*)

FROST: Your boyfriend has betrayed you.

McCALL: Yes.

FROST: As you have betrayed me.

McCALL: Yes. (*A silence.*) Will I at least be allowed to say goodbye to my daughters?

FROST: There are some gentlemen waiting outside for you. (*A pause.*) I'm sorry that this is the way it had to end.

McCALL: Yes.

FROST: I must now face the future without you.

McCALL: You would rather die alone than turn a blind eye to a faithless wife?

FROST: I think I would. Yes.

McCALL: I admire you for that.

FROST: And I admire you.

(*Footsteps. A door is opened.*)

This way, please.

(*The sound of boots on the floorboards.*)

This is she.

(*Footsteps. Handcuffs applied.*)

McCALL: Goodbye then.

FROST: Goodbye, my dear. (*A pause.*) The children will be sent to visit you before...

McCALL: Thank you.

(*Footsteps away. A door is opened and then closed. A silence.*)

FROST: So...this then is what is known as solitude? This. (*A silence.*) It doesn't frighten me. No, I'm not afraid. (*A silence. He then laughs.*) It's nothing...nothing. Just the absence of... (*breaking.*)...the absence of... (*Recovering.*) No. I am a grown man and it is certainly something with which I can quite comfortably deal.

(*The Rachmaninov plays on.*)

Scene Eighteen

The comedy bar. As before.

LAW: Mind if I join you?

ANDERSON: (*Drunk.*) You what?

LAW: Can I get you anything?

ANDERSON: You can fill that up.

LAW: Another for the gentlemen, please.

ANDERSON: You a whore?

LAW: No.

(*A drink is poured.*)

ANDERSON: Then why are you talking to me?

LAW: Because I know who you are.

ANDERSON: I enjoy fame, I have to confess. Which is why I come out at night. I like the recognition.

(*Loud whoops, cheers and laughter.*)

LAW: It is odd that someone as well-known as you should be so successful at playing the role of the snoop.

ANDERSON: I believe people like to be followed. The anonymity of the city sometimes…

LAW: I have been having you followed, Mr Anderson.

ANDERSON: (*Laughs.*) Nonsense!

LAW: You have some despicable habits.

ANDERSON: Please don't make me laugh. I have a weak heart.

(*A drink is placed on the bar.*)

Good health.

LAW: So…you like comedy?

ANDERSON: No.

LAW: Then why…?

ANDERSON: Oblivion tastes sweeter here.

LAW: I see.

ANDERSON: And the people are so young.

LAW: Yes.

ANDERSON: And slender.

LAW: Listen…

ANDERSON: Do *you* find me repulsive?

LAW: I do, yes.

ANDERSON: I see.

(*More loud whoops, cheers and laughter.*)

I've seen you before. You're a socialist?

LAW: I like to think I am. My parents always taught me…

ANDERSON: Yes. I know who you are.

LAW: You almost knocked me off my feet once when…

ANDERSON: By day a leading member of a subversive terrorist organisation, but by night a drama critic who is very much set in her ways.

LAW: I have an opinion which is widely respected. I…

ANDERSON: And you want me to spare the life of your lover, your scrawny, shaghappy little scribblerboy?

LAW: You're very good.

ANDERSON: It is too late. His card is marked.

LAW: He is a great comedy writer.

ANDERSON: I have no interest in writers.

LAW: I implore you to reconsider.

ANDERSON: I'm sorry.

(*More loud whoops, cheers and laughter.*)

But I'm glad he has been enjoying the pieces of silver I gave him. A Judas very eager to bank his abilities. He has, you know, taken to dining in the most exclusive of restaurants.

LAW: Listen…I will do anything if you…

ANDERSON: You are wasting your time.

LAW: Mr Anderson, this boy must live. And I will do anything, anything…to guarantee his safety.

(*More loud whoops, cheers and laughter. A silence.*)

ANDERSON: I have not been touched there since the early 2020s. (*Pause.*) This way.

LAW: Right. Good.

ANDERSON: We shall now get to know each other a little better in the back of my vehicle.

Scene Nineteen

A prison cell. A door is slammed somewhere off. Footsteps. A hatch opened.

A GUARD: Your daughters are here, love!
(*The hatch closed.*)
McCALL: (*Rehearsing her speech at speed.*) You must try not to look so mournful. It is not so bad here as you might imagine. I can think. In this darkness, I can think. Look back on my life and yes, there have been happy moments. You two are my joy but I… I have not been content with what I was given and that…that is unpardonable. Oh, my mind is infested, it's riddled with clichés! So… I need you to be strong. Oh, I don't mean that, do I? But you will have to look after your father when I am gone. You know how incapable he is. But he does love you and he wants only what is best for you.
(*We hear footsteps outside.*)
So, Emily, a hug for you. Live your lives well. Oh, but what does that mean? Just…I am a parent and I must advise but I have no advice to give. It is so hard to sum up these years of anguish in a sentence. To say I love them is not enough for it is so obvious. I cannot think of anything witty, anything of weight, of moment, no pearl of wisdom at all. My vocabulary is deserting me. Hold onto your piano. Yes. And you your cello.
(*She sobs. Then recovers.*)
But to weep is not enough, it's not enough. It is so much…surrender.
(*The door is unbolted.*)

Scene Twenty

A car park. STENNING is setting up his bomb.

STENNING: This is the last one. Definitely the last one. I cannot spend the rest of my days scrabbling about underneath cars like some Cockney garage mechanic. I am an artist and though, it might be argued, an artist ought to be involved with the real world, as it is oddly described, so that he does not become insular and isolated...I have now had my fill of murder. The point has been made. There are other less focused youths who can take my place. And anyway, who is to say that capitalism does not work? I now know what I want to do with my existence and, for an angry young man like me, that is enormously important. The ideas teem around my brain: plots, characters, situations and so, as soon as this Semtex is in its correct position...there we go...I shall consider my time as a freedom fighter...

ANDERSON: (*Muffled, wheezing.*) Come out from under the car.

STENNING: (*Alarmed.*) Who's that?

ANDERSON: It's Anderson.

STENNING: Anderson?

ANDERSON: The fat man.

STENNING: (*Out from under the car.*) What...what do you want?

ANDERSON: Closure. As our leaders say.

STENNING: (*Weak laugh.*) What, the Americans?

ANDERSON: What are you doing?

STENNING: Nothing.

ANDERSON: You have trouble with your engine?

STENNING: No. (*After a pause.*) Yes.

ANDERSON: Get up.

STENNING: What?

ANDERSON: Get up!!

(*STENNING is pulled to his feet.*)

STENNING: What are you doing?

ANDERSON: I normally like to give my victims a little speech before I dispatch them. Give them a few words of...not advice exactly for that would be wasted breath...but rather...

STENNING: Victims? What do you mean 'victims'?

ANDERSON: ...I like to impart a little knowledge. Truths I have gleaned from the journey of my life.

STENNING: Get off me!

ANDERSON: Your friend...your agent...she thinks very highly of you.

STENNING: What do you mean?

ANDERSON: In order to save you, she offered herself to me.

STENNING: You're hurting me!

ANDERSON: I accepted and enjoyed but now, alas, I intend to betray the promise.

STENNING: You're holding me...

ANDERSON: Here is my knife, look.

STENNING: Listen...

ANDERSON: Bought yesterday especially for the job. A virginal, shining blade...

STENNING: Please...

ANDERSON: Unspoilt by the blood of others.

STENNING: I can't breathe. You...

ANDERSON: Quite an honour for you.

STENNING: Please...

ANDERSON: One jab to the heart, one slice for each lung and then a couple of thrusts in the abdomen. How does that grab you?

(A sob.)

You also wept on the film we made together.

STENNING: Please...

ANDERSON: Before I stick this into you...tell me...what *were* you doing under the car?

STENNING: *(Unable to breathe.)* Planting a bomb.

ANDERSON: Sorry?

STENNING: *(Unable to breathe.)* I was planting a bomb.

(A silence. ANDERSON lets out a laugh. This becomes louder until he is bellowing hysterically.)

What's so funny?

(The laughter continues. ANDERSON is now dangerously out of control.)

ANDERSON: *(Struggling for breath.)* He's planting a bomb, he says! ...Planting a bomb!...It's priceless, it's priceless!

STENNING: Why are you laughing at me? I demand an explanation!

ANDERSON: That's irony, is it?!...You have talent!... The critic is...the critic is right! Tal-ent!...Tal-ent!

(*It becomes clear that ANDERSON in now struggling for breath, coughing, wheezing. He has collapsed to his knees. Soon there is silence. The man has died laughing.*)
My God...I have killed a man with comedy. She has a point. I have to admit that she does have a point. Laughter *is* a weapon. And it is I who am the new master, the great, new and much-awaited messiah of the genre. (*He runs off.*)

Scene Twenty-One

A street. There is chaos but not as pronounced as in the opening scenes.

STENNING: No, I didn't say that...I just said I don't know how you could have even offered.

LAW: I did it for you.

STENNING: But the man was so fat!

LAW: But I've already said: his drinking had rendered him unqualified for...

STENNING: I don't even want to think about it.

LAW: What time is it?

STENNING: The civil servant will be emerging from those doors in exactly fifteen seconds.

LAW: You are sure?

STENNING: Absolutely.

LAW: And you won't change your decision?

STENNING: This is absolutely the last time.

LAW: Then I too will renounce violence.

STENNING: And do what exactly?

LAW: Well...be with you. Look after your interests.

STENNING: I can look after myself.

LAW: Your new career will require effective management.

STENNING: Three...two...one.

LAW: As if by magic!

STENNING: Taking his final walk.

LAW: Come on.

　(*They follow.*)

STENNING: He will now begin to quicken his pace.

LAW: Uncanny.

STENNING: And, in a few moments, check his watch.

LAW: Yes.

STENNING: A furtive look around.

LAW: Yes!!

STENNING: And then down to the car-park.

(*They continue down steps for a time.*)

(*Whispering.*) This is the most dramatic moment...when a human being quite obliviously walks towards his inevitable and hideous end.

LAW: (*Whispering.*) I have arranged scores of such deaths but, I have to say, this will be the first time I have witnessed one in the flesh.

STENNING: It will not be pleasant.

LAW: I can take it.

STENNING: He is a man in deep despair.

LAW: He will hear you!

STENNING: He is too absorbed by his own suffering to...

LAW: He is approaching the car!

STENNING: Keep behind me. His hand reaches for the door and...

LAW: (*Excited.*) Hold me!

STENNING: Goodbye, my friend.

(*A long, expectant silence.*)

LAW: What's he doing?

STENNING: He seems to be...crying.

LAW: Why is he running away?

STENNING: He has cheated his destiny.

LAW: Where's he going?

STENNING: There is no precedent for this.

LAW: We must go.

STENNING: Yes.

LAW: Come on.

(*They run off.*)

STENNING: But the bomb will be waiting for him. I now must write.

LAW: Let us leave all this bloodshed!

STENNING: I will strive to be responsible! I will inform, I will educate!

LAW: We must stick together now.

STENNING: I will make the world laugh!

LAW: I will put a deposit on a house for us...

STENNING: But above all I will give a clear meaning!

Scene Twenty-Two

The comedy bar. As the scene unfolds we become aware that it is being played out, sitcom-like, before a live studio audience, who are laughing and applauding deliriously.

FROST: Please officer, am I not allowed to...? I should at least like to say goodbye to my wife in a little privacy?

McCALL: It is time, dear.

FROST: But this is all happening so quickly. It's almost farcical.

(*The audience bays with laughter.*)

McCALL: I am resigned to my fate.

FROST: I ran, for the first time in years, to get here before...

McCALL: You broke your routine?

FROST: I was about to get into the car, to drive to the badminton courts but something, something told me that... Tell me, do you loathe me?

McCALL: No. Of course I don't loathe you.

FROST: I loathe myself.

McCALL: I know.

(*The audience bays with laughter.*)

McCALL: You look older. Greyer.

FROST: I am so alone.

McCALL: You are becoming frail. A little hunched I think. Perhaps you should retire?

(*The audience bays with laughter.*)

FROST: No.

McCALL: Cultivate a hobby or two.

FROST: Please. Don't torture me.

McCALL: I mean only to be kind.

FROST: You were always kind.

McCALL: Yes. I was.

FROST: Our daughters begged to come, to see for themselves how marriages sometimes have to end...

McCALL: The men are waiting for me. The clowns and the jesters, the slapstick merchants. These beaming comedians.

FROST: I want you to know. I tried to raise the money. To release you. I rattled collection tins round comedy bars but...people are less than charitable these days. And I spent all our savings on having you followed.

(An owl hoots.)

McCALL: Isn't it a beautiful night, darling? And a perfect night on which to die.

(The audience bays with laughter.)

FROST: May I kiss you?

McCALL: Kiss me?

FROST: I should like to kiss you.

McCALL: Then do so.

(A kiss.)

Ah. The forehead. You always kissed me there.

FROST: I...

McCALL: But it was nice. I liked it.

(The circus/comedy music begins.)

This is it then. Goodbye.

FROST: It's intolerable, absolutely intolerable! Why? Why? Why is the place so full of these women, these women all dying, all dying willingly, with such smiles on their faces?!

(The audience bays with laughter.)

McCALL: As you say, it's just the way some marriages have to end.

(Thunderous laughter and applause.)

Scene Twenty-Three

The comedy bar. The previous scene is being played to its conclusion to the delight of the assembled crowd.

LAW: And it is this, this bestowing of the message, for which we shall receive the nation's hard-earned gold! (*A pause.*) You must feel so proud, darling.

STENNING: It is your ending.

LAW: Yes, but I can't take the credit away from you.

STENNING: There is something wonderful, is there not, something magical about being able to put smiles on the faces of so many people, to make so many people so very...very...happy.

LAW: And I note that already...already you have begun to put on a little weight.

(The comedy has now finished and the sitcom music plays over the credits. Gradually it fades out and the Rachmaninov takes its place.)

A DIRECTOR'S VIEW

Peter Craze

It is very rewarding to have championed the work of Torben Betts when for so long theatre doors seemed closed to him, and we were beginning to despair at the possibility of ever staging his plays. And now, within a period of just over two years, nine productions of his work will have taken place, seeing him critically acknowledged as one of the country's finest young writers.

I first met Torben in 1991 when he was training to be an actor at the Drama Studio London and I directed him in a production. I did not see him after that for four years. On that particular morning I was off to direct in America when, at London Bridge, I saw a forlorn figure shuffling along the platform. It was Torben and he told me that he was 'fucked off with acting' and that he was leaving England to teach in a then war-ravaged Croatia. He said that he had written a few plays and that he was living near us, in Greenwich. He agreed that he would drop off some of his work and be in touch.

On my return from America, I slept off the jet-lag, and sat down to read Torben's *Pitching In* (later to be retitled *A Listening Heaven*). It is almost impossible to describe that moment when a director recognises a true playwright, but here it happened. His writing, it seemed to me, had a directness, humour and a theatrical energy, combined with a strong sense of structure; the dialogue sharp and colourful. We talked and he informed me that he was working on a verse play, *Incarcerator*.

I found this particular play dangerous and challenging in a way that, for me, transcended his other, excellent, dark domestic comedies. And so began several years of trying to find a London theatre brave enough to stage the play. Eventually, after holding a public reading of the play and developing it with a group of enthusiastic actors, it was the courage of Michael Kingsbury at the White Bear Theatre Club that helped to establish the 'alternative' playwriting career of Torben Betts. The production received glowing reviews and later transferred to the Battersea

Arts Centre. Then followed his sell-out *Five Visions of the Faithful*, again at The White Bear, and this autumn that partnership will be renewed when the darker, Beckettian *The Biggleswades* (a play he wrote back in 1994) will be premiered under Kingsbury's roof.

I consider it a director's responsibility when working with a young, emerging talent to expose the writing to experienced and successful actors. Actors who will help develop and eventually perform the play, contributing to the overall process that will benefit the writer. With Torben's work, people have often asked me how, as in the instance of *Five Visions of the Faithful*, we managed to attract twelve excellent leading actors to commit seven weeks to a 'profit-share' production, by a relatively unknown playwright. I have never had a problem with actors coming on board a Betts play because they too recognise the energy and the vibrancy of the language. He writes for actors in a way that allows them to perform at their highest level. As actor Ian Lindsay said in an interview with *The Stage*: 'I just like the writing. It's absolutely terrific and I would not have cared what part I played. It is intelligent dialogue. It gives the actor width to express himself in all sorts of ways. Like all good writing there is no one way of doing it.' I have found that most brave actors concur with this.

One of our leading critics has advised Torben to resist becoming a 'theatrical poet' and to concentrate on 'what he was born for' – being 'a domestic realist'. How narrow-sighted! And it is interesting to note that the supposedly 'sophisticated' newspapers have been more conservative in their responses to Betts' theatrical poetry, while the more popular press have been very open-minded and enthusiastic, with the *London Metro* giving *Incarcerator* an extremely rare five-star rating. If you have the ability to successfully create in both styles, why not enjoy and celebrate that talent? Why must we pigeonhole the artist? Allow him rather to follow with freedom that special gift, and who knows what he might create?

To a certain extent the frosty silence that greeted the early attempts to stage Torben's work was deeply beneficial to him. It allowed him to create a body of work, unfettered by critical approval and commercial considerations, and now that sense of freedom is so ingrained in his writing that I do not see it leaving him. It also fuelled his anger and cynicism: essential qualities for a radical English playwright.

What I find inspiring about Torben's poetic and form-breaking 'alternative writing' is that, as a director, I start on a Betts play by throwing out all my previous habits and experiences. And anyway these practices can unknowingly inhibit a director, so with Torben's work I am happy to do this. I want to respond to what he has created, to honour and not impose on his text. You give yourself up to this unusual journey, this kamikaze flight. It is scary, but there is a dynamic and a danger in his style that is intoxicating to work with; you have to trust your instincts and your belief in his work. I never know how the play will emerge but I do know that it will be an exhilarating entertainment for actor and audience alike.

This is the great strength of Torben's work: he encourages us to be brave and daring because he himself is. He writes the play he wants to write, not worrying where it will get on, what audience it can be pitched at, nor how it can be fulfilled by director and cast. He simply writes his plays because he must, and this refreshing sense of freedom is apparent in them.

The content of his plays is both historical and contemporary, provocative while pleasing. The work challenges us to explore our social and domestic complacency and our political awareness; to consider the corruption and sexual infiltration of our everyday lives – nudging us, always nudging us. The plays are voiced in a vibrant, strident and often poetic language. Words that resonate long after the experience of hearing them; language that is also a pleasure to read.

Finally, my fervent hope is that Torben will continue to write what and how he chooses, regardless of critical or commercial endorsement, because I sincerely believe that his domestic and poetic styles will one day merge to produce a truly great and major play that will reflect his generation of theatre. We must allow him this freedom.

Peter Craze
London, 2001

AN ACTOR'S VIEW

Nigel Barrett

Torben Betts writes for actors. That is why they love to act in his plays.

This is not to say that other playwrights are neglectful of the people that will deliver their words and ideas, but perhaps they just get so caught up in the worlds they are creating that they forget to consider the real one. And in so doing may create a role one may not always relish playing, even though it is integral to the play. This is never the case in a Betts play.

It's not because he particularly loves us. It is because he loves words so much and luxuriates in language that he wants us to enjoy it too and is aware of the power of live performance when the actors get it right. Yet no matter how brutal or caustic the speech, he will thread it with a beautiful phrase or a shockingly-wasteful poetic throwaway for the actor to entice back the audience.

Also he is very, very funny. Secreted within all the venomous bile are some great gags to soften the blow of his rhetoric on the audience, which also enable the performer to find a humanity in the character and invest it with the truth and energy it deserves.

When you perform in one of his plays you feel you are taking part in an essential cultural and social critique. Whether they are polemic assaults on contemporary mores or abstract dissections of supposedly universal truths, the power of the text challenges you to serve it well. If you manage to master it, it is a wonderfully satisfying feeling.

I have spent painful days watching actors struggle and wriggle over Torben's words (myself included) and then mercifully and suddenly get the connection, to the sound of chuckling from the upward-staring (he listens more than watches), stubble-stroking writer at the back as the actors vocalise the sounds and rhythms he hears in his head.

It is not the arrogance of the writer indulging in his own work but a real joy for him to have actors take the words he has written and shape them to their own ends.

For Torben realises he is just part of a process with many others involved in creating a play, and is always modestly honoured that actors wish to take part in his works. Because of this he ensures that all roles in his plays give each and every performer material to work with.

A writer that not only produces such startling text but also has a caring eye on the people that will perform it; how could any actor not trust his words and want to do them justice?

Nigel Barrett
London, 2001